Mapping the Past

Mapping the Past

*A Search for Five Brothers
at the Edge of Empire*

CHARLES DRAZIN

WILLIAM HEINEMANN: LONDON

1 3 5 7 9 10 8 6 4 2

William Heinemann
20 Vauxhall Bridge Road
London SW1V 2SA

William Heinemann is part of the Penguin Random House group of companies
whose addresses can be found at global.penguinrandomhouse.com.

Penguin
Random House
UK

First published by William Heinemann in 2016

www.penguin.co.uk

A CIP catalogue record for this book is available from the British Library.

ISBN 9780434012183

Typeset in 12.5/16.5 pt Fournier MT Std
Jouve (UK), Milton Keynes
Printed and bound by Clays Ltd, St Ives plc

MIX
Paper from
responsible sources
FSC
www.fsc.org FSC® C018179

Penguin Random House is committed to a
sustainable future for our business, our readers
and our planet. This book is made from Forest
Stewardship Council® certified paper.

For Patsy

Daughter of a Royal Engineer

Contents

CONTENTS

PART III:
UBIQUE QUO FAS ET GLORIA DUCUNT

Prologue

My mother showed no wish to return to the village in Ireland where she grew up until the end of her life. I can fix the time exactly to one evening in a cancer hospital. Until then much of the talk had been of her getting better. But this was the day her life took the final turn. The doctor had seen her during the afternoon.

'He told me that it's hopeless, and there is no cure.'

It was a moment of lucidity in an evening when despair turned into a terrifying phantasm, woven from fragments of the past.

'I won't be happy unless I can go home,' she said. 'I want to go home.'

I tried to explain that we would have to make things right for her so that she could, but the idea of waiting any longer had become intolerable to her.

'I want to go now.'

Frail and emaciated though she was, she swung her legs over the side of the bed. I held onto her bruised, mottled arms to stop her from walking out of the hospital, although in truth she lacked the strength to get even as far as the door of her own room.

'I could climb over the wall,' she said. Home had become a different place now, one that was a simple walk away if only we would help her.

It would be very soon, I said, but no amount of reassurance was enough to calm her. Nothing would budge her from the scenario of an immediate departure.

'So you'll get the car then? I'm ready right now.'

Once again she made to get to her feet only to fall back under my restraint.

'I want to go home!'

At my wits' end, I made an appeal to the only force I knew might contain her. 'Soon you will be able to go home. But now you must pray to God for patience.'

'Something strange is happening here,' she said.

The hospital had become a dark, menacing place that she had to escape at all costs.

'Hurry, Thomas. Jump down.'

She was on a garden wall now with her brother Thomas, slipping back into the house after bedtime. She was back home in Quin, County Clare, from where she had run away to England sixty years before.

When I visited a couple of days later, it was as if that terrible night had never happened. She was cheerful and high-spirited, happy that she was going to be home soon – 'home' now being her house in Hertfordshire – and even speaking of recovery. The only trace of that other night was Ireland.

She spoke about her memories of growing up in Quin, the second oldest child in a family of nine children. Recalling her relations and spelling out names I might not recognise, she went to extra lengths to get the details right.

'You've heard me talk of the McInerneys – M-C-I-N-E-R-N-E-Y. There were no brothers in my mother's family; only girls. There was my mother, Amelia; there was Elena, or Ellie; there was Annie, she was the oldest; and then there was Ettie . . .'

One by one, she listed the members of both sides of the family, the mention of this or that name spinning a web of loosely connected anecdotes. Her father, Patrick Lynch, from Doora, County Clare, had been a military surveyor in the Royal Engineers. She explained how, returning from the war, he had married Amelia McInerney, who was the prettiest girl in the next village. They made their home in a house by the River Rine near Quin Abbey. They called it Bridge House. The property, which Amelia had inherited from her parents, included a cottage and also a pub, one of four in the village.

On the other side of the road was a pub that belonged to Amby Power, who was famous as captain of the Clare team that had won the All-Ireland hurling championship of 1914. His wife, Kathy, had been an old flame of Patrick's, and was madly jealous when he chose Amelia McInerney over her. But she still kept a map of the county that Patrick had drawn for her on display in the bar. 'I think it's still there to this day,' said my mother. 'I remember the pens with which he drew his maps. When I get home, I'll show you some of his writing. He had a gorgeous hand – he was very bright. And he loved the British army – just absolutely adored it. And because of that . . .'

Her face darkened with resentment at a recollected injustice.

3

'Nationalism had raised its ugly head at the time in Ireland. It had been around for centuries before, but it had turned particularly nasty. The IRA were determined to get anyone who had worked for the British. But my father said, "Damn them. They need me more than I need them." Of course they did. There weren't enough trained engineers for the type of work he was doing. So they didn't touch him until he died. Then they refused my mother a pension. Isn't that wicked? Because of his connections with the British army. That's why I never had any time for de Valera's party – "Ourselves". Sinn Féin is "Ourselves". I hated them so.'

With the Royal Engineers, Patrick had travelled around the world, mapping the territories of the Empire. When he returned to Ireland in 1916, after more than two decades of service, he joined the Irish Land Commission, which administered the redistribution of land from the Anglo-Irish landlords to the tenant farmers. It had been established under the nineteenth-century Land Acts, through which the British government had sought to redress one of the great wrongs of Anglo-Irish history.

Patrick was an Irish Roman Catholic, but his experience of Britain was of a country that had given him a livelihood and a career, and also sought to do right by Ireland. He had every reason to look back with pride on his twenty-two years in the corps of the Royal Engineers, and to want to instil in his daughter the same pride.

My mother remembered that when she was a little girl, her father used to say to her, 'Patsy, what are you going to be when you grow up? Well? Let me hear.' Which was the signal for her to shout, 'A Royal Engineer, Daddy. A Royal Engineer!'

For many years Patsy had put the history of her Irish family into a bottom drawer while she brought up a young family of her own. But she began to think about it again when, in the late 1970s, her brother Dermot sent her a cutting of an old obituary that the *Clare Champion* had published on 18 March 1939 of their uncle Jack, who had died soon after their father:

The death has taken place in Melbourne of Major John Lynch, late of the Australian Survey Corps. Born in Deerpark, Quin, he was the son of the late John Lynch. Himself and four brothers were educated in Doora National School under the late Mr. McMascoe of Clarecastle. As they attained the age of 18 years all five brothers joined the Ordnance Staff at Ennis, and later joined the Survey section of the Royal Engineers at Chatham, where they showed a marked aptitude for their work, grasping the technique of military survey work and engineering. As each brother finished his course at Chatham, he was transferred to Southampton, the parent house of British Surveys, for the more advanced courses. Here their ability was quickly realised by the Director General of Ordnance Survey, and John and Patrick were amongst the pioneers selected to survey most of the unmapped lands of British territory in the Gold Coast, the Orange Free State, Transvaal, Cape Territory, Mauritius, Singapore and Canada. In later years, Michael and James were sent abroad on similar work. On the outbreak of the Great War the five brothers went to France, where their work was of a hazardous nature, surveying the lands and laying out trenches over the battlegrounds. John was promoted Colonel on the field from the non-commissioned rank, and Patrick was promoted Major. Michael attained to the rank of Warrant Officer, while Thomas was killed in Armentières. James, whose health broke down, died at home, as the result of the hardships he endured in the war. At the termination of the war, Patrick returned to the Survey Department in Phoenix Park, Dublin, and was subsequently transferred to the Survey Branch of the Irish Land Commission.

She sent the cutting to the Commonwealth War Graves Commission. From the information, they were able to advise her where in France she would find her uncle Thomas commemorated. Like so many other young men in 1915, Thomas had literally vanished into thin air. All that was left of him was a name on a stone wall in Le Touret Military Cemetery.

Patsy travelled to the Pas de Calais to see for herself, but if she had hoped to find out more about her uncle, she was disappointed. A housewife who had had little time for history until then, she did not know how to connect the name to any more significant information. And the digital revolution that would a couple of decades later open up previously remote archives and libraries to anyone with a keyboard and a modem came too late for her to be able to benefit. So when we talked about her Irish family that afternoon in the hospital, she expressed mostly frustration at how very few fragments there were to piece together, her uncle's name in the cemetery serving as a symbol of a wider loss.

'I was very touched when I saw that, but I wish I knew more. I have no idea what he did in the First World War, only that he got killed in the process. Nor what my other uncles did. You should know your family history, but I'm afraid I can't tell you much. I only hope that one day you'll meet someone who will help you to fill in all the gaps.'

Of course it was obvious why she had left it until now to talk about Quin, but we maintained the pretence of the miraculous recovery. We agreed that as soon as she returned from hospital, we would get down the box of old family photographs and go through them together.

'It will be our little project. I'll come bouncing back, please God. God is more powerful than all the doctors. Well, that's true, isn't it?'

Well, she didn't come bouncing back. She died only a few days later, although I am pleased to say that it was at home, in that house in Hertfordshire. She was moved to a downstairs room, where, surrounded by the family she loved, she was able to look at the garden she loved.

The day of her death, Thursday 29 July 2010, was when this book can be said to have begun. I told myself that I would take on 'our little project' in her memory. I found the box of photographs. Found too, hidden away at the back of her brown leather writing case, the cutting from the *Clare Champion* about the five Irish Royal Engineers.

The idea of those five brothers charting the unmapped lands of Empire, of the Irish NCOs being promoted to officers on the field of battle, of my great-uncle Thomas making the ultimate sacrifice, suggested a story of irresistible romance, a family story entwined in a much larger story.

It was a sad irony, I thought, that it should take the loss of my most important witness to begin to write it, but if the sheer finality of my mother's death highlighted the difficulty of the task, I was old enough not to expect to open up more doors than death closes. The goal would be simply to find out what I could.

II

It was with this vague idea that I returned that very afternoon to Hampstead, where I had grown up. I wanted to light a candle for my mother in St Mary's Church, Holly Place, where she used to attend Mass. If I had imagined this act of remembrance as a fitting prologue to my story, it became clear, even as I stepped out of the Tube station, that memory would soon make the story set off in its own direction. There before me, just across Heath Street, was the shop that many years ago had belonged to my father's father – the one grandfather I had actually got to know. I had a sudden memory flash of what it had looked like in the 1960s, before it was rebuilt.

I remembered too the advertisement that faced the Tube travellers arriving at Hampstead as the lift doors opened: 'Only 39 Steps to Drazin's'. My paternal grandfather, Isaac, belonged to a Jewish

family that had fled the pogroms of the Tsar at the beginning of the twentieth century. He had started out at the age of fourteen as a tailor in the East End, but in 1927 he opened an electrical goods store in Hampstead, which became enough of a success that it was still there fifty years later, although that 'fifty years later' is a whole forty years ago, and it is now much more than only 39 steps to Drazin's.

Britain had taken him in as a refugee and enabled him to prosper. Here was the basis for a patriotism of which my Irish Catholic heritage was also a part. Any family or community or nation has a collection of stories, but the challenge is how we bring those stories together. To this extent, Britain, which had successfully reconciled two such different backgrounds, belonged as much to my story as those five Irish Royal Engineers – Britain pulling the different strands of identity into the same weave. Isaac couldn't boast the twenty-two years in the Colours of my Irish grandfather, but he had won a medal for fire-watching during the Second World War. As I set off up Holly Hill, I passed the clock tower, from where he had once looked out over the burning city.

I found Heath Street closed to traffic that day, the road dug up so that the Victorian water mains could be replaced, leaky and beyond repair after 150 years. Passing bollards that had once been cannons, I soon slipped back even earlier through time, almost to Waterloo. A familiar plaque from my churchgoing childhood, 'Holly Place 1816', announced that I had reached St Mary's, this year celebrating its bicentenary. Flush with the town houses on either side, its discreet facade belonged to the early years of Catholic emancipation when the limits of Britain's religious tolerance were yet to be established. The prominent statue of the Virgin and Child above the entrance was only added many years later when the last doubts had gone.

St Mary's founder, the Abbé Morel, had fled the French Revolution. It was a satisfying trick of continuity that the successor of his whom I got to know was called Father Morrall – Morel, only more so – the ninth of the twelve parish priests who have been the custodians of St Mary's two hundred years so far . . . I remember him now with great nostalgia as a down-to-earth, benign presence, a Brummie who was a convert to Catholicism from the Church of England. Every few weeks, he used to drop by the house we then had in Frognal, where my mother, who looked after the church flowers, treated him to tea and whiskey.

St Mary's had been so much part of my early life that I was upset on that day of all days to find the doors locked, in a way I couldn't imagine they would have been when Father Morrall was alive. I took down a number from the parish board so that I could ask to have a candle lit, but I couldn't dispel the sense of having been banished from a foreign country of the past which had nevertheless provided most of my childhood ideas of home.

This book is about mapping that past. The chief topographical features are Ireland, for all my obvious closeness, mostly imagined from a distance; my mother's father and his four brothers, those surveyors of the 'unmapped lands'; and that British Empire on which the sun may have long ago set but whose ruins still underlie . . . not only my past.

Mapping the past is complicated by the way in which the past endlessly amasses new territories. So, to the major landmark of my mother's death, I had to add that of my father four years later, and, with the sale of their house, the disappearance of so many familiar things that had provided me with bearings over the more than half a century of my own personal past. Although the word is not to be found in the title of this book, perhaps the most permanent feature of the landscape that it seeks to map is transience. Whether it happens through the collapse of an empire, or the death of a parent, things fall apart.

III

I feel this most keenly now, in 2016, in the psychic turbulence of a centenary that marks not only the Easter Uprising and the Battle of the Somme, but also — actually two years before the newspaper cutting stated — the return from France of my Irish grandfather, one of the British army's very best topographical surveyors, to a country whose identity, buffeted by the crises of an apocalyptic time, had changed profoundly from the one that he had left twenty-two years before. Six years ago, my story had seemed very simple – a story of Ireland and five brothers who had mapped the British Empire, but whose own lives remained unmapped to their family. Today it feels as much a story about losing the past as discovering it.

My mother's father, Patrick, had died too early for his children to have any more than the scantiest memories of him. The only possession of his that my mother had managed to keep was a torn old leather suitcase with the initials P.B.L. printed beneath the broken handle. A label inside revealed that it had been bought from Moore's Travellers' Depot, Dublin, purveyor of 'trunks, bags, suit & attache cases, & all travelling requisites'. One day it was accidentally thrown into a skip after a clear-out of the attic. We had to climb in to fetch it out. My mother was furious that we could have got rid of such a precious object with so little regard for its associations.

As the case was not 'regulation issue', I supposed that it belonged to a period of my grandfather's life after he had left the Royal Engineers. Although there seemed to be nothing else that could be deduced about its history, it became even more of a precious heirloom when my mother died, charged with the memory of my grandfather and now her too.

It was too broken to be used for its original purpose, but, as I set out on my journey of mapping the past, it became a suitcase for a different kind of travel, containing the bits and pieces I discovered about P.B.L., his brothers and the Empire they once served, having only the most hazy idea of where they might take me.

PROLOGUE

PART ONE
IRELAND

I

Carrying the Flame

The candle I had wanted to light for my mother reminded me of that afternoon in the hospital with her when she told me, not for the first time, about the day her father died. A neighbour, John Brown, who had a pony and trap, fetched her early from school and dropped her off outside Bridge House. 'Be sure to go straight in, Patsy,' he told her. 'Your daddy will be waiting for you.'

Patsy slipped past the front door and ran into the downstairs room, which had been turned into a bedroom when her father had become ill some months before. The first thing she noticed on entering the room was candles. 'I thought, "What's this? Candles?" Then I looked at the bed, and there was my father laid out.' She was so shocked that she didn't talk for days.

'My mother had been used to money and a successful husband and suddenly he was snatched. Can you imagine what it was like? It was just awful. And I think that blighted my early years. Because I was always thinking, "If only . . ."'

Patsy grew up idealising her father and wanting to find out

everything she could about him. A lifetime later, she was still trying to assemble a coherent image of him out of the scraps of memory. Had we been able to go through the family photographs together, then 'our little project' would have been the continuation of an enquiry that had begun long before I was even born.

My grandfather's very name was a subject of investigation. I had always thought that I had been given my middle name of Bernard after his middle name, but I learned from my mother that afternoon of a doubt over whether it had been his name at all.

'All I know is that he's very much P. B. Lynch. Patrick Bernard. Or Patrick Bennett. My mother told me, "Your father's name is Bernard, not Bennett," but one of my O'Neill cousins said, "No, your father's Bennett." Anyway, I ended up on the wrong side of the argument and I refused to discuss it.'

Soon after her father died, Patsy was sent to stay with her aunt Ellie in Tulla, who was married to Patrick O'Neill. During the week she would go to the Sisters of Mercy convent school in Tulla, then cycle home to Quin for the weekends. With the death of her father, the idyllic life she had known gave way to hardship. Her mother may have been the prettiest girl in the village, but she struggled to cope with nine children on her own, the oldest of whom, Breda, was a seriously ill invalid who needed constant nursing. The family was held together by her much more staunch and practical older sister Annie, who had lost her fiancé during the Great War.

Whenever Patsy met her father's army friends, she would ask them to describe to her what he had been like. She remembered particularly Stephen O'Dea who had grown up in Quin and worked with her father at the Irish Land Commission's headquarters in Merriam Street in Dublin.

'Your father was a gentleman,' he told her. 'Far too good for the bloody Irish government.'

There was only one small correction Patsy received to the picture she had built of her father as a kind, honourable, cultivated man cruelly stranded on the wrong side of Ireland's politics.

'Yes, when he wasn't on the bottle,' Aunt Annie said one day.

'What do you mean?'

'He liked his whiskey, he liked his beer.'

'What's wrong with that?'

'In his job, you have to make only one error . . .'

'But he *never* made any errors,' my mother said to me. 'I couldn't bear the people who didn't like the English. I thought, "Good God, where would they have been without the English army?" They just did not want them there, but they were able to take advantage of English rule, and I was very happy with English rule. I loved it.'

During the war, in which Ireland remained neutral, Patsy followed the radio broadcasts of the BBC closely, rooting for a cause that was inspiring thousands of Irishmen and women to volunteer for service with the British forces, and that she knew would also have been her father's cause.

I think she would have enjoyed Churchill's wartime joke about Eamon de Valera. A British bomber is over Berlin. As one engine catches fire and the rear-gunner is wounded, the Irish pilot mutters, 'Thank God Dev kept us out of this bloody war!'

She had no patience for the careful calculation of small-nation politics with which de Valera abstained from a struggle against obvious evil. She wanted to belong to a big nation that played its part in the affairs of the world; that – floating free of narrow nationalist sentiment – fought for what the Irish writer Oliver

St John Gogarty had called 'the existence of human beings'; and that, finally, had been the country her father had loved. She made her own contribution to the war effort when she baked a cake with deadly laburnum seeds as a welcome gift for any German paratroopers who were foolish enough to invade the village.

With its ruined Franciscan abbey that went back to the time of the Normans, Quin was the kind of picturesque place that de Valera would have regarded as a model for the mythical Old Ireland to which he seemed to want to return. But Patsy found it suffocating. She remembered a place where what mattered was not who you were but who you knew. 'You were nothing without money and influence. And the most influence was with the Church. It made me cross the way the Church courted people who had money, and if it looked like you didn't have any money, they dropped you. That's why although I love the Lord and I depend on Him, I felt very often let down.'

After convent school, she went to a technical college in Ennis and trained to be a secretary. She liked fashion and clothes, so her mother had a word with a family friend, Dr Moylan, who owned the Ennis Cash Company, the town's largest draper's store. He found a job for Patsy in the millinery, napkins and furs department.

'But I thought he was a nasty fellow. When my father died, he didn't lift a finger to help. I said, "I don't want to work in his silly old shop." But my mother said it would be very insulting not to take the job.'

After three years at the Cash Company, she left Quin to work at Clery's department store in Dublin. Across the sea, England beckoned. A distant cousin, Mary Kelly, worked as a nurse near London. Patsy would often see her when she returned home to

Ireland, and loved to listen to her stories. 'I remember thinking that's the country that my father loved.'

Mary nursed at Chase Farm Hospital, which during the war had been part of the Emergency Hospitals Scheme. It was where casualties of the London Blitz and wounded servicemen were treated. 'She knew an awful lot of what had gone on, and I was very taken by it.' The tales of wartime valour made Patsy feel even more proud to be her father's daughter, yet at the same time impatient with what she perceived to be a narrow, parochial Ireland, so she begged her mother to allow her to go to England.

The London of the early 1950s may still have been a city of drab austerity, picking itself up from the war, but for a young woman from the west coast of Ireland, it was a magical, miraculous place, full of possibility, which Patsy loved all the more because she remembered that her father had so often talked of it – this great city, larger than any other, which was home to the world.

Over the years that followed, she became too caught up in the bustle of life – 'the existence of human beings' – to learn much more about her father, but I think she remained close to him through some kind of synchronicity. When she first began to work at Chase Farm Hospital, like her cousin Mary, there were still many soldiers who were having long-term treatment there. But also, to become a nurse in early-fifties Britain, when you had to be single and live in a dormitory, must have been a little like being in the army yourself. And when she did leave nursing to get married, there was another coincidence. For it was to an Admiralty psychologist on permanent secondment to the Royal Aircraft Establishment at Farnborough. Fifty years before, when her father was still with the corps, the Royal Engineers had established the

School of Ballooning there, the direct ancestor of the Royal Air Force.

Now I was taking on the flame that had been lit many years earlier. My first big discovery was the service records of the five Lynch brothers. They had had an even luckier escape than P.B.L.'s suitcase. In September 1940 a German bombing raid set ablaze the War Office archives in London, destroying more than half the files of the seven million men who had served in the British armed forces during the First World War. The surviving documents, water-soaked and badly charred, were microfilmed at the National Archives and then digitised. The World Wide Web has brought the past closer, although my mother, who remained firmly of the analogue age, died just a little too soon to see questions that she had spent her whole life puzzling over settled by the click of a mouse.

Her O'Neill cousin had been right about her father's name. The top of the very first page of P.B.L.'s service record solved that mystery: 'Attestation of No. 28423, Patrick Bennett Lynch, Corps of the Royal Engineers.' Bennett, not Bernard. Bennett: short for Benedict, 'the blessed'. Gathered into one document about twenty-five pages long was a collection of papers that included his attestation, his military history sheet, his medical record, and letters to and from the War Office concerning the award of various medals, certificates and commendations. Every stage of his career from enlistment to discharge was documented:

Special qualifications for employment in civil life: Very superior surveyor . . . Conduct exemplary during his service of 22 years at Home and in Gibraltar, West Africa, Ceylon, Malay States and France.

'West Africa' fell at the end of a line that had been eaten up by one of the many tears and burn marks that riddled these blitzed documents. A lick of flame carried off the word 'Canada'. Patrick had served there between Ceylon and the Federated Malay States, receiving a commendation from the governor general for his work. The exact date of his discharge had also been obscured by fire and water, but from elsewhere in the document I was able to work out that it would have been 31 August 1916. It was exactly twenty-two years earlier, on 1 September 1894, that Patrick joined the Royal Engineers with his older brother John, known as Jack. The attestation stated that he was twenty years old, born therefore in 1874, the same year as Winston Churchill. His brother Jack was nearly twenty-two. A year later, on 30 September 1895, James joined the corps. It was Michael's turn in January 1899, and finally the youngest of the five, Thomas, in January 1904.

The three older brothers, Jack, Patrick and James, enlisted with the stated trade of 'surveyor', the two younger as 'clerks', but I think that the *Clare Champion*'s glamourised account of them in Jack's obituary – wrong, I was finding, in so many details – had been right at least when it stated that all five had worked at the Ordnance Survey's regional office in Ennis. It was the obvious path into military service, because at the end of the nineteenth century the senior management of the Ordnance Survey was still drawn from the Royal Engineers.

The Lynch brothers were first-rate soldiers, but – somewhat at odds with my mother's memories – they were definitely not 'officer class'. They belonged to a poor Catholic family from the west of Ireland. Their father had been a gardener, their mother a servant. While the Anglo-Irish gentry in whose houses their parents had worked could trace their history through family papers accumulated over generations, the Lynches were only a generation beyond Catholic Ireland's catastrophic history of confiscation, famine and eviction. Their own time then added plenty of disruption of its own.

While I should not have been surprised that there were so few family documents to supplement the bare facts of their service, any disappointment I felt soon melted away in my sense of the much bigger story of which they were a part. Their military records provided an emblematic network of connections relating to the British Empire that they both served and mapped.

Indeed, the challenge now seemed less the absence of a story than the presence of too many. These records, which I retrieved through the World Wide Web of the twenty-first century, made up a kind of World Wide Web of the British Empire in the nineteenth, the brothers' travels functioning as hyperlinks to its history. The digital revolution had brought within my reach countless previously unobtainable answers, but the sheer infinity of connections raised so many more questions that I risked being left even more confused than I had been in the beginning. The service records, at least, had the advantage of imposing the limit of the brothers' careers. Their paths diverged widely over twenty-five years but passed through stages that were so carefully catalogued as to offer some basis for order. Whatever the chance and serendipity involved in their various individual journeys, it was finally the War Office that decided their postings according to the underlying strategy of Empire.

I was able to follow the five brothers around the world in the *Handy Shilling Atlas* that once belonged to my grandfather – returned to the suitcase he must surely once have put it in – but the one place I knew I had to see for myself was County Clare, where all their journeys began. The 'Questions to be put to the Recruit before Enlistment' open with the age-old enquiry going back to the time of Ulysses, 'Where are you from and who are your people?' The form of attestation (Army Form B 265) asked: '1. What is your Name?' Then: '2. In or near what Parish or Town were you born?'

Five times over, the Lynch brothers gave the same answer: 'In the Parish of Doora, near the Town of Ennis, in the County of Clare.'

In the box of photographs that my mother and I would have gone through together had she lived, I found several of Ennis, Doora and County Clare, but many more of other stories and other lives. Irish faces from the west, but also Jewish faces from the east. The pictures of Jewish weddings and bar mitzvahs were as numerous as those of first communions. Some faces I could identify, but most of them I couldn't, even though they must have belonged to close relations. All the photographs were mixed up in the box beyond easy disentanglement.

Endless paper wallets – filled with glossy 4×6 colour prints and strips of negative in cellophane – formed a topsoil of the more recent past. Going down through the strata of memory, I reached back to stiff studio photographs of the early twentieth century when everyone dressed for the occasion and no one smiled. Starched collars and formal poses offered an index of social constraint that seemed to stretch through most of the black-and-white age to a sudden liberation in the age of the Instamatic. Suits, hats, ties and uniforms, after an *annus mirabilis* – of about 1963 – gave way to the Kodachrome time of long hair, T-shirts and jeans.

Among the thousands of photographs, I could find only two or three of my mother as a child in Ireland. But she is instantly

recognisable in this picture of a small girl of about five or six, sitting on a chair dressed in a dark skirt and pullover. She looks wet, bedraggled and cross. Standing next to her is her younger brother, Thomas, immaculate in a smart jacket and tie, with a folded handkerchief in his top pocket. A caption on the back explains that their father had taken the picture soon after Thomas had thrown a jug of water over his sister's head.

My mother lived in Ireland before casual picture-taking had become commonplace. The only photographs I know for certain that show her village were taken in the mid-1950s when she was about to say goodbye to it for good. She had brought her fiancé over to Ireland to meet her family. While they were there, she and her brothers showed him Quin Abbey, where she used to play as a child. They climbed to the top of the tower and posed for photographs. There's one of my mother, and another rather

ghostly picture of my dad sitting by the parapet between my mother's brothers Jim (on the left) and Dermot, where some quirk of processing repeats their faces as though they belonged to the departed spirits that they have all since become.

The pipe my dad holds to his mouth fixes the moment even more firmly in a long-ago time, although maybe to smoke a pipe was old-fashioned even then. Ireland itself was another step away from modernity. That night they ate dinner in the Lynch home by the light of an oil lamp, as electricity had yet to arrive in the village.

Sixty years on, the only relation I knew who still lived in the area was a second cousin, Pat Murphy, whom I had met for the first time at my mother's funeral. His grandmother was Ellie O'Neill, the aunt that my mother had stayed with when she went to the Sisters of Mercy school in Tulla. Pat had offered to show me Tulla, Quin, Ennis and all the other places in Clare that my mother would have known, but by the time I was ready to take him up on the offer two years had passed by, so that when I finally got round to sending him an email, it seemed a presumption. At the funeral, there had been the usual exchanges of regret among relations that meet only on such occasions, the usual resolves to see one another more often, but in my Englishness I didn't seriously imagine any such meetings would really happen until the next funeral (although that didn't turn out to be long), or that a distant cousin who had met me only once would necessarily even remember me. Twelve hours later, I received this reply:

I remember meeting you very well and it was a pleasure to do so, other than to say it would have been much more preferable to have met in better circumstances – something in fairness that goes without saying. I will only be delighted to come and meet with you or indeed you are most welcome to call to see me if you so wish, as indeed anybody who may be travelling with you is as equally welcome to drop by. I look forward to meeting you and showing you about. *Slan leat mo Culcathair.* (Best to introduce you to a little Gaelic – translates to 'Goodbye, Cousin'.)

I got in touch with my uncle Thomas about my planned trip. While my mother had stayed away from Quin for good, Thomas had an easier relationship with the past, which meant that, although he too had settled in England, he had returned to Clare several times. He talked of a place that remained 'home'. He told me where to look for the family graves in the grounds of Quin Abbey with the familiarity of someone who had not so long ago seen them himself. He took in his stride the passage of years that my mother had turned into an unbridgeable gulf. Indeed, it was Thomas who had told Pat Murphy about my mother's funeral, making the kind of connection that my mother had shown no wish to encourage until her very last days.

I spoke also to my aunt Joan, who was able to recall the people and places with a dispassion that my mother never had. 'You'll have to go to Deerpark in Doora,' she told me. 'That's where our cousins lived. When you go to Quin, you can go to the abbey and the church, then go over the River Rine and you'll come to our home. The Marlboroughs live there now, they're old family friends – friends of my mother. Then there's that fellow Pat Murphy. You'll find him very informative. Anyhow, it will be relaxing. Nobody worries there. This is what I've discovered. They don't seem to worry about anything at all.'

2

An Irish Village

A week later I was driving through the quiet Clare country-side. When I saw the Shannon for the first time from the plane, I recalled some long-ago kitchen conversation with my mother about how the lands along the river had in ancient times belonged to the Lynches but had been confiscated by the accursed Cromwell.

She gave me the impression of a family that had once been among the great chieftains in wealth and power. Was this really true or just her romantic nature? In the land of the beggar kings, I learned, truth and legend are inextricably entangled. Beyond the motorway of a Celtic Tiger that had retreated only a little while before could be seen ruined castles of an older Ireland that, in the aftermath of the crash, was reasserting itself.

I took the turn-off for Quin and tried to match the features of the landscape to my aunt's description. Where was the bridge? Where was the River Rine? Fields gave way to a development of newish houses, Celtic Tiger houses, but they were no more than a curtain, beyond which the heart of the village remained much the same as it had been when my mother left it in 1950.

Mine was the only car driving up the high street. I reached a small stone bridge, beneath which ran the Rine on its way into the grounds of Quin Abbey. Many years ago this quiet stream had swollen into a torrent of flood waters that had swept away a small child. It was one of the stories that my mother told me: how her older brother Dermot ran along the bank, shinned up an over-hanging tree and pulled off a daring rescue. The old home of the Lynch family, Bridge House, must be somewhere close. I passed the village hall, where my mother used to go to dances, and parked close to the gate that led to the meadow by the abbey. A little further up was the entrance to St Mary's Church. A painted statue of the Virgin stood by the stone wall that separated the street from the meadow. Her blue and white robes picked up the hues of the sunny, cloud-speckled sky behind the abbey in the distance. It lent a gaiety to the idolatry that He-Who-Must-Not-Be-Named had failed to crush in spite of efforts that had included the sacking of the abbey. Roofless, ruined but proud, the cluster of buildings – cloisters, chapel and tower – exerted an immense romantic power that soon had me walking in their direction.

It wasn't difficult to find the Lynch graves. They are almost the first you come to, once you pass through the kissing gate into the friary yard. I couldn't help thinking of my mother whose favourite playground these ruins had once been. The day after her father died, he was moved from Bridge House to lie in repose at St Mary's Church, and on the next day he was buried here only a few yards along the path from the gate. It was an abrupt, nasty end to her childhood.

A Celtic cross, heavily spotted with lichen, marked a grave that contained the remains of three generations of Lynches:

In loving memory of John Lynch, Deerpark, Doora, who died 23rd Sept 1913, aged 73. Also his wife Bridget who died 8th June 1914, aged 70.

And their son, Thomas Joseph, Royal Engineers, who was killed in action in France, 15th May 1915, aged 29.

Patrick Lynch, Quin. Died 14th March 1938, aged 59 years. His daughter Bridget A, died 25th June 1941, aged 17 years. His wife Amelia B, died 30th Jan 1972, aged 73 years.

A little further along, on the other side of the path, I came upon a second headstone which lay flat on the ground. Great splashes of lichen had spread across the face so that only isolated words of the inscription could be deciphered – and that with more guesswork than certainty. 'Here lies . . . Michael Lynch . . . Also James Lynch, Ordnance Survey, who died . . . Deerpark . . .' It wouldn't require too many more years to pass until the rain, falling directly on the slab, would wash away the letters completely.

Some months later I found a record of the full inscription that my uncle Dermot had written a long time ago before the rain had carried away the words:

> Here lies the remains of Michael Lynch, Drim, who died 22nd May 1819 aged 30 yrs. May his soul rest in peace, Amen. Erected by his father, James Lynch, for him and posterity. Also James Lynch, Ordnance Survey, who died 23rd September 1920 of Deerpark, Doora.

'Michael Lynch' was not one of the five brothers, as I had assumed when I saw the stone in the graveyard, but another Michael born a hundred years earlier. And obliterated completely – lost to posterity had it not been for the trouble that Dermot had taken to write out the words – was another James, from the eighteenth century, the oldest known of the Lynches, although beyond his simple existence nothing was known about him at all. Two more graves contained the remains of members of my grandmother's family, the McInerneys. The most recent addition was Aunt Annie, who had died, still a McInerney, in the same year as my grandmother, 1972.

I passed into the halls and cloisters of the abbey to find the gravestones as plentiful there. There were more Lynches and McInerneys, but also all the other families of the village – the Clunes, the Hassetts, the MacNamaras, the O'Hallorans . . . In this place, where there was still a powerful connection between the past and the present, the one became effortlessly the other. Buried beneath the stone slabs of the cloisters are the Franciscan monks who had lived in the abbey. Their inscriptions sketch out the history of the abbey from the fourteenth century, when the MacNamara clan built a church, sacristy and residence in the ruins of an Anglo-Norman castle, to the final extinction of the order in the nineteenth:

Here lies the body of the Revd JOHN HOGAN, of Drim, who departed this life A.D. 1820, aged 80 years, the last of the Franciscan Friars who had their residence at Drim, the place of their refuge when driven from the Abbey of Quin. He was supported by the pious donations of the faithful, and served as an auxiliary to his neighbouring parish priests in the vineyard of the Lord. He knew how to abound and how to suffer want as the Lord was pleased to send. He died in holy poverty, respected for his strictness in religious discipling and venerated by all.

The first time the friars risked being 'driven from the abbey' was when Henry VIII ordered the dissolution of the monasteries, but they stayed on under the protection of the powerful O'Brien clan. During the reign of Elizabeth I, English troops stormed the abbey. Their commander, Sir John Perrot, had one of the O'Briens, Donough Beg, half hanged from a cart. His bones were then broken with an axe and, still alive, he was hanged from the steeple. A handful of friars dared to stay on. They even opened a college, but then, in 1651, Cromwell's soldiers arrived. They shot and beheaded one friar, and hanged two others. This time the monks did not hesitate. They left, but returned again about fifteen years later. When they were expelled a second time, during the years of the Ascendancy, they took up residence in the nearby townland of Drim until they came to the end of the line with John Hogan.

Patrick Lynch's grandfather would probably have been one of the old friar's neighbours. The Lynches lived in Drim until they were evicted from their home at the time of the Great Famine of the 1840s. They moved on to the nearby townland of Doora, and then, after Patrick married into the McInerneys, established themselves in Quin, just a stone's throw from the abbey.

It was while playing in these ruins as a little girl, reading the inscriptions, that my mother received her first lessons in Anglo-Irish history. She would have climbed into the abbey grounds over a stone wall at the end of the garden of Bridge House. The present owner, Anne Marlborough, whose family bought the house from the Lynches in the early 1960s, took me down to see it. Anne had climbed over the same wall when she was a child.

'Nowadays you can't go up in the tower,' she explained, 'but when I was a child that's where we would have spent our lives.'

She showed me round the house in which my mother had been born – the large front room that in the Lynches' time was the lounge of the pub, the room on the other side of the hallway where Patrick spent his last days, and then upstairs.

'There used to be handbasins in all of the bedrooms,' she pointed out. 'It was a very progressive, modern house for its time.'

I had met Anne Marlborough in that special dimension of invisible connections that is peculiarly Irish. With me was Lena O'Loughlin and her daughter Niamh. Lena was the sister of Eddie Hughes, whom I knew in London. When I told Eddie that I was going to visit a little village in Ireland called Quin, where my mother came from, he told me that his sister Lena was married

to a farmer there, and I should look her up. This kind of seem-
ingly fantastic coincidence is the ordinary way in Clare, where
everyone seems to know everyone. So Lena then introduced me
to Anne.

Sitting at a table in my mother's old garden, I leafed through
a book of local history that Anne had fetched for me. 'Despite
the counter-influences of the modern era,' began the foreword, 'it
is still good to be part of a parish community in rural Ireland. It is
good to know your neighbours and to be known by them; to
share a concern for each other's welfare, to have a sense of place
and to identify with it, to feel you belong.' The book included
memories of the village from local people that went back to the
time when the Lynches still lived in Bridge House. There was also
a reproduction of a torn and creased photograph with the caption:
'Girls attending Quin National School in the 1930s'. At the left
end of the second row stood my mother: Patsy Lynch, only seven
or eight years old. In the first row was Patsy's sister Joan, and
her brother Jim, who was the only boy in the picture but – as I
learned from my aunt later – had been allowed that afternoon to
join the girls because he was her twin. On the next page was the
photograph of all the other boys at the school, with my mother's
brothers Dermot in the back row and Thomas at the front.*

I was thinking that the words RIP, which had been scribbled
on the chest of one of the girls, could now be wished to almost
the entire class, when Anne interrupted: 'Good news!'

She pointed to a girl called Carrie Clune, who was in the same
row as Patsy.

* 'Ancient times!' my father replied when I emailed a copy to him. 'I have
never seen these photos, nor known of their existence. Your mother was just
the same as ever.'

'This woman's still alive. She lives here in the village. You could try and meet her. She's one of those people who have time on their hands.'

'I think this must be her house,' said Lena a little later, knocking on the door.

An old lady with a plump, rosy face answered.

'Carrie?' asked Lena.

'Hello.'

'Carrie, I'm married to Rory O'Loughlin out in Corbally, Duckle's son.'

'Come in, now. Come in.'

'This is my daughter Niamh, Duckle's granddaughter.'

'Hello, my dear.'

'And this is Charles.'

'How do you do, Charles.'

'Charles's family – '

'Come and sit down. I'm just finishing my dinner and having a glass of wine. Will you join me? Of course you will! What a lovely surprise to find some of my people coming to see me.'

Carrie went into the kitchen to fetch a bottle of wine and glasses.

'Now then, we're sitting down. You can tell me why you're here.'

'*Slainte!*' said Lena.

'*Slainte*,' replied the old lady. 'And welcome, whoever you are!'

'My mother grew up in Quin,' I began. 'She was Patsy Lynch. And I think you were in the same class.'

'Patsy Lynch?'

'Yes.'

'Now who was her brother?'

'Dermot.'

'I can't believe it! Yes, I remember the Lynch girls. And Mrs Lynch. But I'm very old now, so my memory is not good. But it's funny, the name I remember most of all is Dermot, who would have been your uncle. A very imposing boy, very tall. You know, there's a book of the village with pictures.'

'Yes, we've seen it. Anne Marlborough suggested we called on you because you appeared in a photograph of the school, with Patsy Lynch.'

Carrie fetched her own copy of the book and sat down beside me. We turned to the page with the school picture.

'That's my mother. That's Patsy Lynch.'

'Now she was in the same class as me.'

One by one, Carrie went through the faces in the row. 'Ciss MacNamara, Betty O'Halloran, I remember her. And Winifred

Meaney. Is that Winifred Meaney? That's right. And the fat little one is me.'

'Philomena Clune. Is that your sister?'

'No, she's another Clune. She's still around, but she's a nun. When she comes home, she always comes to see me. I have to get the afternoon tea ready. She likes a little bit of the best china.'

She went back over the faces, recalling what she could of them. 'They were my classmates, that group.'

The infants at the school were taught by a Mrs Clune, and the older children by the principal, Stephen Clune. Two more Clunes who were not related to her. The thing she remembered most about Stephen Clune was his cruelty.

'What is a quarter of a penny?' he asked her once.

'A quarter of a penny is a quarter of a penny.'

He slapped her for giving a wrong answer. 'What is a quarter of a penny?'

'Twenty-five per cent.'

He slapped her again.

'0.25.'

And again.

After several more whacks, the answer that he was looking for dawned on her. 'A quarter of a penny is a farthing.'

'We were different politics, and maybe that accounted for it.'

'Politics back then would really have carried a lot of weight,' said Lena. 'It was one or the other. Ireland in towns and villages was very split politically.'

Carrie had retired home to Quin only a few years before after spending her working life as a teacher in England. At about the same time as Patsy Lynch's father died, Carrie lost her mother. Her father, who struggled to look after a family of five children, sent her away to a convent school in Gort. From there, she went to university in Galway, where – in spite of Stephen Clune – she studied mathematics. By the time she graduated, her father had also died. Since there was now no need to stay in a poor country where it was so difficult to find employment, she crossed the Irish Sea to become a maths teacher at a girls' school in Gravesend, Kent. It was the familiar Irish path. Her school was only a few miles away from Chatham, where a generation earlier the Lynch brothers had begun their training with the Royal Engineers.

It was nearly dark when we said goodbye to Carrie. We had stayed much longer than we had intended.

'I hope I've been of some help,' she said.

'You were very gracious to receive us,' Lena replied.

'You're a bit of my youth. It was so strange that I'd been looking at that picture only yesterday.'

3

Only Yesterday

When I googled the name of Clune some time later, I came upon not only a glowing tribute from the schoolgirls of Gravesend to 'Carrie Clune, a legend in her own Maths class!', but also a feature story on Quin, 'A Village in Ireland', that *Life* magazine had published in July 1939. Accompanying a photograph of the Irish tricolour flying from the tower of Quin Abbey was the headline 'A NEW FLAG BRINGS HOPE TO AN OLD AND PIOUS LAND'. The headline on the following double-spread, split between the two pages, read 'THE VILLAGE OF QUIN ...' on one page, and 'BELONGS TO THE CLUNES' on the other. An aerial photograph was labelled with the owners of the houses and various plots of land.

It was true. The Clunes were everywhere from Dan Cider Clune next door to where the recently bereaved Lynch family lived – their property labelled simply 'Pub' – to Stephen Johnny Clune opposite the post office on the Tulla road. You could tell the story of the whole village through the Clunes, and the story of the whole country through the village. They seemed to

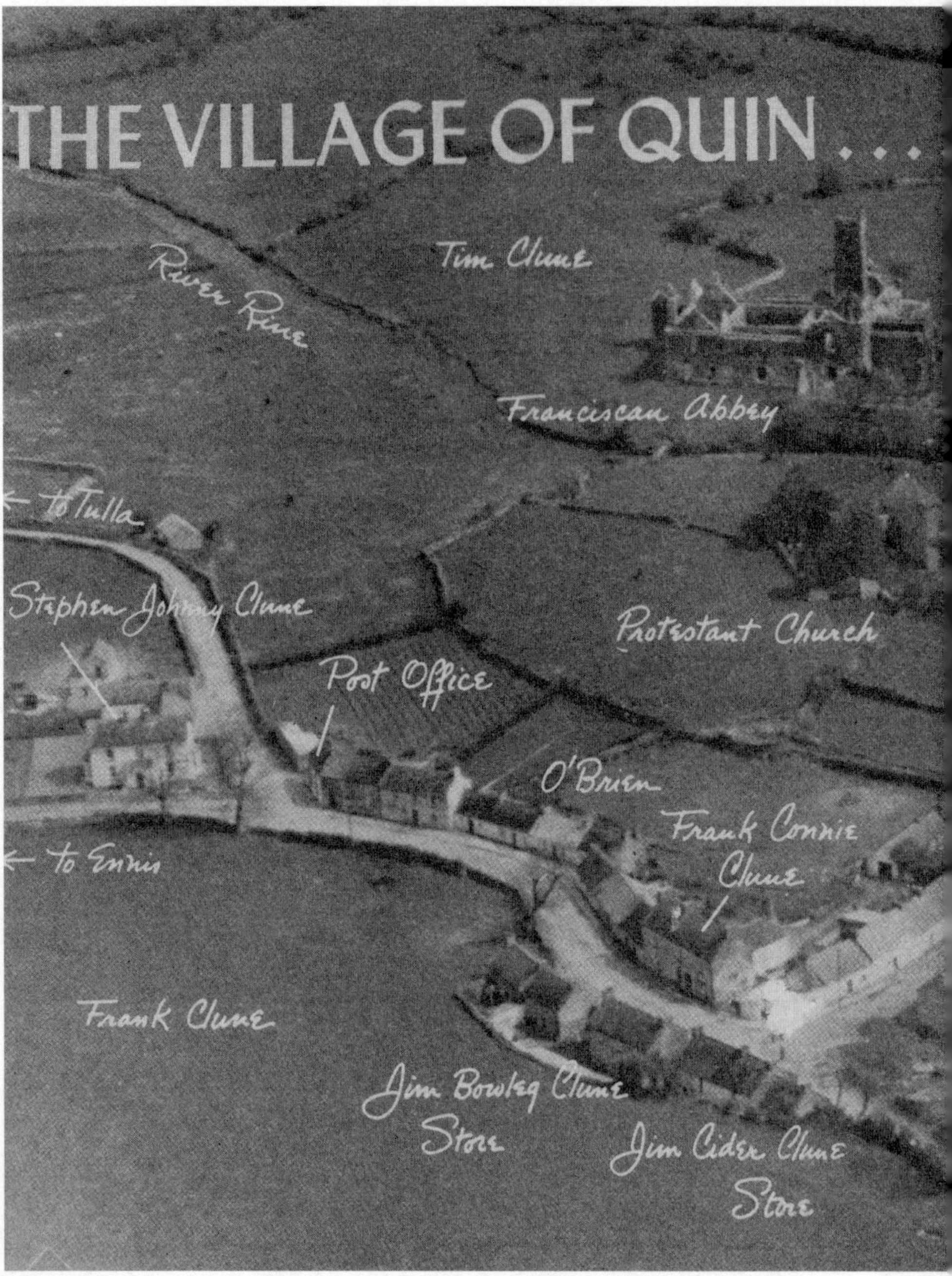

THE VILLAGE OF QUIN...

River Rine

Tim Clune

Franciscan Abbey

to Tulla

Stephen Johnny Clune

Post Office

Protestant Church

O'Brien

Frank Connie Clune

to Ennis

Frank Clune

Jim Bowleg Clune Store

Jim Cider Clune Store

BELONGS TO THE CLUNES

to Kilkishen

Priest

Police

Catholic Church

River Rine

Pub

Dan Cider Clune

Bridge

Pub

Power

Pub

Baker

Corbett

Power's Pub

Paddy Johnny Clune

Willie Johnny Clune

Patrick Corbett

Jim Johnny Clune

Jim Johnny Clune

occupy every walk of life, the Clunes. Teacher, nun, shopkeeper, even rebel.

A year later, the village became representative of Ireland again when *Picture Post* devoted most of its issue for 27 July 1940 to the country. At a time of national crisis when France had just fallen and the Battle of Britain was about to begin, the magazine asked how a neutral Ireland could be defended in the face of a possible Nazi invasion. In considering whether Britain might come to Ireland's aid, it summarised the troubled relations between the two countries that made the question so difficult and ran several articles offering a profile of contemporary Irish life. Quin appeared in an illustrated feature called 'An Irish Village', which included pictures of the church, village store, a farmer tilling

the fields, Mrs Flaherty with her spinning wheel, and, inevitably, the abbey, with some of Quin's cows chewing the cud in the foreground.

'A Memorial to a Past Invasion,' declared the caption that accompanied the picture of the abbey. 'Quin's Franciscan Abbey, built in 1402, was sacked by Oliver Cromwell's men in 1649. The ruins dominate the village, a monument to a faith that still lives, and a national grievance that has never died. Generations of Clunes are buried in its grounds.'

There was national grievance but also division. One of the Clunes was Conor Clune, for whom a commemorative plaque had been erected near the abbey entrance. While my grandfather and great-uncles had helped to map the British Empire, Conor Clune was among those on the other side of the divide who had fought the Empire.

He was killed during one of the most notorious episodes of the Anglo-Irish War of Independence, when IRA leader Michael Collins ordered the assassination of members of the 'Cairo Gang', a group of British undercover intelligence agents. In the early hours of 21 November 1920, Collins's hit squad killed fourteen men. The British reaction later on ensured that the day would go down in history as Ireland's bloodiest Bloody Sunday. In the afternoon, the security forces turned up at a Gaelic football match in Dublin's Croke Park stadium looking for suspects. Opening fire indiscriminately on the crowd, they left fourteen dead. But there was still the evening to come, when Conor Clune was one of three prisoners to be killed after being interrogated in Dublin Castle. There is conflicting evidence about exactly what happened, but the Republican version that they were murdered after refusing to reveal what they knew about the IRA attacks on the British intelligence agents seems plausible. At a post-mortem, Conor Clune was found to have been shot thirteen times in the chest.

The Gaelic inscription that marked his grave in Quin Abbey said that he had 'died for Ireland', but really he was just in the wrong place at the wrong time. A member of the Gaelic League that promoted the use of the Irish language, he was a Republican supporter, who had on the day before the attacks turned up at Vaughan's Hotel, Parnell Square, to see Piaras Béaslaí, the publicity director of the revolutionary Irish Parliament. Unknown to him, Michael Collins and other IRA leaders happened to be there putting the final touches to their plans. When the British, who had received a tip-off, raided the hotel, they escaped but Clune was arrested.

In the *Life* and *Picture Post* photographs, there was much intelligence to be gleaned about the reality of a 1930s village in Ireland, when the mass of its people had, in the words of *Life*, to 'grub for a living'. In this poor rural community, there were no gardens, only extra land to be cultivated. In one picture, Amby Power, former captain of Clare's victorious All-Ireland hurling team of 1914, could be seen planting potatoes behind his pub, 'a little behindhand', according to the caption, because the potatoes should be down by St Patrick's Day when the 'hard' days begin. On the other side of the street, the Lynches would probably have been doing much the same on the land behind their pub.

The road that ran past the Lynch home led to a Protestant church, which the massive presence of the ruined abbey behind made look rather small. Only three families of the dwindling Anglo-Irish gentry continued to use it, driving in once a month from their big

houses in the surrounding countryside. A few years later it was taken down and its bricks used to build a wall in nearby Clarecastle. The spirit of the Franciscans never left the land. The principal source of authority and power in Quin, appropriately situated across the road from the police station, was the Catholic church.

Missing from the aerial photographs was Fineen's Hall, which in 1942, soon after the photo-journalists had departed, was built with some of the Church's wealth just a few yards up the road from the Lynch pub by the River Rine.

The family box of photographs provides some supplementary evidence of the way the village was. Two pictures, which must have been taken during that 1950s afternoon when my mother and father climbed the abbey tower, show the massive Catholic church of St Mary's, which would years later be renovated beyond all recognition, and the back of Fineen's Hall, stretching almost to the Protestant church behind – tiny enough to be easily carted away in a few wheelbarrows.

The new hall may have offered a place where young people could dance, but it wasn't enough to make up for the lack of opportunity. The photographs also help to explain why young people like Carrie Clune and Patsy Lynch felt they had to leave Quin to find a better future. It was an achingly beautiful land, but one where the only decent employment prospects were for priests and farmers.

The next morning I visited nearby Ennis, the county town, where Patsy Lynch got her first and only job in Clare before leaving for good. I found the Cash Company, still in business a lifetime later on O'Connell Street. As Quin was the typical Irish village for *Life*

magazine, so an astonishing amount of Ireland's history was funnelled through its nearest town. Just that one street was a close mesh of the personal, local and national.

At the top is O'Connell Square, where the 'Great Liberator',

49

Daniel O'Connell, stands on his pillar. The monument was built on the site of the old courthouse. It was here that in 1828 O'Connell became, as the parliamentary candidate for Clare, the first Catholic in modern history to be elected to the House of Commons, although it wasn't until the passage of the Emancipation Act in 1829 – and after he had stood for election a second time – that he was allowed to take his seat. Another landmark election took place here in July 1917, after Major Willie Redmond, MP for East Clare, was killed in action at the Battle of Messines. Brother of the nationalist leader John Redmond, he must have been one of the oldest soldiers on the Western Front. The photograph I found of him, in the online collection of the National Portrait Gallery, in which he is wearing the cap of the Royal Irish Fusiliers, suggests a kind of Irish Colonel Blimp. He believed that

the war against Germany was a fight for the greater good which would also help to win Home Rule for Ireland and reconcile the division between Catholics and Protestants. But when Sinn Féin won the by-election that was called to fill his vacant seat, it confirmed a ruthless new militancy that had no faith in the constitutional path. Their candidate was one of the rebel leaders who had fought in the Easter Rising and been released from prison only a few months before: Eamon de Valera.

In the Clare Museum, just off O'Connell Square, this most sulphurous period of Ireland's history is kept behind glass. I looked at a cabinet which contained some representative artefacts from a hundred years ago: a Webley revolver that had been used in the War of Independence during an IRA attack on an RIC barracks; a constable's spiked helmet, which could easily have belonged to an Irishman who had been on the receiving end of the Webley; and, between the two, the 'Proclamation of the Provisional Government of the Irish Republic'.

This particular copy was torn and stained enough to make it easy to picture the week of bloodshed that it provoked. On Easter Monday 1916, Patrick Pearse stood between two columns of the imposing GPO building that the rebels had seized and began to read out the declaration. 'Irishmen and Irishwomen,' he began, 'in the name of God and of the dead generations from which she receives her old tradition of nationhood, Ireland, through us, summons her children to her flag and strikes for her freedom . . .' A few passers-by would have stopped to listen, but I imagine that in this first moment of the Rising the number of people would have been no more than might have clustered around a harebrained zealot in Speakers' Corner. By the time the rebellion had been crushed six days later, the city centre had been devastated by shelling and over four hundred people had lost their lives. Compared to the blood-letting of Flanders it was really rather minor, but while no amount of munitions could help Britain break out of the stalemate of the trenches, the 'terrible beauty' of Easter 1916 was to show how completely violence could change the mood of Ireland, whether it was the original blood sacrifice of the rebels or the harsh retribution of the British. Spared the death by firing squad that was meted out to sixteen of the other leaders of the rebellion, the shrewd new MP for East Clare knew how to take advantage.

The most eye-catching exhibit in the cabinet was a large emerald-green Sinn Féin banner, as heavily decorated as the Book of Kells. 'A NATION ONCE AGAIN,' it declared. In the bottom half was the image of a phoenix with outstretched wings rising from the fire. Above were the Gaelic words '*Eirim chun mo ghníomh a chríochnú*'; below, their English translation: 'I arise to complete my task'. Incorporated into the top half was a photograph of the man my mother cursed almost as much as Cromwell. As I looked at a young Eamon de Valera in his Irish Volunteers uniform, I recalled the bitterness with which she talked of a man whose hold over Clare was so strong that he was still the parliamentary representative for the county when she left Ireland. It was known as 'Dev's County', and Dev's Ireland was the country she was thinking of when she said to me, '*So now you know why I came to England.*'

Standing before the glass, I shivered with an inherited, unthinking, visceral dislike. But then the odd thought occurred to me: I would not be alive were it not for this man, whose vision of Ireland served only to hasten my mother's departure across the sea.

It was actually Patsy's brother Thomas who was the first to make the journey. It's no longer there now, but when Patsy was

working for the Cash Company in Millinery, Napkins and Furs, Thomas had a job at the O'Connell Bar just across the street.

A victim of the same Stephen Clune who had whacked Carrie Clune's hand, Thomas left school at fourteen. His mother had wanted him to follow his older brother Dermot to the Christian Brothers' school in Ennis, but he had no patience with an education that had to be beaten into you with a strap. After odd jobs helping the local farmers, working in the village post office, or putting up posts in the surrounding countryside for the electricity that had still to arrive in Quin, the job in the bar was Thomas's longest stretch of employment in Ireland. The fact that he had stuck it out for three years – long twelve-hour days for only thirty shillings a week – was some measure of the stagnant economy in County Clare. When his cousin Tommy O'Neill came into the bar on a visit back from England, he told Thomas that he would help him get a proper job 'beyond'. Sooner than expected, Thomas would take him up on the offer, when one night the O'Connell was raided by the Guards for after-hours trading.

I continued on down the street until I came to the Old Ground Hotel, where the Sinn Féin leadership stayed when it campaigned for de Valera in 1917. One of its members was Countess Constance Markiewicz, whose hotel registration form was another exhibit in the Clare Museum: 'Surname: Markiewicz. Nationality: Irish. Birthplace: Ireland. Business: Irish Republic's. Trade or occupation: Rebel.' A year later the rebel became the first woman ever to be elected to the House of Commons, although she refused to take her seat. Renouncing Westminster, the successful Sinn Féin candidates, who won 73 out of 105 Irish constituencies, formed the Dáil Eireann, the Irish Parliament, in Dublin and declared a republic.

The short walk from the O'Connell monument at the top of the street to the Old Ground Hotel at the bottom had taken me from emancipation to revolution in not even a hundred years. I couldn't doubt that the final outcome of independence was right, but as a son of a daughter of an Irish Royal Engineer, I wished it had happened in a different way. The 'terrible beauty' seemed, to me, a very ugly twist of history that had perpetuated the bitterness and the bloodshed. While rebels became Founding Fathers, men who were no less patriotic or brave were forgotten and reviled.

A tissue of contested facts and feeling, the past cannot be mapped with any precision. The history of ordinary families, where there are no 'Great Men', exists even more in the realm of speculation.

When my mother talked about 'Deerpark', where her father and brothers had grown up, she gave me the impression of a big house of the kind that the local Anglo-Irish gentry might have lived in, rather than a cottage with only three rooms that the family didn't even own. It was only after she died that I discovered that 'Deerpark' was not a mansion but a 'townland', an ancient, pre-Norman division of land that included both pasture and dwellings. The parish of Doora was made up of thirty townlands, each not more than about two or three hundred acres at most.

I found the vagueness of the word appealing. In denoting a place that was neither town nor county but something in between, it reflected the organic interaction between a land and its community. There was a human scale to it that seemed typical of a country still relying on local knowledge rather than postcodes to deliver the mail.

The cottage where the five Lynch brothers were born had long ago been pulled down. The last living connection with the place had been my mother's cousin, Father Paddy Lynch, whom I remembered from occasional visits he had made to London, but he had died just a few weeks before my mother.

In the graveyard of St Brecan's Church, Doora, I found his tombstone, which also remembered his younger brother Barney:

In Memory of
Father PATRICK (PADDY) LYNCH
Deerpark, Doora
died 2 June 2010
aged 90 years
His Brother
Father BENEDICT (BARNEY)
Interred in Canberra, Australia
died 5 July 2008

aged 87 years
Requiescat in Pace

Close by I found a second family monument:

MICHAEL LYNCH, Deer Park,
who died 8th June 1927
His daughter MARY MONICA
Died 15th Aug. 1927 aged 7 weeks
and his wife ELLEN JOSEPHINE (née CAHILL)
died 18th March 1960
Also their son MICHAEL KEVIN
who died in New Guinea Aug 1943

Michael Lynch was my mother's uncle, the second youngest of the five Lynch brothers who had joined the Royal Engineers. His son Michael Kevin had died of blackwater fever when he was with the Australian Army fighting the Japanese during the Second World War. The Lynch family certainly seemed to exemplify Ireland's tradition of producing soldiers and priests. There were the brother priests Paddy and Barney, but their sister too, Agnes, who had joined the Poor Clares, a contemplative order of nuns in Belfast. My mother remembered her aunt Ellen as an 'old bag', whom she disliked visiting. She couldn't understand why her uncle had married her. One reason might have been for her money. The Cahills were the most prosperous family in Deerpark, who had made a fortune in the Australian gold mines.

Michael was around long enough to give Ellen four children who survived to adulthood, but otherwise he spent most of his last years in Australia, where the oldest Lynch brother, Jack, had settled before the First World War. The explanation passed down within the family was that he had hoped that the dry air would help him to recover from the tuberculosis of which he eventually died, but it seems strange that he left his young family behind in Ireland.

Whatever the real reasons were, they were not something that his children wanted to talk about. While I had met Father Paddy only once or twice, one of my Irish cousins, Paula, got to know him quite well, often visiting him at the Cahill house in Deerpark to where he retired. Although he was happy to reminisce about the past, she remembered that the mood darkened at the mention of his father, whom he refused to discuss.

But he made up for this reluctance with the most glowing memories of his uncle Patrick – Patsy's father, and my grandfather. After Michael died in 1927, Patrick did his best to look out for his brother's children. It was Patrick who bought Paddy his first bicycle. He often used to walk across the fields from Quin with his dog and gun to Deerpark, and take his nephew with him on trips across Clare. His work for the Irish Land Commission involved him surveying the countryside, which he knew better than anyone.

The immense affection with which Father Paddy talked of Patrick was all the more striking to Paula because it was so very different from the account she had had of her grandfather from her own father, Dermot, who remembered a stern man with an often fierce temper.

'To hear Father Paddy talk about Dad's dad, he was the most wonderful man in the world. So I think maybe Dad and his father just didn't hit it off.'

But I wondered to what extent it was simply the vagaries of time and chance that accounted for such differences of recollection.

Born in 1926, Dermot was six years younger than Paddy. So much would have changed by the time that he was old enough to go out with his father. Between 1924 and his death in 1938, Patrick and his wife Amelia had twelve children, of whom three died in infancy. To add to the cares of a growing family, he also had the worry of his eldest child Breda. Paralysed with poliomyelitis, she breathed with the help of an iron lung. All sorts of efforts had been made to cure her. She had even been taken to a doctor in Edinburgh that the family knew through the Clunes. But nothing had worked. Then there was the fact that Patrick spent most weeks in Dublin, where he worked at the headquarters of the Land Commission in Merriam Street, returning to Quin only for the weekends. There was no longer the leisure of earlier times that his nephew Paddy had benefited from. Perhaps, too, in those last years, which coincided with a period of particularly bad relations between Britain and Ireland, his British army background was held against him. I could imagine that there were plenty of reasons to make him more than usually fond of his drop of whiskey, easily available to him in the lodgings he took at the Brazen Head Inn.

The only certain thing was the uniquely different experience of their father that each child had. If Dermot suffered from some weight of parental expectation as the oldest son, his sister Patsy, three years younger, was indulged, but old enough, at the age of nine, to take his loss as a shattering blow. The next sister, Joan, was four years younger. She had only the most shadowy memories of her father putting down his bags and sweeping her up in his arms when he arrived home at the weekends. Once, when he bought a toy pram for Patsy, he bought a smaller pram for her. It was navy blue with a little doll that she could put inside, and small enough that she could push it along a garden seat. She remembered too the big car in which a chauffeur called Brody used to drive her father across the county. On one occasion it was used for a family trip to Kilkee. Her four-year-old self had been so frightened of the sound the engine made that, running round and round the car, she refused to get in. These were the sum total of memories that she had of her father, but their very scarcity spared her the pain of losing him, and, with no strong impression of life ever having been much different, she adapted more easily than Patsy to the reduced means that his death entailed. The youngest child, Theresa, was only an infant when her father died. She had no memory of him at all, but she felt that she had known him very well, because her mother, past the years of greatest crisis, often used to talk about him. 'I'll be seeing you tomorrow, Mum,' Theresa said when she saw her mother in hospital the day before she died. 'I don't think so, Theresa. I'll be with your dad.' Out of these different recollections, you could weave no one account that could actually be called 'history'; your idea of the past depended on who you were, what you had suffered and what you wished for.

4

Across the Banner County

It was Friday 27 July 2012, the first day of the London Olympics, when the world was looking at Britain. The opening ceremony offered a vision of a country that had at last moved on from the role – so familiar to my generation – of the nation that had lost its Empire.

In a feel-good version of history, the Britain that my grandfather and great-uncles had served was airbrushed away. The only hint that the Empire might even have existed was a carnival version of the SS *Windrush*, which had brought the Caribbean immigrants to England. Moving from the Industrial Revolution to the NHS, a national pageant wove a tapestry of a compassionate, confident, multicultural and egalitarian Britain, building Jerusalem in its own green and pleasant land rather than possessing other lands. The director of the show happened to be the son of Irish Roman Catholics from the west of Ireland, while one of the most successful British athletes in the Games had come to Britain as a child refugee from Somalia. A defining image was to become Mo Farah wrapping himself in a Union flag that was no longer a symbol of imperial might but represented a tolerant, inclusive society.

This was the day on which my cousin Pat Murphy gave me a tour of the county.

'*Céad míle fáilte,*' he said as I got into his car. 'Now you're wondering what that means.'

'A hundred thousand welcomes.'

'Very good.'

Soon we had worked out the family connection. My grandfather Patrick was one of the five Lynch brothers and my grandmother Amelia was one of the six McInerney sisters. While Amelia married Patrick Lynch, her sister Ellie married Pat Murphy's grandfather Patrick O'Neill. So here we were, by some pleasing symmetry, grandsons of the two Patricks.

Céad míle fáilte. Only a few weeks earlier Martin McGuinness, a former commander of the Provisional IRA but then deputy prime minister of Northern Ireland, had wished 'a hundred thousand welcomes' to the Queen of England when she made a Diamond Jubilee visit to Northern Ireland. These were astonishing times for Anglo-Irish relations, where we saw the unimaginable happen before our eyes. The previous year the Queen had visited the Republic for the first time in her sixty-year reign. Then she had spoken of the 'importance of forbearance and conciliation, of being able to bow to the past, but not be bound by it'. Thirteen months later, she showed her own readiness to loosen what she had called the 'knot of history' by shaking hands with a man who had fought the British state for the best part of thirty years. Her apple-green coat and dress matched McGuinness's green tie. The spirit of forbearance and conciliation seemed to generate a genuine warmth. *'Slán agus beannacht,'* said McGuinness when they parted. 'Goodbye and Godspeed.'

No one who witnessed that moment, either there or watching on TV around the world, could doubt that the words were meant. A long, difficult but close relationship was on the right road at last. The clenched fist of Ulster had been turned into a handshake.

As we drove across Clare, Pat and I talked about an extraordinary gesture that was still fresh in people's minds.

'I'd be no more than fair in saying that it surely took much more for the Queen and Prince Philip than it did for McGuinness,' said Pat. 'Because, after all, their uncle had been killed.'

In 1979 an IRA bomb blew up Lord Mountbatten while he was on holiday in Ireland. A cousin of the Queen as well as Prince Philip's uncle, Mountbatten had not only played an important part in bringing the royal couple together, but had also been a mentor to their son Prince Charles.

'Their uncle was killed by people that McGuinness represents. Not easy. Maybe they did it out of a sense of protocol, but you have to be fair now. Forget who they are. They're human beings like you and me. It required an enormous effort.'

It wouldn't have been difficult to turn Mountbatten into a symbol of the British military presence in Ireland – last Viceroy of India, First Sea Lord, Chief of the Defence Staff . . . but on a human level he was just somebody's uncle. The Queen's special achievement, in her visit to Ireland, was to reach the individual closeness beyond the contested history:

There are other stories written daily across these islands which do not find their voice in solemn pages of history books, or newspaper headlines, but which are at the heart of our shared narrative.

Many British families have members who live in this country, as many Irish families have close relatives in the United Kingdom.

These families share the two islands; they have visited each other and have come home to each other over the years. They are the ordinary people who yearned for the peace and understanding we now have between our two nations and between the communities within those two nations; a living testament to how much in common we have. These ties of family, friendship and affection are our most precious resource. They are the lifeblood of the partnership across these islands.

We passed the disused railway station at Ardsollus townland, in the countryside outside Quin. This is where the Lynches began their journey to the other island. It would have been quite a walk through the countryside, whether you were the five brothers coming from Deerpark, in Doora, or my uncle Thomas who made the same journey from Quin village fifty years later. You would be lucky if you knew someone with a pony and trap to take you there.

'Tom walked there carrying two suitcases,' said Pat. 'Most likely your mother did the same. There were no cars, no buses, no taxis. So most likely she walked out exactly the same as everybody else walked out. This was the walk. There was nobody to drive you.'

He pointed to a green postbox in the wall. 'The first postboxes in England were that colour. They painted them green. So they were green in Ireland too. It was the standard colour. But then there were so many accidents with people bumping into them all the time that they did a study and decided to find a more visible colour. So everywhere, including here, they were changed to red.

But when the country became independent, our new leaders painted them green, not realising that the Brits had painted them green first. Anything rather than what the Brits did, even if there had been a good reason.'

We took the road to Tulla, where Patsy had been sent to live with her aunt Ellie after her father had died; and where Pat himself – one of Aunt Ellie's grandchildren – had grown up.

After a failed effort, on the outskirts of Quin, to find a gate where my uncle Tom had got into trouble with a fierce dog, Pat drove on into the open countryside. A few minutes later, he stopped and got out of the car. Pointing over a stone wall, he said, 'That is where the High Kings of Thomond were crowned before the English came to Ireland.'

All I could see was a grassy mound.

'And that is Hell Bridge. There is a legend that the Devil flew over the country one night and landed right here.' He pointed at two cracks in the top edge of the wall. 'They're called the Devil's marks. He then flew off in the direction of Killaloe and took a bite out of a mountain, which they call the Devil's Bit.'

He was about to explain further, when we heard the sound of a van coming towards us from the Tulla direction. It stopped next to us and the driver wound down the window.

'Meet Tom O'Loughlin,' said Pat, 'the brother of Rory O'Loughlin who you were having dinner with the other night.' He then explained to Tom how I had come to know Rory through his wife's brother Eddie Hughes in London.

'Ah, he knows the Hugheses.'

'He knows the Hugheses. That's it. On the button. It's a small world.'

'My God, it is, Pat. That without a doubt.'

'He's originally from Quin – the Lynches from Quin.'

'Ah, the pub.'

'On the button!'

'I was in there as a young lad.'

'You remember?'

'All I was getting that time was lemonades.'

'You were there, though.'

'That would have been up to the sixties. Was it '62 or '63?'

I told him that I thought it was '62. By that time, the Lynch children were either in England or had moved to Dublin. Their mother and Aunt Annie were on their own, so Dermot persuaded them that it would be better for them to move to Dublin too. The house and pub were sold to the Marlboroughs.

'Do you come home often?' asked Tom O'Loughlin.

'This is the first time I've ever been to Quin.'

'Oh, good God Almighty, that won't do at all.'

'His mum passed away two years ago,' explained Pat. 'So for her sake, he came to Quin.'

'Ah, why wouldn't you?'

'He wanted to tie down the roots.'

'You were related to the Lynches, Pat?'

'That's right.'

'Your mother's side?'

'My mother was first cousin of his mother.'

'My God.'

'Sure, they spent all of their youth together. They were always together. Small world. And Tom Lynch, his uncle now beyond, worked along this road. If you look in the fields there, you'll see a line of poles. Tom put those up when the electricity came to

Tulla. When I came along this road with him, he was able to tell me who owned all the farms. If he's over again, I'll bring him in to you.'

'I'd love to meet the man.'

'Because he'd know all the people along the road now, left and right.'

'Ah, he would.'

'They used to walk to Tulla this way.'

'Do you know, it's a funny thing now, it was the same in Tulla – on your ten fingers you could count all the families that were in Quin.'

'That's the way it was.'

'Towns and villages were smaller.'

'They were different times.'

'Are you looking at the kings?'

'Wouldn't you think they'd make something of it?'

Coming from over-merchandised England, I found a charm in the fact that they hadn't, and was pleased to be in a place where the present lives side by side with the past without feeling the need to show it off. In Ireland you stumble across wonders that astonish all the more for the lack of announcement.

'There's a stone over there where they used to wash their hands.'

Tom climbed down from his van to show us. For a brief while that evening the Quin to Tulla road was completely blocked.

'On the mound? The kings used to wash their hands?'

'Yes.'

'It was found somewhere?'

'It's always been there.'

'Jaysus!'

'You see the tree? There's a basin inside there.'

'A stone basin? Was it always there? In your youth now, was it always there to be seen?'

'For about eight or nine hundred years. If you stood it up, you'd find the print of their fingers. At one time it was probably a sundial. There would have been a ring of them around.'

'But it's terrible to think they don't do it up and make something of it,' said Pat. 'But we have no money, and Mrs Merkel is very reluctant to give us any more. We may have to go to the Queen and ask her for a few quid. After all, we did bring her over.'

'We did, we did,' agreed Tom O'Loughlin.

'And in truth now, there was no couple ever that could have been happier to have got to Ireland.'

'Aye, the sense of achievement.'

'They had been all over the world, but the joy of at last being able to come to Ireland was the crowning glory. It was their age that made it so special. Nobody else would have been able to do what they did.'

One more moment that the history books would not record – the healing of the Anglo-Irish wound being celebrated on a warm summer's evening by a field where Ireland's kings had been in-augurated. Fifteen minutes had gone by with the two vehicles still blocking the road, and no one had come along in all that time. Were they watching the Olympics or was the road always this quiet?

Having said goodbye to Tom O'Loughlin, we continued on our journey to Tulla. 'That place where the kings were inaugurated is known as Magh Adair,' said Pat. He spelt it out: 'M-A-G-H ... A-D-A-I-R. It's a small world now,' he marvelled. 'There you'd be in London, related to us, know a brother of his brother's wife and then arrive here in a small village to run into him on the road.'

We reached Tulla after dusk. 'This is an important place for you to see,' said Pat, as we pulled up outside a long, low whitewashed building that loomed out of the darkness. 'It's the convent that housed the nuns that educated the town.'

It looked like a barracks. Although the Sisters of Mercy convent had recently begun a new life as a Comhaltas Ceoltóirí Eireann cultural centre, there was still a crucifix above the entrance to remind you of what it had once been.

Patsy attended school here when she went to live with Aunt Ellie after her father had died. And Pat went to school here too when he was growing up in Tulla.

'Your mother came from a time and place where the Church ran your life,' said Pat. 'It was bred and hammered into you. She did a huge, marvellous thing in marrying a man outside her faith, but that would never have happened if she had not gone to England. Not a prayer now. The Church ostracised anyone who didn't fit in. They ran society.'

We sat in Pat's car in the darkness, across the road from the convent – the convent that was no more. Irish society had made huge strides since Patsy's time. In the aftermath of the sexual abuse scandals, it had at last thrown off the Church's shackles. It was thinking for itself in a way that would have astonished the young Patsy. Our next station was Flan McArthur's pub on Main Street. We parked by a building with large bay windows that would originally have formed the open arcade of a market house. At the time of independence it was the barracks of the Royal Irish Constabulary. We walked down the other side of the street to a red door set in the whitewashed wall of a terraced house. On the lintel above the door, which was flanked by a pair of matching grilled windows, were the generously spaced letters, red on white: M. M^CA R T H U R.

'Now you'll have a pint of Guinness,' said Pat, 'because, incredible Flan McArthur is open at this time of night, Flan McArthur – oldest publican in town.'

As a terraced house, it wasn't even a two-up two-down. There was just a single sash window on the floor above. It was a pub in a parlour, like the one that the Lynches had run in Quin. From the front salon, where there was space for not more than about six people, a step led to the back, where there was a tiny bar on the left and, against the wall opposite, two or three tables.

An old man, in jacket, waistcoat and tie, stood behind the bar.

'I didn't expect you to be open, Flan. The last night you weren't open.'

'Well, I have different hours now.'

Pat introduced me.

'Now does he look like anyone you ever met, Flan, in your entire life?'

'It will take me a while . . .'

'You drank porter over at his family's pub.'

'Is that right?'

'Now you told me so yourself.'

When further scrutiny failed to produce an answer, Pat directed him back the half-century to when there still was a Lynch pub, explaining that I was Patsy Lynch's son over from beyond. Even if I wasn't recognised, the Lynch pub and the Lynches were well remembered. I told Flan how much my mother had talked about Quin in her last days.

'Ah yes, she would. Wherever you're born, you'd like to go back again.'

Unusually, Pat let me buy the drinks.

Two men in their sixties, John and Michael, were talking at the other table. Once it had been established to which of the Murphys in Tulla Pat was related, we joined their conversation.

Michael had been watching the Olympics opening ceremony. 'It was such a jumble,' he said. 'They went back over the years – lots of aspects of Britain. And you know, they sang the Scottish national anthem, the Welsh one and the English one. Then it was the turn of Northern Ireland and they played some tune from the North.'

'Oh, did they?' said Pat.

'They should have left Northern Ireland out.'

'That was stupid now.'

'It was stupid, yes, but they played some kind of tune – I forget what it was now.'

'That's silly, because you're going to alienate one side or the other when you do that.'

Now John spoke: '"Danny Boy" is the one that doesn't alienate.'

'But the strange thing is that then they showed several people in the British Lions team getting a try,' Michael went on. 'They showed a Scottish fellah, a Welshman and an Englishman, but when it came to Ireland, it was the Northern Ireland player that got the try.'

'But you'd let that go,' said Pat. 'The fact they showed the Irish team was good.'

'But they didn't show the team. They only showed the man getting the try. I didn't agree with that, you know. Oh, they showed real division tonight.'

The conversation turned to the continuing divisions in Northern Ireland of which most people in Britain were unaware. 'They have no concept in the UK about the North,' said Pat. 'None whatsoever. They don't realise that the Northern Ireland soccer team is a totally Unionist team. That most Catholics would not support it. They don't realise how fragmented Northern Ireland still is. It's going to take donkey's years to fix.'

'In the South, it's not much better,' said John. There are still some diehards. I remember when I was at school, I'd get six of the best if I didn't turn up for a GAA match.'

'What's the GAA?' I asked in my English ignorance.

'The Gaelic Athletic Association,' explained Pat. 'Hurling, Irish football, camogie. It's part of Irish life. You have to play.'

'Because of a guy called Cusack,' said John. 'Michael Cusack. I was annoyed with him, because if it wasn't for him, I wouldn't have got six of the best.'*

'There was a cracked national fervour that was allowed to go unchecked. If you competed in an English-based game, played it or even looked at it, you were in trouble.'

'How do you mean – "an English-based game"?'

'Any game the English invented. Rugby or soccer. If you played an English game, you'd be banned from playing your national game. You'd be thrown off the teams. The GAA was the country's national identity. It still is, but soccer and rugby have been allowed to grow in the last probably twenty-five years. Would that be about right?'

* Born in the Burren, Clare, in 1847, Michael Cusack was an Irish nationalist who championed the revival of Irish language and culture, and founded the Gaelic Athletic Association to promote Irish sports.

'Aye,' said John. 'Because in this country you had the one dance, the one song, the one game. Everything was one.'

'People are more relaxed now?'

'It's getting into the past, but it caused an awful lot of trouble. People couldn't speak out because they were intimidated. They had to keep it quiet. They had to keep it under. It was like living in Germany under Hitler.'

Hundreds of years of contested history had created a cauldron of endless recriminations, cooling maybe, but still hot enough to need careful handling. Michael now took us back to one of the notorious flashpoints of more recent times. 'With the GAA now, did you see the troubles in the North, when they wouldn't let the people play in Crossmaglen? Even when they were playing a game, the helicopters used to dive down. That was pure provocation.'

'Crossmaglen is a little village that is literally just over the border,' explained Pat. 'It is absolutely, totally Irish. There was a GAA club there. The British army took over half of the field the lads used to play in. But before that, they had helicopters, which would swoop down on the lads playing. You would literally run for your life with the helicopters coming down. This was total intimidation now, but if you tell people in the UK, they would never believe that their army would do such a thing. This would never happen in Her Majesty's land. There's wrong on all sides.'*

Behind the bar, Flan listened quietly, too wise and experienced

---

* There was another 'side' in the casualty figures. Crossmaglen was considered to be one of the most dangerous postings in Northern Ireland for a British soldier. Troops were flown in by helicopter because it was too risky to enter the base by land. During the Troubles, 124 soldiers and 58 police officers were killed in the surrounding countryside.

a publican to offer, on this particular issue, any opinions of his own.

Pat got up to buy the next round of drinks.

'I don't know if you'll remember my mum's brother, Tommy O'Neill. He worked most of his life in the UK. You'll remember Tommy, Flan? Well, Tommy told me this story at the height of the Troubles. He told me so that I would remember and not go down the wrong road. He said, "You remember when you were over with me as a young lad?" "I do." "You remember the people who used to live next door?" "I do. How are they?" "Wait until I tell you. I owned the site they built their house on, sold them the land. They were a Catholic family, with twin boys. Remember, you used to play with them? Well, when the kids were born, I was there for their baptism, I was there for their communion, I was there for their confirmation, I was there for every birthday party. When they grew up, they joined the British army. One week after their twenty-first birthday, they went into Northern Ireland on their first tour of duty. They had not a single clue what they were heading into. Northern Ireland might as well have been in Saudi Arabia. They knew nothing about it. In they went, and one week later, they came home in two pine boxes. Both of them." Their parents never ever spoke to Tommy again. So bad did it get, he told me, that he sold up and left. He got out because he couldn't live with it any more. But his point to me was that there was wrong on all sides. Those two young lads didn't deserve to die. They were just two grand young fellahs that were reared beside me. They were an Englishman's sons. Did they deserve to get a bullet in the North?'

'Well, except the training of the British army was in the North.' The unyielding edge to Michael's voice stood out all the more for the silence that followed it. The conversation had entered an uncomfortable zone of uncertainty. Then all of a sudden it fizzled harmlessly away.

'But the Queen now,' said Michael, 'it was quite something to see her shake hands with Martin McGuinness.'

'That's right,' said Pat. 'We were talking about this earlier.'

'That was huge,' said Michael.

'It was a huge thing,' agreed John.

'And the Queen spoke Irish,' added Michael.

'You see, it is all gelling together,' said Pat. 'There are a lot of years to go yet, but we are getting there.'

'There's an awful lesson in all of this,' said John, 'which is that it is sometimes easier for two real enemies to make up than it is for neighbours who have fallen out.'

'Yes, that's true, sure enough,' agreed Michael.

On the drive back to Ennis, Pat and I reflected on the kaleidoscope of shifting identity. Irish, English, British, Catholic, Protestant . . .

'I'm going to be honest with you now,' he said, 'I have often thought that your mother's life in London had made her forget about Quin and Clare, that she was embarrassed to go back to her roots.'

'I think it was just too painful to go back to her roots. Losing her father changed everything. From that point on, she said, her life was blighted.'

'I find that particularly sad because my life was blighted the exact same way.'

Pat's father had died when he was six years old.

'In that pub where you were just in, my father gave me his last sixpence to buy a Cadbury's Crunchie bar one hour before he died. In front of that man that's there to this present day, who couldn't have been kinder to me over the years. I let you buy the first drink, because Flan would not take the money from me. No matter who I bring in, Flan will never take the first drink from me. I'll buy another round, or you'll buy a round, but he'll never take the first one from me. It's a recognition that I was there on that day. But the blighting of your life is that you feel you were deprived of your father, and all that he would have given you. I had the intellect to go anywhere in life, but not the direction that a father would have provided. So even now when I look back, I feel that life cheated me. And your mother would have felt the same.'

The tour resumed early the next day. We drove across the rocky limestone landscape of the Burren, as forbidding and austere as it is beautiful. One of Cromwell's generals said, in words that every Clare man and woman seems to know by heart, 'It is a country where there is not water enough to drown a man, wood enough to hang one, nor earth enough to bury him.'

This was where Brody often drove my grandfather, who surveyed it when he was with the Land Commission. The commission may originally have been set up by the British to redress the wrongs of Anglo-Irish history, but the timeless landscape, scattered with megalithic cairns and standing stones, made such grievance seem of only the most fleeting significance. The Poulnabrone dolmen, whose stones form a giant table, is estimated to be about five thousand years old.

We passed the cliffs of Moher, rising four hundred feet above the ocean, and saw in the distance the three low-lying humps of the Aran Islands. We came around by Hag's Head, passing through the seaside resort of Lahinch, where the Lynch children used to spend their holidays, and turned back inland towards Ennistymon. Stopping on a quiet road outside the town, Pat said, 'You're about to see the famine.'

A Fáilte Ireland information board, written in Gaelic and English, explained the *Leacht an Ghorta Mhóir*, the Memorial to the Great Hunger.

A pair of doors, hewn from limestone, stood slightly apart on a stone terrace, their massive scale all the more imposing for the absence of any surrounding structure. Against the Clare countryside behind, they reminded me of the great slabs of Poulnabrone. A small, emaciated boy, sculpted in bronze, stood against one of the doors, his head and hands pressed against its unyielding surface, while out of the other door reached the grieving head of a shawled woman and her two clenched fists. Beneath was the following inscription:

> Gentlemen
> There is a little boy named Michael
> Rice of Lahinch aged about 4 years
> he is an orphan, his father having died
> last year and his mother has expired
> on last Wednesday night, who is now
> about being buried without a coffin!!
> unless ye make some provision for
> such. The child in question is now at
> the workhouse gate expecting to be
> admitted if not he will starve.
>
> Rob S. Constable

Rainwater had trickled down from the woman's neck and the boy's hands and the hinges of the two doors, leaving long, white streaks. It was as if the whole monument was weeping.

'The worst part of it is there was enough food to feed the people but the landlords took it out of the country and sold it. There need never have been starvation.' The landlords also evicted the tenant farmers who could no longer afford to pay their rent – as many as half a million people. Meanwhile, the world's wealthiest nation did little to address the crisis. Sir Charles Trevelyan, the British civil servant chiefly responsible for administering the government's relief policy, believed that the disaster was a stroke of providence that taught the feckless Irish a necessary lesson in self-reliance. Posterity, he wrote, would consider the famine to be 'the commencement of a salutary revolution in the habits of a nation long singularly unfortunate, and will acknowledge that on this, as on many other occasions, Supreme Wisdom had educed permanent good out of transient evil'.

Pat had tried so hard over the past days to be even-handed, to see the history from all sides, to reach for a fairness, but now we stood before the unforgivable. 'If you want to understand where the Irish come from, the Irish come from the fact that the British allowed them to die. There were lots of things bad, but this was the worst.'

Exhibition signs explained the famine story. 'Read as you go,' said Pat.

To the extent that an individual can identify with a nation, it was impossible not to feel ashamed. 'It's really important to understand what the British did wrong here,' I said.

'That's all,' answered Pat, the warmth returning to his voice. 'It has to be acknowledged.'

What was left of the workhouse could still be found on the other side of the road. A small cottage hospital now stood on the site. If the little boy Michael Rice had managed to get past the workhouse gate, he would have found conditions inside little better than they were outside. Over a thousand people died of hunger and disease in the Ennistymon workhouse, and were buried without any ceremony in an unmarked, mass grave.

As one of the signs explained:

During the Famine the Ennistymon Union Workhouse and its auxiliaries became a byword for the most extreme conditions of human suffering and misery. Families who sought refuge there from the horror stalking the countryside were separated, and fated often never to meet again alive. Crowded into filthy and unhygienic surroundings, where a poor and sometimes revolting diet hastened their deaths, human beings in their hundreds, men, women and children, whose bodies were already fatally weakened from lack of food, fell easy victim to disease: typhus, relapsing fever, dysentery. Those who survived the workhouse existed for years in conditions which were intolerable and where human anguish and despair reached depths that we cannot begin to imagine.

Over three successive years of potato blight in the 1840s, the famine resulted in the deaths of more than a million people, with Clare being one of the worst hit regions in the country. Many more people left Ireland for good, establishing the pattern of emigration that, with the occasional lull, has continued to this day. Ireland's population fell from eight million immediately before the Great Famine to half that by the end of the nineteenth century.

Totting up the catalogue of Ireland's grievances against the English would give you quite a list, but even the time of Cromwell struggled to match the sheer scale of the famine. Nor was it so long ago. My grandfather's parents were small children when it began.

'The famine was the worst,' said Pat. 'Probably number two would be shooting the boys in 1916. And then the Black and Tans. They would rob, shoot, plunder, on sight. And there was no one going to correct them, because they weren't there. They were the law. Now if you had a force like that coming into your home tomorrow morning, wouldn't you be inclined to hate who was behind it for a long, long time?'

In the politics of a confusing, dangerous age, chance mattered as much as loyalty. Pat told me the story of Tom Crean. A member of several Antarctic expeditions, including the Scott expedition of 1911, Crean had received three Polar medals and a bravery award for saving a comrade's life. In 1920, he returned to Kerry, where he opened a pub called the South Pole Inn. One day, the Black and Tans searched his house. 'They took him and his family out and put them up against the wall, had them there waiting to get the order to fire. The officers were inside with two or three boys, when they found his pension book and medals in a drawer. One of them ran out. "Jesus Christ! Put down your weapons!" Tom Crean and his family survived only because they had found these things in the drawer.' His brother, Cornelius Crean, who was a sergeant in the Royal Irish Constabulary, was not so lucky. A few weeks later, he was killed in an IRA ambush.

There was one last place I wanted to see before my return to England – Drim, where the Lynches lived before the Great Famine, and where the Franciscan friars of Quin had taken refuge after having been driven from the abbey. I wondered whether there might be any traces of either.

In the twenty-first century you can google, but it will take you only so far. In the west of Ireland the quickest way to get an answer to such questions is to knock on a door. The network of kinsfolk still has an edge. Through knocking on doors, we learned that there was an old lady in Drim, Mary Conlan, who might be able to help.

Bright, lucid and delighted to see us, she turned out to know the Lynches very well. 'My mother told me that one of the Lynches married a Hickey from Drim,' she said. 'Father Barney used to say we can't locate where the Lynches lived in Drim but they were there in years gone by.'

'I know that my great-grandfather, John Lynch, married a Bridget Hickey,' I said.

'Now, look at that!' replied Mary with a chuckle. 'My grandfather was a Hickey. So we're related! They were a lovely family, the Lynches. A lovely family. I always think of the Lynches when I'm saying my prayers. I think of Mrs Lynch — and Annie also, her sister who helped rear them. They were a big family — like steps of stairs, the children.'

'How do you remember Patsy?'

'Oh, Patsy was a lovely little chubby-faced girl.' She chuckled again at the marvel of having this conversation. 'Isn't it a small world?' Then she added, 'But sure, my sister Cissy would be able to tell you much more than I can. She and Patsy were best friends when they were little. Every other Sunday without fail Patsy came up here after Mass. Then the next Sunday Ciss would go down and the two of them used to go into Quin Abbey. There was an old window there with bars and they used to slip between them and climb up to the top. Oh, Ciss would love to tell you all this now. She was so fond of Patsy Lynch. And then they never corresponded afterwards, you know.'

'And where is she now?'

'She lives in Derreen, over towards Clarecastle.'

Half an hour later we were knocking on Cissy's door in Derreen. Mary's daughter Una had rung ahead to announce our arrival.

'Oh, we were bosom pals we were,' said Cissy. 'Oh dear, dear, dear, I can't believe it. We were great friends, sure, and it was only recently that I remarked to my own daughter that I had a friend in Quin that I used to go down to see every second Sunday. But then she left and I never heard from her again. Honest to God, it was only a short time ago, and to think that she was dead. Oh, I often wondered where Patsy was indeed. Oh, my my. That's the hardest thing – you die in wonder. She never came back to visit. But I suppose you put your roots down somewhere else, then you stay, thinking of your house and home.'

'When her dad died,' Pat explained, 'she was hit very badly. She was so upset that in later life it was too painful for her to think about Quin.'

'And did you know,' said Cissy, 'that she had a sister that died, Breda? Patsy took me upstairs one time to show her to me. Breda was about seventeen at the time, and she was in bed. She didn't live too long after that. Oh, I remember that well, that she took me up to see her. Oh, we were so sorry that they left Quin. They sold their land, a small bit from Quin towards Ennis. They used to keep a few cows in it, and Aunt Annie used to come up on her bicycle with a bucket to milk the cows out in the field.'

Pat was able at least to reassure her that both Aunt Annie and Patsy's mother had been brought back to Quin to be buried. 'You were probably at those funerals, and I was too, but I didn't know who you were.'

'Oh, look at that.'

'I remember coming down from Dublin after one of those funerals. The hearse broke down on the road from Tulla to Quin. The undertaker got out to explain to the brothers that the hearse had run out of petrol. "We perfectly understand," they said. "She would have wanted to stop, anyway." I suppose in a funny way it was meant to happen.'

'Isn't it nice to piece things together, all the same?' said Cissy. She brought out a bottle of Paddy whiskey. 'Success to temperance,' she said, pouring me a glass.

'To you and Patsy,' I said.

'I am sorry that she is gone,' said Cissy. 'She took the lead of me.'

'You couldn't tell a better toast,' said Pat, regretfully declining the glass that was offered to him, 'but unfortunately the villains of the Gardai won't allow me to join you.'

'No, they will not,' lamented Cissy, putting the cap back on the bottle.

'They have no mercy any more. There was a day when you could have it and drive out.'

'Oh gosh, they've ruined it for us!' agreed Cissy.

'To Patsy.'

PART TWO
EMPIRE

5

Esprit de Corps

Back home, in London, I opened the battered suitcase and took out the service records of my grandfather and his four brothers. The technology with which they had been brought to me – laser prints of the downloads of the scans of the microfilm in the National Archives – offered some measure of how far the world had moved on since nameless clerks filled in the original documents by fountain pen.

The handwritten entries of my grandfather's military history sheet enumerated the twenty-two years of his service as follows:

COUNTRY	FROM	TO	YEARS	DAYS
Home	1.9.94	29.10.99	5	59
Gibraltar	30.10.99	11.6.00	0	225
Home	12.6.00	30.10.03	3	120
Passage to Sierra Leone	31.10.03	8.11.03	0	9

COUNTRY	FROM	TO	YEARS	DAYS
W. Africa	9.11.03	26.6.04	0	229
Passage home	27.6.04	8.7.04	0	12
Home	8.7.04	25.4.07	2	292
Canada	26.4.07	14.12.07	0	233
Home	15.12.07	21.5.08	0	158
Ceylon	22.5.08	16.7.11	3	56
Home	17.7.11	16.5.12	0	304
Malay States	17.5.12	19.12.14	2	217
Home	20.12.14	30.9.15	0	285
B.E.F. France	1.10.15	24.8.16	0	328
Home	25.8.16	31.8.16	0	7
			22	

He went to so many places that the clerk couldn't squeeze them all into the correct box at the top of the form. They cascaded over sections below that addressed other aspects of his military history such as 'Whether educated' (he was), 'Campaigns' and 'Effects of wounds'. The sheet had become such a dog's dinner of crossings-out, overlapping and barely legible entries that the postings were written out again on a separate card, certified by an officer – although I'm sure some mistakes still slipped through.

Here was the military equivalent of William Blake's grain of sand – a world on a sapper's index card. But for all the far-flung places, the beat of my grandfather's career, both opening and closing his service, and punctuating all the journeys, was 'Home', the one posting that he and his four brothers all shared. 'Home' was a general military term for the United Kingdom, but most of all for a Royal Engineer 'home' was the School of Military Engineering at Brompton Barracks, Chatham, a training camp for recruits but also a melting pot in which to forge a new identity of Britishness, which owed as much to the endeavour of Empire as it did to that strange, uncertain union of England, Wales, Ireland and Scotland.

Many of the fragments of that identity were still around when I was growing up in the 1970s and the Empire had all but fizzled out. At school, there was an old music teacher, Mr Kim, who taught the class to sing sea shanties and marching songs which I suppose have long since been removed from the curriculum. It was a testament to their catchiness that I continued to hum them long after the last lumps of the Empire had melted away.

> Some talk of Alexander,
> And some of Hercules
> Of Hector and Lysander,
> And such great names as these.
> But of all the world's great heroes,
> There's none that can compare
> With a tow, row, row, row, row, row,
> To the British Grenadier . . .

'The British Grenadiers' was the tune that over the years I found myself humming most of all, so I was pleased to discover that it was one of the marching songs of the Royal Engineers. Some small part of me had been sharing in the *esprit de corps* of the sappers without my even realising.

The Lynch brothers would have heard the Royal Engineers

band play the same tune as they marched back and forth across the parade ground at Brompton Barracks. It was the *tabula rasa*, where men from many different backgrounds put aside their previous lives to learn how to become British soldiers.

During my visits to the corps library, which is housed in the old Royal Engineers Institute building by the parade ground, I beheld a line of monuments that included a Crimea arch, an obelisk to the Great War, a South African memorial arch and a statue of General Gordon at the steps of the institute itself. Hardly changed in a hundred years, they helped me to slip back to the time of my grandfather and great-uncles. As I read inside the library about the training that created a sapper, I tried to imagine the five of them among the ranks of the new recruits at the turn of the last century.

Reveille at 6.30. Drill on the parade ground until 3.30, then physical exercises in the gymnasium. The routine was repeated day after day after day until the will of the men had become the will of the corps. This was a time when the way soldiers marched in formation was still a basic battle tactic, the square still a favoured tool of the British army.

When the men weren't being taught how to march, they were taught how to use and look after a rifle – the new bolt-action Lee-Metfords that were replacing the Martini-Henrys. The iconic weapon of Empire, which Kipling had even written a story about, was old technology that the new recruits were much more likely to face than use in the colonial wars that continued to erupt around the Empire.*

* 'The Martini-Henry rifle may be taken as a guide to the power of weapons likely to be used against us by an uncivilised enemy,' notes the *R.E. Field*

One recruit who passed through Chatham not long after the Lynches remembered the instructor's drill resembling 'a High Priest offering an incantation at the altar'. Many decades later, he was still able to recite the first verse:

> On raising the bolt-lever, the bolt rotates to the left and the stud on the cocking-piece moves from the long to short cam groove withdrawing the striker one-eighth of an inch at the same time the stud on the underside of the bolt moves down the inclined slot withdrawing the bolt one eighth of an inch which is the first loosening of the cartridge in the chamber.

After about three months of such prayers, the men marched ten miles to the Royal Engineers rifle ranges, which were located on the Kent marshes about a mile downriver from Gravesend. Here, they underwent a fortnight of shooting trials, at the end of each day dining and sleeping in the casemates of Shornmead Fort, which had been built during Napoleonic times. They practised with live ammunition at ranges from one hundred to four hundred yards, then took part in a final day's shoot-off which determined their classification.

The most insistent sound of these months of training was the call of the bugle, barking out an unvarying diet of commands from reveille in the morning to Last Post at the end of the day. Lights out at 10.15.

As precious as the vestments of any priest was the Royal Engineers' dress uniform: a scarlet tunic with blue and yellow facings;

Service Pocket Book of 1894, while the Lee-Metford offered a measure of what to expect from 'civilised foes'.

ROYAL ENGINEERS.

HISTORY AND TRADITIONS.

The British "Military Engineer" is first mentioned in the Domesday Book compiled shortly after the Norman Conquest. and until 1715 the Chief Engineer had charge of all engines of war—including guns. In 1716, however, a Royal Warrant established the Royal Artillery to superintend the "King's Guns and Ordnance," whilst the Engineers, as a separate Corps, undertook special charge of the "King's Works." A company of Soldier Artificers, raised at Gibraltar by Sir William Green in 1772, was the origin of the rank and file of the Corps. Every Sapper is an Artisan and receives Engineer Pay, in addition to Regimental Pay, regulated by his skill at his trade. The motto, "Ubique" —"Everywhere,"—best explains why the Royal Engineers have neither Colours nor Battle Honours. Both Officers and Men are trained at the School of Military Engineering. founded at Chatham by Sir Charles Pasley in 1812. Their work comprises fortress, field, survey, railway, telegraph, bridging and ballooning duties. Officers of the Corps were originally ineligible for military command, but in 1868, Sir John Burgoyne was created a Field Marshal, and since then many of the highest Army Commands have been held by Royal Engineer Officers. Finally, the importance and duties of the Corps constantly increase with the increased application of science to military operations.

a pair of blue trousers with broad red stripes; a blue helmet, with brass badge and brass top spike. To keep these immaculate, a regulation set of brushes and polish was issued to each recruit. The two suits of white canvas, the standard issue for hauling guns and building bridges, and the two suits of working service dress, were also meant to be kept spotless.

The intensity of training escalated day by day, reaching its last pitch with the passing-out parade. Marching in full ceremonial dress to the strains of the corps band, the soldiers were expected to give a flawless display of drill, ending with the general salute.

While a soldier in the infantry would at this point be sent to join a battalion, recruits to the Royal Engineers now had to embark on a three-month course of military engineering. Issued with the Royal Engineers' jackknife, with its distinctive marlinspike, they were taught how to splice, knot and unknot ropes. They then learned how to use their new skill to make derricks, trestle bridges and aerial ropeways. They also learned how to use explosives, how to site and dig trenches, how to build dugouts and machine-gun posts; and, practising on the Medway, how to construct bridges with spars, boats and even beer barrels.

After they had mastered the general skills of the Engineer, it was time to choose a trade. The Lynch brothers took the six-month course in military surveying. It was an obvious return to the trade they had already embarked upon at the Ordnance Survey office in Ennis. Other sappers were becoming engine drivers, or mastering the use of underwater explosives in the School of Submarine Mining, or joining the School of Ballooning.

The Royal Engineers were the ultimate jacks of all trades. A sapper could build a bridge, blow it up, put down a temporary pontoon, and then start all over again – but also, if need be, pick up a rifle and fight with the infantry.

They were both sportsmen and scholars. An Engineers team took part in the first FA Cup Final at Kennington Oval in 1872. Although they lost 1–0, they reached the final on three other occasions, and won the competition in 1875. Exploiting a style of play that demonstrated the tactical advantage of combination football, they were pioneers of the modern passing game.

They pursued the same excellence in the lecture hall. The Royal Engineers Institute building (designed by Lieutenant Montague Ommaney, RE) was first home to the Institution of Royal Engineers, which was founded in 1875 to promote the science of military engineering. The pursuit of knowledge was encouraged among the rank and file as well as the officers. A new 'Soldiers' Institute', built at Chatham Barracks in 1861, included a reading room and a library. When a military theatre was added to the building in 1872, the opening ceremony included a lecture from Captain Brackenbury, professor of military history at the Woolwich Royal Academy. Speaking on the subject of 'Moral Force in War', he contended that it was the lack of this quality that had accounted for the reverses of the French in their recent war against Prussia.

The idea that moral force counted for as much as physical force was at the root of the corps philosophy. When in 1910 the commander of the Training Battalion, Colonel Ward, compiled a handbook of notes for the NCOs who drilled the recruits, he set out – with the characteristic certainty and decision of the time – the five maxims that every British soldier ought to remember, and which would guide him through life:

The first of these maxims is LOYALTY. – Every true Briton is rejoiced to perform an act of service to his King and Country. A soldier who has no such desire is of no value and is not worthy of the name of Soldier. Upon the loyalty of the troops depends the safeguarding of the rights and the prosperity of the country.

2. COURTESY. – From the General to the private there exist ranks and orders. Commands from seniors must be obeyed, and such are to be regarded as the King's commands. Courtesy must be paid not only to seniors in all branches of the service, but also to one's equals and juniors.

3. BRAVERY. – There are two kinds of bravery; one kind actuated by rashness and folly, the other kind by thought. Soldiers must think before they act, neither despising an inferior enemy nor fearing a powerful one.

4. UPRIGHTNESS. – Without this no community can have a lasting existence. Be a man of your word, and before promising anything, consider first your power to perform it, lest you find yourself in such a position that you fail to keep your word, and thereby possibly let down a comrade.

5. MORALITY. – The vice of immorality makes men become feeble in spirit, careless of their promises, extravagant, selfish, and unworthy of being British Soldiers.

Bad habits contracted by soldiers spread like an epidemic, and lower the spirit of an army.

The training of recruits placed an emphasis on the soldierly spirit, *esprit de corps*, which the NCO instructors inculcated through teaching the history and traditions of the corps. All recruits attended a lecture illustrated with lantern slides in the Royal Engineers Institute, which traced the origin of the military engineer all the way back to Domesday.

At the end of the eleventh century, Gundulph, the Bishop of Rochester, built a keep by the River Thames, the 'White Tower' in the Tower of London, which became the Engineers' first home. It was a notable coincidence that the modern School of Military Engineering stood within sight of another stronghold of Gundulph, Rochester Castle. The nearby cathedral contained monuments to military engineers who had served at Waterloo, but also the more recent campaigns in Afghanistan, Egypt, the Sudan and South Africa.

It was in these lantern-slide lectures that the Lynch brothers learned how the modern Royal Engineers came into existence. With the introduction of a standing army after the Restoration, a regular corps of officer engineers was created in 1716. At first, it hired labour as the need arose, but shoddy work by civilian craftsmen during the fortification of Gibraltar led to the formation in 1772 of a 'Company of Soldier Artificers'. During the Napoleonic Wars, the company grew into several companies and, in 1813, acquired the new name of 'Royal Sappers and Miners', which reflected the increased importance of field engineering and siegecraft. Finally, after the Crimean War, the officers in the corps of the now Royal Engineers were merged with the rank and file of the 'Royal Sappers and Miners' to become one body, with the privates of the combined force continuing to be called 'sappers'.

The prime purpose of the lantern slides was to encourage imitation. For as Colonel Ward pointed out, 'it is chiefly by the example of the actions of our forefathers that we are guided in our own course of conduct'. The actions of this particular breed of soldier were entwined in the larger life of the nation to a striking degree, since the corps drew its strength from the trades that were the backbone of the nation – bricklayers, masons, carpenters, clerks, printers, smiths, wheelwrights, engine drivers, surveyors . . . 'Craftsmen of all sorts are invited to enlist,' its recruitment posters declared. While other regiments in the British army were formed through an association with a particular part of the country, every sapper – whether from England, Wales, Scotland or Ireland – passed through the Training Battalion at Chatham, this common home moulding their wider concept of home.

6

Everywhere

I had started out wanting to find out more about my mother's father and his family, but as he and his four brothers disappeared into the ranks, I found myself more and more pulled along by the lure of the bigger story. I wondered if they had felt the same, marvelling at the sheer scale and enterprise of Empire. After all, they were there on the parade ground marching along to its tune.

Standing on the same spot a hundred years later, I felt I had only to turn my head to see them. Astonishingly complete, the monuments of Brompton Barracks were a time capsule, offering a measure of the Empire at its highest point of pride. Inscribed over the great Crimea arch was the corps motto, '*Ubique Quo Fas et Gloria Ducunt*', 'Everywhere, whither right and glory lead'. The Royal Engineers were at the heart of the imperial project, whether it was building the Empire in the first place or mapping and taming the vast wildernesses that it encompassed.

In this place where pomp and ceremony were part of the everyday routine, the sheer weight of Portland stone suggested the thirst for grandeur that inspired the Romans. The Victorian passion for the classical suddenly became clear to me. All those *Kennedy's Revised Latin Primers*, with their Empire-red covers, were part of the imperial enterprise, belonging to a time when the public schools were nurseries for the Empire's administrators, and knew the inspirational value of ancient heroes. The wandering Aeneas, a fugitive of fate, founding a new settlement far from his original home of Troy, struck a chord with imperial, colonising Britain. It wasn't Rome or Troy that mattered, but Britannia. While the Romans had their straight roads that took you to the edge of civilisation, the British had their shipping lanes girdling the globe.

If the Royal Engineers provided a handy mirror of the British Empire, their greatest hero, General Charles Gordon, was the personification of what that Empire aspired to be. The statue before the steps of the institute depicts him mounted on a Sudanese camel, in the act of 'over-awing', to use Colonel's Ward's term, a crowd of Arab slave dealers. He is dressed in the Egyptian general's uniform that he had worn as Governor General of Sudan. 'Pasha Gordon' he had been called then. The extraordinary outpouring of grief and adulation that greeted his martyr's death in Khartoum could perhaps best be understood as a response to a man whose life resonated with a time that was much more comfortable than our own with such lofty words as 'virtue' and 'morality', and who seemed to justify the Victorians' faith in the Empire as a force for good.

THE PRINCE OF WALES UNVEILING THE STATUE

The statue at Chatham, which had been unveiled in 1890, was not the first memorial that the Engineers had put up to Gordon. In the same effort of commemoration, General Wolseley, who had been in command of the relief force that had arrived only two days too late at Khartoum, unveiled the Sudan windows in Rochester Cathedral, in honour of Gordon and all the other Royal Engineers who had served in the Sudanese campaign.

'Neither in this Cathedral, nor in any other Church that I am aware of within this Realm, has there been tabulated upon its walls a name more worthy of being remembered for ever by the people of this country,' said Wolseley, delivering a eulogy that, in the usual Victorian way, treated memory as an instrument of action. 'I cannot wish any future generation, or future body of men, any higher blessing than that they may follow the example of the noble man to whom I have referred.' It offered a rationale that had never previously occurred to me for all those statues I passed on my evening commuter's walk from central London to Waterloo Station. They included, inevitably, one of Gordon, brooding on his high plinth in the Victoria Embankment Gardens.

Perhaps no other Victorian, other than Victoria herself, has been celebrated in so much stone, such was the extraordinary hold that he had over the Empire's imagination. Long before he had earned the name of 'Pasha Gordon' in the Sudan, he was known as 'Chinese Gordon', already a national hero for his exploits as the leader of the 'Ever Victorious Army', which had crushed the Taiping Rebellion. 'Walking at the head of his troops, with nothing but a light cane in his hand, he seemed to pass through every danger with the scatheless equanimity of a demi-God.'

The hymn, 'Onward, Christian Soldiers', which had been composed around this time, might have been written for him. He captured perfectly the curious mix of the military and the evangelical that was such a feature of the High Empire. When Gordon returned to England from China in 1865, Queen Victoria made him a Companion of the Order of the Bath. He was the most famous person in England. But with a soul that 'revolted against dinner parties and stiff shirts', he gladly fled London society to become Commander of the Engineers in Gravesend, with responsibility for renovating the lower Thames forts.

At a time when Britannia really did rule the waves the assignment could have had little military value, but the years in Gravesend were as indispensable a part of the Gordon legend as his exploits in China or the Sudan. Appalled by the local poverty in the area, he threw himself into doing whatever he could to relieve it. He visited the poor in the local workhouse, bringing with him food, tea and tobacco. He spent as much time in the town's infirmary, administering to the sick and dying. He opened up his garden to the deserving elderly. He taught evening classes at the Gravesend Ragged School, buying hundreds of suits of clothing for the destitute children out of his army pay.

When a Jewish teacher, Henry Berkowitz, who had set up several soup kitchens in the town, came under personal attack from some Church leaders, Gordon came to his defence. Urging the different denominations in the town to work together, he declared, 'The Church is like the British Army, in it is One, only different regiments.' The endless charitable deeds he undertook were at the expense of his own comfort. As Lytton Strachey observed, 'The easy luxuries of his class and station were unknown to him; his clothes verged upon the shabby; and his frugal meals were eaten at a table with a drawer, into which the loaf and plate were quickly swept at the approach of his poor visitors.' When an appeal was made during the Lancashire famine, having already given away all his money, he sold his Chinese medal as an anonymous gift.

It has been suggested that Gordon's acts of charity at Gravesend were the result of a spiritual conversion that had been caused by the deaths of his father and brother soon after his arrival in the town. But the more I discovered about the corps, the more I wondered whether there was also something about being a Royal Engineer itself that made a difference. These were the men who went everywhere. They had no battle honour other than their motto, *Ubique*, in recognition of the fact that they were present in every campaign, and often long after the campaign was over. In any operation they were famously the first to arrive and the last to leave. Their reputation was to be able to meet the need of any situation at war or in peace. Gordon helping out the poor and sick in Gravesend was a good sapper following his instinct.

Even if my grandfather and great-uncles had not served in the corps, I would have found it hard not to be filled with admiration for the sheer breadth and variety of their achievement. But to be the son of a daughter of a Royal Engineer filled me, the most unmilitary of all the Lynches, with the extra pride of a personal connection.

'Patsy, what are you going to be when you grow up? Well? Let me hear.' 'A Royal Engineer, Daddy. A Royal Engineer!'

Well, through blood, loyalty and association, I had grown up to be a Royal Engineer too.

The pre-eminent poet of the Empire, Rudyard Kipling, inevitably wrote about them, in fact more than once. His poem 'Sappers' captures well the epic dimension of what they did:

> When the Waters were dried an' the Earth did appear,
> ('It's all one,' says the Sapper),
> The Lord He created the Engineer,
> Her Majesty's Royal Engineer,
> With the rank and pay of a Sapper!
>
> When the Flood come along for an extra monsoon,
> 'Twas Noah constructed the first pontoon
> To the plans of Her Majesty's, etc.

And onward march the verses, enumerating all the things a sapper does, so many that Kipling does not even get round to mentioning the maps that my grandfather and his brothers made.

The non-commissioned ranks of the Royal Engineers published a monthly magazine called *The Sapper*. An early issue, which I looked at in the library, from October 1895 when the third Lynch brother, James, began his training at Chatham, addressed the question, what is a sapper?

> The question is one which it would puzzle the uninitiated to solve, for he is represented, at one and the same time, in a hundred different capacities, and takes as many shapes as Proteus. He seems in fact to be equally at home afloat or ashore . . . But as to defining his functions – as to saying precisely what a sapper is – we hardly know how to set about the task; for he appears, like Buckingham, to be, 'Not one, but all mankind's epitome', condensing the whole system of military engineering, all the arts and sciences, and everything that is useful and practical under one red jacket. He is the man-of-all-work of the Army and the public; and the authorities, by a wave of the official wand, may transform him into any of the various characters of – astronomer, geologist, surveyor, engineer, draughtsman, artist, architect, traveller, explorer, commissioner, inspector, artificer, mechanic, diver, soldier, or sailor – in short, he is a Sapper.

I spent my lunch hours at Chatham, when the Royal Engineers library was closed, wandering around the corps museum. Many of the sapper's hundred different capacities were on display there. I lingered longest in the section that was devoted to the Survey. This was the trade, after all, that had turned my grandfather and his brothers into Royal Engineers in the first place, so I wanted to find out what I could about it.

'The story of the Ordnance Survey starts in Scotland with the suppression of the Jacobite Rebellion of 1745–1746,' explained a wall panel. 'In order to aid the Army's control over the Highlands, Colonel David Watson RE suggested mapping the area, thereby undertaking the first comprehensive survey of a part of the British Isles.'

In a nearby cabinet the gleam of a strange brass contraption caught my eye – a telescope fixed to a spindle suspended over a disc. A label explained that it was a Ramsden theodolite. 'This belonged to General William Twiss RE who oversaw the construction of the Martello Towers built along the Kent and Sussex coast during the Napoleonic Wars.' Britain's leading instrument-maker, Ramsden had built an even bigger version for Major General William Roy RE, who masterminded the network of measurements that led to the first accurate and detailed map of the entire country.

In 1783, Roy, who was then director of the Royal Engineers, had soldiers pace out a baseline of five miles from King's Arbour on Hounslow Heath to the Poor House at Hampton Court, choosing the terrain because of 'its great extent, and the extraordinary levelness of its surface, without local obstruction whatever to render measurements difficult'. To get the measurements as accurate as possible, he used a set of glass tubes to minimise any contraction or expansion with the change of temperature. From each end of the line, Roy then used Ramsden's theodolite to take bearings on a distant object. It enabled him to calculate through the measurement of the angles the precise length of the other two sides of the triangle formed. The completed triangle then supplied the base from which further triangles were plotted, radiating outwards, over the next sixty years, to complete the Principal Triangulation of Great Britain.

This Principal Triangulation provided the framework for a

secondary triangulation that criss-crossed the land with smaller interior triangles. The result was an immensely accurate skeleton that surveyors like the Lynch brothers then clothed with the topographical detail of the country – the hills and valleys, the rivers and lakes, the roads and railways, the villages, towns and cities. Here was the entire United Kingdom of Great Britain and Ireland in all its variety. But the wonder, I thought, was how everything had sprung from that first line – how, through the magic – no, science – of triangulation, a relationship was found between things that had no obvious connection – the church in the village, the watermill by the river in the valley, the top of a hill . . .

In the museum, there was a life-size dummy of a surveyor, in pith helmet, khaki uniform and jodhpurs, and with regulation moustache, lining up the kind of theodolite my grandfather would have used. The uniform had belonged to a Captain Talbot, who was a surveyor with the Afghan Boundary Commission of 1885. It was the time of 'the Great Game' when Britain and Russia jostled for influence over the region. After a long and dangerous rivalry, the two countries were cooperating to mark out a northern boundary. Yet, straying far from the frontier, the Royal Engineers surveyors still used the opportunity to gather information for the next war. They reported on the defence of Herat in the west and explored routes to the south between Nushki and Helmand, the obvious place to drive through a railway from India if only the Amir of Afghanistan would allow it (he never did).

Whichever part of the globe one looked at, the sustained effort of Empire was striking. 'From the mid 18th century until 1906 the Royal Engineers served in Canada without a break,' a museum label explained. 'At first they were there to fight the French, then to fortify the frontier against the Americans, then to mark it and finally to maintain British naval bases on the Atlantic at Halifax, Nova Scotia and on the Pacific at Esquimalt, British Columbia . . .'

The military history sheets of the Lynch brothers offered their own terse catalogue of this particular continuity. Three out of the five served in Canada. The longest posting belonged to Michael, who was in Halifax, Nova Scotia, from 18 September 1901 to 15 March 1906 – to be exact, as the service records always were, 4 years, 179 days. But here at Chatham, it was the bigger picture of Empire that most commanded the attention. I would look more closely at the brothers' military history sheets later. For now it was enough to take in the epic nature of the army's man-of-all-work.

A sapper's military history sheet divided his service into the distinct categories of Home and Abroad, but the trick of the Royal Engineers was to dissolve the difference between the two. Everywhere at home, whether afloat or ashore. In the museum, the exhibits of their achievements came from all four corners of the earth, and as I read about their exploits in the library, I put aside critical objectivity and, at the core of the corps, became a helpless fan. Everywhere I turned, I saw their genius for Everywhere and Everything. Wanting to capture at least some of those shapes of Proteus, I buried myself in myriad sappers' tales of extraordinary feats and journeys.

In my imagination, I went aboard the *Thames City*, the clipper that carried a detachment of 120 Royal Engineers, along with their wives and children, to Vancouver Island, a six-month voyage that took them around Cape Horn. Seventeen thousand miles. The steamship had already been invented some time before when they set off from Gravesend in October 1858. So perhaps the mode of travel was some economy of the War Office, but it only made the fortitude and endurance of the travellers seem all the more extraordinary.

To alleviate the tedium of their long journey, the Engineers put together a weekly newspaper called the *Emigrant Soldiers' Gazette and Cape Horn Chronicle*. Beneath the title and the royal coat of arms, the corps motto, *Quo Fas et Gloria Ducunt*, opened the first issue.

Offering a compendium of news items, riddles,* songs and poetry, as well as nature notes on the voyage, the newspaper made a conceit out of the ship's name, suggesting that the voyagers occupied a real town, albeit one floating on the ocean. It carried reports from such neighbourhoods as Longboat Crescent, Laundry Lane and Fire Bucket Arcade. About as far away as it was possible to be from the streets they had once known, they created an

---

* An example from the second half of the voyage: Why is the *Thames City* in a heavy sea like the black dog brought on board at the Falkland Islands? Answer: Because she is a horrible lurcher.

alternative home on the high seas, decorating it with all that was comforting and familiar. A column called 'Market Intelligence' kept the inhabitants up to date with the latest commodities: 'Mutton – Scarce. Porter and wine – In great demand still; a fresh cargo is expected shortly.' When the ship's cook slaughtered one of the sheep, the newspaper reported a murder in Longboat Alley: 'The name of the deceased is at present unknown. One of the witnesses said that he had formerly been known by the name of lamb, and was about to pass as mutton.'

The lost and found advertisements displayed the extra style of a community with time on its hands. When someone lost a bunch of keys, the following verse was published in the *Gazette*:

> I've lost a bunch of bright steel keys,
> A bunch that numbered seven,
> If you've found them, oh! return them please,
> You'll find reward in Heaven.
> For know you friends these keys have locked
> The lids of all my trunks;
> I lost them on the fourth of March,
> In the neighbourhood of the bunks.

There were jokes and amusing stories, too, of the kind that might appeal to a sea-bound community – the one, for example, about Lord Nelson being transported back to England in a barrel of brandy after the Battle of Trafalgar. Towards the end of the journey, the stopper fell out, causing the admiral to offer his hand to an old seaman, who exclaimed: 'Hang me, old boy, if you are not in better spirits than any of us!'

The commander of the detachment, Captain Henry Luard, read

the newspaper to the assembled company every Saturday night. It was then left on the lower deck, until the appearance of the next week's issue, for anyone who wanted to read it at their leisure.

The editor was 2nd Corporal Charles Sinnett, who compiled the newspaper in the 'Editor's Office, Starboard Front Cabin, *Thames City*'. He not only edited the newspaper but also wrote it out in long hand. Hence the smock that he invariably wore, to protect his clothes from ink. The newspaper contained no bylines to reveal the identity of the contributors, but I assume that Sinnett composed most of the pieces himself.

It wasn't until the *Thames City* was approaching the equator* that an editorial set out the reasons behind the voyage, expressing the hope that 'our readers will bear with us, and not think us too egotistical, if we make a few remarks suggestive of the importance of the expedition'. Formerly known as New Caledonia, British Columbia was an uncolonised wilderness in British North America, where the only European presence was the Hudson's Bay Company, whose representatives carried on an extensive trade in furs with the Indians. But then gold was discovered along the Fraser River, and many thousands of prospectors from California flocked to the area.

The British government feared that these 'motley adventurers' would use armed force to overcome opposition from the natives who hunted along the river. It was also concerned that the situation might offer the United States a pretext to annex territory. So it established the colony of British Columbia, appointing as its representative the governor of Vancouver Island, James Douglas

---

* At the time of publication of the third issue, on 20 November 1858, the ship's position was Lat. 2.54 N. Lon. 23.38 W. The equator was 174 miles away, with Lizard Light 3,036 miles behind, and Cape Horn 4,200 miles ahead.

(who also happened to be head of the Hudson's Bay Company west of the Rockies). And as the *Emigrant Soldier's Gazette* explained, this was where the Royal Engineers came in:

> It being also necessary that the Governor should be supported by a proper military force, it became incumbent on the Colonial Minister to select and send out a body of men on whom proper trust and reliance could be placed. It at once occurred to Sir Edward Bulwer Lytton, the Colonial Minister, that great advantage would accrue to the Colony, could a body of men be sent out possessed at once of military and scientific requirements, inasmuch as, while in their military capacity they could give all necessary support to Governor Douglas, their mechanical and scientific labours would contribute in a most important degree to the improvement and colonisation of the country. For such a body he turned to the corps of Royal Engineers.

Although it took six months to reach the scene, the *Thames City* was to some extent a nineteenth-century-style rapid reaction force. Fighting had already broken out that summer between the natives and the prospectors. The phrase 'a good Indian is a dead Indian' summed up the practical attitude of many of the miners, who were prepared to go to any lengths in their frenzy for gold to drive the natives off their hunting grounds along the Fraser River. The only military forces immediately available to the governor were marines on board the Royal Navy survey ship HMS *Satellite* and a party of Royal Engineers attached to the joint British–US boundary commission that was then marking out the border between British North America and the United States. While a fragile peace had been restored, the arrival of the Royal

Engineers on the *Thames City* was urgently needed to keep that peace and to build the infrastructure of a civilised society. Their mission was in effect to prevent the Wild West from repeating itself north of the 49th parallel.

The *Thames City* finally arrived at Vancouver Island on 12 April 1859. Over the next four years, the Engineers built schools and churches, laid out towns (including the city of Vancouver), and explored an area that was nearly four times the size of Britain. All the early maps of the colony were made from surveys that the Engineers had carried out.

While the officers who arrived with the *Thames City* eventually returned to England, most of the men settled with their families in the new country they had helped to build. The British government gave each of them 150 acres of land in recognition of their service. *Tantae molis erat Romanam condere gentem.* 'So great was the task to establish the Roman people.'

When Aeneas left Troy to found a new city, he took with him the 'lares and penates', the household gods that contained the spirit of the home he hoped to rebuild across the sea. For the British Empire's soldiers the lares and penates were their memories of home and the sort of songs and stories that got set down in the *Emigrant Soldier's Gazette*. The further away from home they found themselves, the more important it became to perpetuate the idea of home and to understand what it meant. I suppose a similar logic accounts for my wish to write this book, with its attempt to trace roots that I did not feel any need to explore while my mother was still alive, but it is quite a challenge to define the place of the sapper in my personal heritage.

In the Royal Engineers library, I couldn't help but ponder the immense gulf to be bridged. At the age my grandfather was

learning to use rifle and theodolite at the School of Military Engineering, I was studying Latin and Greek Literature at Oxford. I
could have told you a lot about the wanderings of Aeneas and
Ulysses but had no idea what a theodolite was, let alone how to
use one. But the more I learned about the Royal Engineers, the
more I appreciated that the wanderings of Aeneas and Ulysses
had their relevance.

A warrior and a seafarer, Ulysses was also a workman capable
of the most exquisite artistry. Homer describes him as *polymetis*,
a man of many talents; as *polymechanos*, a man of many devices;
as *polytropos*, much-wandering. The emigrant soldiers of the
Thames City would have recognised a man of their own kind, an
accomplished jack of all trades, who, to quote the corps motto,
went 'where right and glory lead'.

While the Royal Engineers from the *Thames City* were building
the towns and roads of British Columbia, other sappers were
taking part in the Boundary Commission that was surveying and
mapping the border between the United States and British North
America. They cut out of the virgin forest a twenty-foot-wide
strip from the summit of the Rockies all the way to the Pacific
coast, building great pyramid-shaped cairns to mark a line that
zigzagged as close to the 49th parallel as the terrain allowed.

Whether it was the 49th parallel abroad or the prime meridian
line at home, the same system of endeavour underpinned both, the
British Empire offering a practical measure of nineteenth-century
optimism, enterprise and progress. The Engineers recorded their
work, as well as the landscape and the inhabitants they met along
the way, with the new science of photography. Two sappers dedicated themselves full-time to the care and use of the equipment.
They turned a tent into a darkroom in which to prepare the wet

collodion plates, and, to meet the challenge of giving a still-cumbersome process mobility, attached the heavy camera to the tailboard of a cart. The grave faces of the Indian tribesmen, who helped the Engineers along the way, were less an index of the arduous nature of their work than the fact that, at this early stage of photography, it took about thirty minutes for a smile to set.

It was yet one more example of the sapper's hundred different capacities. 'All roads lead to Rome,' it was said of that other great Empire, but when one's motto is 'Everywhere', then the road can lead anywhere. The only proviso of the sappers was that it should lead to right and glory.

The men who had taken the first snapshots of the 49th parallel had received their training from Charles Thurston Thompson, official photographer at the South Kensington Museum (later to become the Victoria and Albert). In the year 1857 alone, Thompson had taught and issued certificates of proficiency to eighty-seven sappers. Trained photographers were dispatched to Royal Engineers stations around the world, where their accumulated efforts amounted to the first systematic attempt to photograph the planet.

Thompson had got to know the Engineers when he was preparing the photographic exhibits for the Great Exhibition in 1851. It was the moment when the corps first began to emerge from military anonymity into a position of national renown. With the support of the royal patron Prince Albert, the commanding officer of the Royal Engineers at Woolwich, Lieutenant Colonel Reid, was appointed in February 1850 to be chairman of the exhibition's executive committee. Turning to his own corps for the trained manpower required to guarantee a punctual opening, he enlisted the services of twelve officers and two companies (over four hundred men), who helped not only with the construction of the Crystal Palace but also the organisation of the exhibits inside.

To take the pulse of Empire in its most confident phase, it was enough to stay with the corps of the Royal Engineers at home in London. When the proceeds from the Great Exhibition were used to purchase fifty acres of land on which to build new exhibition halls in promotion of the arts and sciences, a party of forty sappers cleared the ground. A Royal Engineers captain, Francis Fowke, was appointed to be Superintendent of Buildings for the site. He possessed the skills of a first-class architect, but was also the inventor of the bellows camera, an improved umbrella and a portable pontoon bridge of waterproof canvas. Embracing an age of rampant technological progress, he not only masterminded the vast complex of museums and public galleries that would transform South Kensington into what can be seen there today, but also figured out how to light them, with a machine that could ignite hundreds of gas burners in a few seconds.

After designing the galleries, courts and lecture theatre for the South Kensington Museum, Fowke began work on a Hall of the Arts and Sciences, inspired by a visit he had made to the Roman amphitheatres at Arles and Nîmes. Tragedy became an inseparable part of the enterprise. First, Prince Albert died in 1861 at the age of only forty-two. Then four years later, also at the age of forty-two, Fowke himself died. His fellow Royal Engineer Lieutenant Colonel Henry Scott took over a project that had now become an accompaniment to the monument that was being built for Albert across the road in the park. When the Queen was invited to lay the foundation stone, she asked that the words 'Royal Albert' be added to 'the Hall for the Arts and Sciences'.

Having no shortage of achievements themselves to commemorate, in 1889 the Royal Engineers published a history of the corps, which was dedicated to the memory of the Prince Consort, 'as a humble and grateful tribute'. Commemoration itself was one of the great achievements of the Victorian age.

7

The Queen's Shilling

There's a saying that the Irish know their history too well, and the English too little. My journey through life so far offers some embodiment of the adage. While my mother was alive, I had been cheerfully indifferent to my past. I knew the Irish and the English had often been at odds, but I couldn't even begin to explain why. Yet when I came back to London from Clare, I found myself gulping down history in great, long draughts, trying to unravel centuries of Anglo-Irish enmity that previously I had found far too tortuous to want to think about. After all, my Irish family had been nurtured in the cradle of such enmity, so I thought I had to make some effort to understand it, but hopefully without bearing the grudges that my mother begrudged the Irish. To wear history lightly so that it does not hamper you, surely that was a good English quality.

Whether it was William of Orange, or Cromwell, or Elizabeth I, or Henry VIII, the centuries of wars and confiscations created the pattern of ownership that gave Clare its nineteenth-century complexion: a handful of Protestant landowners lived in the big houses, while a multitude of Catholic farmers eked out a subsistence on land they did not own. According to the *Parliamentary Gazetteer of Ireland*, in 1834 there were forty Protestants in the parish of Quin, and 3,093 Catholics, yet those Catholics were still required to contribute to the living of the local vicar. It was an obvious grievance which lay behind the tithe wars of the 1830s and ended only with the disestablishment of the Church of Ireland in 1869.

Although there were still massive disparities in fortune and privilege, it became possible in an improving climate to foster relationships of mutual regard between the two communities and to begin to forgive the past. Perhaps my mixed heritage predisposed me to look for the stories of conciliation.

Captain Blood, for example. After my grandfather Patrick Lynch died, one of the people who tried to help his widow get back his missing pension was Captain Charles Blood of Ballykilty Manor. The Bloods were an old Anglo-Irish family, whose ancestor Colonel Thomas Blood was famous for having stolen the Crown Jewels. When the colonel was caught, he was brought before Charles II.

'What if I should give you your life?' asked the King.

'I would endeavour to deserve it,' answered Blood.

The King not only gave him his life but also an estate in Ireland. Whether or not Colonel Blood did make any effort to deserve his fortune, I like to think that at least the help that his descendant offered the Lynch family was some small restitution for all the land that the English had stolen from the Irish over the centuries. But otherwise the Bloods made recompense through the more conventional means of service to the Empire. One of Captain Blood's relations was General Sir Bindon Blood, who in 1897 had been the commander of the campaign that had lifted the siege of Malakand on the North-West Frontier. At the time of my grandfather's death in 1938, he was the Chief Royal Engineer, although he was then well into his nineties. An admiring Sir Winston Churchill had dedicated a book to him.

Giving land in Ireland had once been a favourite way for an English King to reward a subject, although that land was really no more his to give than the Crown Jewels had been Colonel Blood's to take. Not far from the Blood manor at Ballykilty was Hazelwood House, where the Studdert family lived. According to *Burke's Landed Gentry*, their ancestor, the Reverend George Studdert, was awarded his land in Ireland after preaching a particularly good sermon in William of Orange's camp at Limerick during the Jacobite Wars.

At the end of the nineteenth century, when the five Lynch brothers were growing up, Britain was making serious efforts to redress the injustices of the past, with the introduction of the Land Acts and even the promise of Home Rule.

Although my fuzzy childhood picture of my Irish forebears owning an estate called 'Deer Park' was not true, the Lynches and the McInerneys knew the big houses well, having worked in them as servants. The Anglo-Irish gentry might have enjoyed immense privilege, but they were a source of employment in a countryside that otherwise offered few opportunities. The McInerneys were stewards at Hazelwood House, until it was set on fire by the IRA in 1921,* while my mother's grandfather, John

---

* The IRA destroyed the house in a reprisal against its Loyalist owner, Francis Hickman. My aunt Joan remembers seeing its burnt-out husk as a small girl in the 1930s after the land had passed into the possession of the Butlers, who were distant relations of the family. 'There was a beautiful barn and stables, but there was this old ruin. It always used to puzzle me how old Butler had got the land. I don't know if he had anything to do with the fire, but I know he had been IRA. I guess that must have had something to do with it.'

Lynch, had been a gardener for a Church of Ireland vicar who owned land near Doora.

One day, according to a family story, my great-grandfather John Lynch put down a fountain pen and a shovel side by side on the table and told his sons to take their pick. The fact that there was even a choice was due to the vicar he worked for, a Studdert, who helped to give the boys a good education, but it was a necessarily narrow choice in a rural community that offered so few prospects to its people. That all five Lynch brothers should have become soldiers was less a coincidence than a reflection of this fact. Soldier, priest, farmer, rebel – the choice was not much wider than that.

When they were old enough to do so, each of the five brothers, John, Patrick, James, Michael and Thomas, joined the Ordnance Survey office in Ennis, one of four offices that had been established in Ireland in 1824. Responsible for both the civilian and military mapping needs of the United Kingdom since its establishment in 1791, the Ordnance Survey was under the direction of a Royal Engineers officer, who would recommend promising surveyors for enlistment in the Survey companies of the corps.

This was how the Lynches came to join the British army. The earliest document relating to their service was the official note of recommendation that the director general of the Ordnance Survey, Colonel Sir John Farquharson, wrote for the oldest of the five brothers, John Lynch, on 21 August 1894. I found it included with his service record:

A description of this man is given in the margin, and certificates of Character and Trade Proficiency are attached, together with certified specimens of his 'writing from dictation' and 'arithmetic'.

He is well developed and apparently suitable for the Corps. He is reported to be a Fair Surveyor and as such I recommend his enlistment.

Ten days later, both John and Patrick had enlisted together. I wondered whether they had joined at the Ordnance Survey office on the Kilrush Road, but when I went there during my visit to Clare I had only the sense of a trail going cold. Housed in a modern municipal building, the office seemed to have long ago lost any meaningful connection with its past. There was nothing there, I thought, that the Lynch brothers would have recognised.

The electric bell I pressed at the public counter made no sound, so eventually I began to knock on office doors in search of help. When at last I found someone, he told me that the prime role of the office was to update maps and it had no record of its history. For that kind of information I would need to visit the head office in Phoenix Park, Dublin.

I returned to the street, disappointed not to have found any trace of the two brothers. But as I began to walk towards the town centre, I noticed, on the other side of the road, a stone statue of a soldier kneeling on a wall that ran along the edge of a housing estate. I crossed over to look more closely. A plaque explained that the wall had once belonged to an old military barracks that had been built on the site of a fever hospital dating back to the time of the Great Famine. 'In 1855 the military authorities took possession of the fever hospital which became the headquarters of the Clare Militia . . . To the end of the century officers and men who were quartered here served with distinction in many overseas engagements with the British army.'

It can only have been in recent years that anyone would even have dared to put up such a statue. Here at last – of all places in Dev's County – the experience of the Irish soldier in the British army was being commemorated. It was most likely here that John and Patrick began their service in the army, although only a week later they would both be transferred to the Royal Engineers' headquarters in England.

8

The Shadow of This Time

Leaving the Royal Engineers Museum was like walking out of a dark cinema at the end of an epic movie. I had to adjust to the daylight, so at odds was the spectacle with the reality of contemporary Britain. Just as few people came to the museum, Chatham itself had long ago become a backwater. Once, the town was home not only to the Royal Engineers, but also a division of Royal Marines, and a dockyard that for more than four hundred years had built the Royal Navy's ships. But the marines left in 1950 and the dockyard was closed in 1984.

When I first walked from Chatham railway station to Brompton Barracks, the sign that I was heading in the right direction was a statue of Lord Kitchener. After Gordon possibly the Royal Engineers' most famous old soldier, the field marshal sat astride a horse on Dock Road. Beyond were the barrack blocks named after him, which had recently been sold off for redevelopment. Was that why he was looking away from them, I wondered, towards St Mary the Virgin on the other side of Dock Road?

Although there was not much more comfort to be had there.

In the late nineteenth century, the tower of Chatham's former parish church was restored and eight giant bells cast to mark Queen Victoria's jubilee. But now the building was disused and derelict, boarded up against thieves and vandals, while the bells that used to sound across the town had been taken down and moved to Cornwall. The Avenger of Gordon was no more able to save the church from this different age than the soldiers who lay in its graveyard.

I found myself thinking of the film *Jubilee*, of the magician John Dee, who conjures up the spirit Ariel to transport Elizabeth I into the jubilee year of her twentieth-century namesake. In a vision that contrasts starkly with her own golden age, Ariel shows the Queen the 'shadow of her time', a future England mired in anarchy and violence. But in mapping the past, it seemed to me, whenever we put aside the bias of nostalgia or patriotism or kinship, we soon find that the 'golden age' is a dark age too, that its shadow is already there. In returning to the times of my grandfather and his brothers, perhaps especially as a British Jewish Irish Catholic, it behoved me to look at the two sides of the Queen's shilling, the two pasts that existed side by side.

In my mind's eye I turned the clock back to a day in 1890 when Gordon had yet to be avenged (although the Empire was already planning that he should be). Chatham had turned out to celebrate the unveiling of his new statue at Brompton Barracks in an event that involved the *esprit de corps* of an entire nation.

The Prince of Wales, who was the guest of honour, arrived from London at Chatham railway station. The dignitaries who accompanied him included the Duke of Cambridge and the minister for war, Edward Stanhope. From the station, the Hussars accompanied the royal party a mile and a half to the barracks along a route that was thronged with cheering spectators several lines deep. Nearly every house displayed some form of decoration for the occasion. The town was a sea of Union Jacks, floral garlands, bunting and banners, with slogans such as 'TO THE HERO OF KHARTOUM', 'HONOUR TO GORDON' and 'HONOUR OUR PRINCE, WHO HONOURS GORDON'.

Along the way, the procession passed under a series of triumphal arches erected by the various civic and military institutions of the town. The first, representing the Freemasons, featured two castle towers of wood and canvas, with the Masons' motto, *Audi, Vidi, Tace* (Hear, See, Be Silent), suspended from the summit of the arch high above the road. Half a mile further along, the fire brigade had put up an arch that comprised two fire-escape ladders stretched between flanking towers, which were decorated with coils of hose and pictures of the firemen at work.

The Royal Engineers of course made sure that their display should be the most splendid of all. A phalanx of gleaming brass howitzers and torpedoes stood before an arch that was decorated with equipment demonstrating every aspect of the sappers' craft. On top were three self-righting boats guarded by life-size models in full diver's dress. The afternoon was a pageant of gaudy enthusiasm that today would perhaps most resemble a Mardi Gras carnival. Feeding on the pride of an Empire that, for all the loss of one more hero, had yet to suffer any serious challenge, it defied any sense of measure or good taste.

A salute was fired and the national anthem played as the royal party passed into Brompton Barracks. Three battalions of Engineers, over two thousand men, were drawn up on the outer parade, while a guard of honour stood at the entrance to an enclosure of stands that surrounded the new monument. Hidden beneath the drapery of several Union Jacks, the statue stood on a base surrounded by blue forget-me-nots, with clumps of lilies at the four corners.

After the Prince of Wales had spoken in tribute to 'brave General Gordon', a name that 'will be honoured and esteemed for ever by all Englishmen', a young bugler gave him a cord, which he tugged to unveil the statue. The corps band then played Gordon's favourite hymn, 'For Ever with the Lord', and the three battalions ended the formal ceremony with a march past.

The royal party stayed on for lunch in the officers' mess, where they were given a guided tour of the various spoils of Empire that the corps had brought back from the four corners of the earth. Of particular interest that day was a wooden throne General Gordon had sent back from China thirty years before. Featuring decorative panels of the most beautiful, intricate carving, it stood on the claws of a dragon. Three sets of cushions of imperial yellow silk rested on a triple seat . . .

But now the other side. *Ubique* did not always lead to right and glory. Here it had led to a plundered, oriental throne. What kind of justice was there in that? In nineteenth-century Britain there were very few shades of grey. *Ubique* meant a chiaroscuro world of 'good' and 'bad', in which the murky reality was often lost in the dazzle and darkness. Gordon had first arrived in China during the last days of the Second Opium War, when an Anglo-French force was on the point of forcing the Emperor to yield to demands for a free trade that was a major cause of China's endemic drug addiction.

In October 1860, he took part in the British siege preparations that forced the Emperor to open the gates to Peking, winning promotion from Captain to Major for his contribution. He took part, too, in the last act of the war when the British high commissioner, Lord Elgin, ordered the burning of the Emperor's Summer Palace, Yuen-ming-yuen, in reprisal for the Chinese execution of members of a deputation that had been sent to negotiate a truce.

'It makes one's heart burn to see such beauty destroyed,' he wrote, 'it was as if Windsor Palace, South Kensington Museum and British Museum, all in one, were in flames: you can scarcely imagine the beauty and magnificence of the things we were bound to destroy.'

He regretted the fact that the sheer number of palace buildings meant that there had not been an opportunity to 'plunder them carefully'. This was a time when prizes of war were recognised as an established perk of the soldier's profession. The French soldiers, who had first taken possession of the palace, had already enjoyed several days' start on the British, who had to work very hard to catch up.

British complicity went up to the very top. When Queen Victoria was presented with a Pekinese dog that had been found in the Summer Palace, she named it Looty. Mentioning Looty now reminds me that when I was very small, my mother – daughter of a Royal Engineer that she was – had a Pekinese called Snooty, presumably a descendant of the original beast of plunder.

A century and a half later traces of the theft are still percolating through the world's auction houses. In 2008 a cache of letters that Gordon wrote to a fellow Royal Engineers officer turned up at Christie's.

'I have got such a piece of plunder which I think will be for the mess,' he wrote from Peking on 25 October 1860. 'It is part of a throne out of the Summer Palace. It is of iron wood and some red wood beautifully carved. There was a splendid screen behind, which I took for Mitchell the General and I kept the throne.' Mitchell was the commander of one of the two divisions that had formed the British military expedition. Three weeks later Gordon complained about some Royal Engineers officers who wanted to share in his gesture of giving the throne to the mess. 'I am rather sore at some of the other fellows taking such very good care not to present any of their own plunder and yet so willing to join in presenting mine.'

Gordon may have expressed disapproval of the wanton destruction that the looters left behind them, but it paled in comparison to the fires that Elgin ordered, which razed to the ground a man-made marvel that offered an embodiment of Coleridge's opium-inspired vision of Xanadu: 'a stately pleasure-dome' that 'twice five miles of fertile ground with walls and towers were girdled round'.

Not such a marvel was the arrogance with which the British were able to commit this act of barbarism, which far exceeded any cultural crime Elgin's father might have been guilty of when he removed the marble sculptures from the Parthenon.

Viscount Wolseley – the same Wolseley who had unveiled the memorial windows in Rochester Cathedral – had served as a staff officer in the campaign. He remembered that the French had protested against the British putting 'the coup de grâce to their work', but it was, he argued, a 'vengeance' that had served to secure the Emperor's complete submission, thereby saving many lives. The assumption of British superiority spared him the trouble of considering whether there might not have been another, less destructive way to achieve the same outcome.

Yuen-ming-yuen may have been beautiful, but Wolseley dismissed it as the product of a decadent, less significant culture, with China's five thousand years of civilisation reckoned of little worth. 'In their thirst after decoration, and in their inherent love for minute embellishment, the artists and architects of China have failed to produce any great work capable of inspiring those sensations of awe or admiration which strike everyone when first gazing upon the magnificent creations of European architects,' commented Wolseley. 'Taking Yuen-ming-yuen all in all, it was a gem of its kind, and yet I do not suppose there was a single man who visited it without being disappointed. There was an absence of grandeur about it, for which no amount of careful gardening and pretty ornaments can compensate.'

Such philistine contempt made anything possible. Elgin returned home to London in triumph. After all, he was the first Englishman ever to make the Emperor of China kowtow. He had an opportunity to explain the destruction of the Summer Palace when he attended a banquet held to open that year's Summer Exhibition of the Royal Academy of the Arts, which then occupied the east wing of the National Gallery in Trafalgar Square. Many prominent members of the British establishment attended, including the prime minister, Lord Palmerston, and most of his Cabinet.

After dinner, the president of the Academy proposed a toast to Britain's army and navy, who provided the security that made the appreciation of the arts possible. The First Lord of the Admiralty and the commander-in-chief of the army were both present to express their thanks. Then it was Elgin's turn to be honoured.

'The toast which I have next to propose is in some degree connected to the last,' said the president. 'It is, at all events, connected with a universal feeling of admiration and respect. That toast is: "The Health of his Excellency the Earl of Elgin."'

The room broke into loud, continued cheering as the entire company raised their glasses to his health. When the applause finally began to die down, Elgin gave his thanks in a speech that was full of the pompous circumlocutions of the age. This was the age of steam, after all, in which expansion seemed to take every form, from the monuments that were going up in the capital to the new territories that were being acquired for the Queen; from the florid ornamentation that decorated public buildings to the Ciceronian rhetoric that embellished the least speech with an endless series of clauses. In this context, Elgin's words seemed almost modest.

'I am especially gratified,' he said, 'because I trust that I may infer from it that in your judgement . . . I am not so incorrigibly *barbarous* as to be incapable of feeling the humanising influences which fall upon us from the noble works of art by which we are surrounded.' There was an eruption of laughter at the word 'barbarous'. It was a word that China's rulers had been using of England and her merchants for many years, but now the tables had been turned. The cheers carried Elgin forward to a second pun. 'As I have ventured to approach so nearly to the margin of a *burning* question, I hope I may be allowed to take one step more in the same direction, and to assure you that no one regretted more sincerely than I did the destruction of that collection of summer-houses and kiosks, already and previously to any act of mine rifled of their contents, which was dignified by the title of Summer Palace of the Chinese Emperor.'

Before imperial Britain's rulers, he made one of history's greatest desecrations seem as though it were just a matter of a few beach huts, arguing that what he had done was the necessary act to avoid another year of war. 'I trust that there is no man serving the Crown in a responsible position who would not hesitate when it is presented to him as to the decision at which he should arrive.'

No one contradicted him.

Amid further cheers, he quickly passed on to the question of whether British art would benefit in any way from the opening up of China. He acknowledged that the country deserved credit for an ingenuity of mind that had, centuries before anyone else, produced gunpowder, the mariner's compass and the printing press. 'But in the hands of the Chinese themselves the invention of gunpowder has exploded in harmless crackers and fireworks. The mariner's compass has produced nothing better than the coasting junk. The art of printing has stagnated in stereotyped editions of Confucius; and the most cynical representations of the grotesque have been the principal products of Chinese conceptions of the sublime and beautiful. Nevertheless, I am disposed to believe that under this mass of abortions and rubbish there lie some sparks of a diviner fire, which the genius of my countrymen may gather and nurse into a flame.'

More cheering greeted this justification of the imperial mission. The president then offered a toast to the commander of the Chinese expedition, Lieutenant General Sir Hope Grant. When he made the customary response, Grant kept his speech short, saving his greatest praise for the new breach-loading Armstrong gun, which had flattened any defence that the Chinese had cared to put up against it.

The pride in British military supremacy on display that evening outshone the paintings in the exhibition that the banquet had been meant to inaugurate, so many of which were portraits of British viceroys, generals and admirals. A cartoon in *Punch* a few months previously, soon after the news of the Chinese surrender, captured this highpoint of jingoism. Under the caption of the 'New Elgin Marbles', it depicted a stern Lord Elgin dictating terms to a cowering Chinese Emperor. Cradling a large cannonball against his chest, and with a heap of more cannonballs at his disposal, the British high commissioner demands that the Emperor honour the terms of the trading treaty that had been one of the causes of the war. 'Come, knuckle down! No cheating this time!'

In the Britain of 1861 there were few artists or writers who had not been carried away by the triumphalist mood, but the French writer Victor Hugo, who had been living in exile in the Channel Islands ever since Napoleon III had overturned France's Second Republic in a *coup d'état*, offered this more independent voice:

> One day two bandits entered the Summer Palace. One plundered, the other burned. Victory can be a thieving woman, or so it seems. The devastation of the Summer Palace was accomplished by the two victors acting jointly. Mixed up in all this is the name of Elgin, which inevitably calls to mind the Parthenon. What was done to the Parthenon was done to the Summer Palace, more thoroughly and better, so that nothing of it should be left. All the treasures of all our cathedrals put together could not equal this formidable and splendid museum of the Orient. It contained not only masterpieces of art, but masses of jewellery. What a great exploit, what a windfall! One of the two victors filled his pockets; when the other saw this he filled his coffers. And back they came to Europe, arm in arm, laughing away. Such is the story of the two bandits.

NEW ELGIN MARBLES.

Elgin to Emperor. "COME, KNUCKLE DOWN! NO CHEATING THIS TIME!"

We Europeans are the civilized ones, and for us the Chinese are the barbarians. This is what civilization has done to barbarism.

But to judge from the headlines, most people would have agreed with Wolseley's audience in the Royal Academy of the Arts that the Chinese needed to be 'taught a lesson'.

It does not take long to find a modern parallel for what the British and French did to the Summer Palace. A recent example is Islamic State's destruction of the ancient town of Palmyra. In our own chiaroscuro age, it is difficult to speak of progress with any great confidence, but I suppose it is some kind of progress if we now can recognise the racist arrogance of the Empire we built; can even express – without feeling totally out of step – discomfort that items looted from the Summer Palace should continue to come up for sale in auctions, or that friezes levered off the face of the Parthenon should continue to sit in the British Museum.

Some talk of Alexander / And some of Hercules . . . Of all the world's great heroes, the Royal Engineers certainly provided a few, though how many of them can we still proudly talk of today?

9

None That Can Compare

'*When you did Irish history, you wouldn't have done it in the detailed way that I did it,*' said my mother as she enumerated the endless grievances that went back centuries. Growing up in England, I didn't do Irish history at all. But its legacy was impossible to ignore. I just had to stand before the Great Famine monument in Ennistymon to appreciate the impossibility of ever leaving Irish history behind. The challenge was how to come to terms with it.

I had first come across Captain Thomas Drummond when I was reading about the early days of the Ordnance Survey – he had been one of its pioneers – but it was only later, when I found an old guide to the School of Military Engineering in the corps library, that I began to realise how unique he was, even among the men-of-all-work of the Royal Engineers, with their 'hundred different capacities'. In the final chapter, the former director of the school, Lieutenant Colonel Ward, gave the reader a tour of the pictures and statues that could be found in the headquarters' mess. Among seven statues in the North Annexe was one of

Drummond. 'His name is far less well known in our Corps today than it deserves to be,' Ward wrote. 'When we consider first his character, and in the second place his achievements in both science and politics, we may well question whether an officer of greater or even equal promise ever wore the uniform of the Royal Engineers.'

Although Ward's guide did not include a picture of the statue, it reproduced the words that had been inscribed at its base:

CAPTAIN THOMAS DRUMMOND, R.E.
2nd Lieut., March, 1816.
2nd Captain, August, 1837.
Private Secretary to Chancellor of Exchequer, 1833.
Under-Secretary for Ireland, 1835.
Commissioner, Irish Railways, 1836.
Died 15th April, 1840.

I was intrigued by the discontinuity of his career. How, I wondered, did one go from being a second lieutenant in the Royal Engineers to the Chancellor of the Exchequer's Private Secretary? But even more intriguing for me was what could it have been that Drummond had achieved as Under-Secretary for Ireland?

The more I found out, the more I was pulled into a life that had ended before the five Lynch brothers were even born, yet demanded to be a part of my story because it justified a small Irish girl's pride in the Royal Engineers. Drummond had risen no higher in rank than captain and had not a single battle honour to his name, but he was the hero beyond compare.

I wondered whether my grandfather and great-uncles had seen his statue during their training at Chatham when Saturday-morning fatigue duties required sappers to polish the floor of the head-quarters' mess. The thought made me realise with a jolt that their time was actually much closer to Drummond's time than my own, a time that did not even have photographs to help me through the degrees of separation.

When Thomas Drummond was born in Edinburgh in 1797, the very idea of 'Briton' was still taking shape, albeit as much through violence as any sense of common destiny. The 1800 Act for the Union of Great Britain and Ireland followed on the heels of the notoriously bloody 1798 rebellion of the United Irishmen. Nor were the rebellions of Drummond's own native Scotland so very far in the past. But his own life offered a model for a different kind of relationship, in which to be a 'Briton' might really be a way to 'flourish great and free'.

The two Victorian biographies that exist of him were motivated by the politics of their time. The first was written in 1867 by John Ferguson McLennan, a Scottish anthropologist and social reformer, who called Drummond's period as Under-Secretary of Ireland the 'only great effort yet put forward for the renovation of that unhappy land'. The second was written in 1889 by an Irish Catholic, Richard Barry O'Brien, who was a supporter of Home Rule. He described his book as 'a labour of love', but it must have had the practical purpose of contributing to the Home Rule campaign, which was then near the beginning of its long, difficult path, before the disillusionment set in.

O'Brien was born in Kilrush, County Clare. When his book was published, my grandfather would have just started out as an apprentice at the Ennis Ordnance Survey office. Perhaps this was when he first heard of Drummond, before he even began his sapper's training at Chatham.

If the Ennis office took any pride in the fact that it was a Clare man who had written the biography of a great pioneer of the Irish survey, I could imagine my grandfather reading about Drummond's contribution to the Survey only to find himself even more astonished by the multitude of other things that, Royal Engineers-style, Drummond had achieved in Ireland. If you wanted an argument that it was no disgrace for a young Irish surveyor to take the Queen's shilling, it would have been hard to find a better example.

According to the *Genealogical Memoir of the Most Noble and Ancient House of Drummond*, which was published during Drummond's lifetime, his father James, the last laird of Cromrie, 'was a gentleman of great ingenuity', who 'new modelled entirely the village of Cromrie', but died when Thomas was only three, leaving debts that forced his family to sell the estate and move from Edinburgh to the nearby town of Musselburgh.

Here Drummond's mother, Elizabeth, made the best of the family's suddenly reduced circumstances, eking out a tiny income to provide for her five children. A well-off family friend, Mr Aitchison of Drummore, who had admired Drummond's father, paid for Thomas's schooling and became a kind of informal guardian, providing the advice and means to help him to make his way in the world.

It was clear from early on that the young Drummond had inherited his father's ingenuity if nothing else: he showed an extraordinary aptitude, as a sister put it, for 'making things'. His childhood enthusiasm for tin soldiers may have been unremarkable for a boy growing up during the Napoleonic Wars, but the miniature castles they fought over showed an impressive eye for authentic detail, with drawbridges that could be lowered or raised and cannons that really fired.

Clearly destined to be a military engineer, after study at Edinburgh High School, he became a cadet at the Royal Military Academy at Woolwich and received his commission into the Royal Engineers in July 1815.

To join the Engineers immediately after the Battle of Waterloo, when the corps had yet to develop its full repertoire of versatility, must at first have seemed rather bad timing. There was little to do beyond routine training exercises. Incapable of being idle, Drummond took advantage of the spare time to work on an idea for an improved pontoon bridge. For the want of any obvious military need, it received little encouragement, but his flair for invention found a peacetime use when he was posted in 1820 to the Ordnance Survey, under the command of its new director, Lieutenant Colonel Thomas Colby.

The Survey was still engaged in the Principal Triangulation of Great Britain, which had begun with Sir William Roy's baseline on Hounslow Heath thirty years before. One of the most obvious needs was for better lights so that triangulation points could be observed more quickly in the murky English weather. Drummond dedicated himself to the problem. He rose early every morning to study chemistry before turning up to work at the Ordnance Survey, which, as an organisation originally founded to produce maps for military use, was then housed in the headquarters of the Board of Ordnance at the Tower of London.

Learning about the incandescence of lime at one of Michael Faraday's lectures at the Royal Institution, Drummond began to experiment with the substance until he had developed a lamp of unprecedented brightness. To demonstrate the new invention he borrowed the armoury room of the Tower, which was three hundred feet long. When the audience of scientists had taken their seats between the pikes and shields that decorated the windowless walls, he had the room darkened and then, one by one, exposed three lights. First, a standard British lighthouse lamp. Second, the new Fresnel lamp used in French lighthouses, which was magnified by an ingenious multi-prism lens to make it much brighter than its British rival. And finally . . . the limelight.

'[A] glare shone forth,' wrote the astronomer Sir John Herschel, 'overpowering and, as it were, annihilating both its predecessors, which appeared by its side, the one as a feeble gleam, which it required attention to see; the other like a mere plate of heated metal. A shout of triumph and admiration burst from all present.'

Drummond's light received its first field test not in England

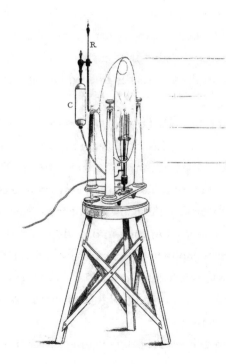

but Ireland. Following the Act of Union, the British government had to integrate the Irish taxation system into that of the United Kingdom. Since the accurate mapping of the Irish townlands was required to provide a basis for a fair valuation, the Ordnance Survey switched its resources across the Irish Sea and, in the summer of 1825, began the systematic mapping of the country on the scale of six inches to the mile. From the outset, the surveyors had to battle with what their director Colby called the 'inveterate haze and fogginess' of the country. The first of the great triangles was to be created by observing the 2,100ft peak of Slieve Snaght in Inishowen, Donegal, from Divis Mountain, near Belfast. A persistent mist had prevented a successful sighting for many weeks, so that it was already late October when Drummond and a team of seven sappers were dispatched from Belfast on a two-day trek to Inishowen. Setting up camp on the summit of the mountain, they had to battle fierce winds that made pitching their tents impossible. They built stone huts instead, where they sheltered for several days until the weather offered enough of a respite to set up their equipment.

It was long after the end of the surveying season. Colonel Colby had already returned to London, leaving two Royal Engineers officers on top of Divis Mountain to look out for Drummond's light. In this time before radio, telephone or even telegraph, there was no means of warning them ahead of time. They had no alternative but to gaze at the far horizon day after day, the immensity of the remote, misty landscape lending their vigil a biblical quality. 'The earth was without form and void, and darkness was over the face of the deep . . .' But then the light appeared like a bright new star in the firmament.

'Your light has been most brilliant tonight for three hours and twenty minutes,' Lieutenant Hastings Murphy, one of the two observers on Divis, wrote to Drummond. 'I must most heartily congratulate you, my dear friend, on the complete success which has thus crowned your very ingenious and laborious exertions for the good of the service.' The distance between Divis and Slieve Snaght – in the straight line that the light itself had made it possible to calculate – was sixty-seven miles.

After the successful sighting, the weather closed in, and the surveyors' stone shelters were buried in deep snow, so that several days were spent perched on the punishingly cold hill before they could begin the gruelling journey back to Belfast.

What impressed Drummond's contemporaries in Ireland was how his engagement with the country went far beyond simply charting its mountaintops. He wanted to know about its people too. '[E]ngaged in the Ordnance Survey,' commented the writer Daniel Madden, 'he had abundant opportunities for seeing the Irish character in all its native force. Lying on the mountainside at night in some savage wild of Antrim or Tyrone, with the stars over his head, and with no vestiges of civilisation in the neighbourhood, he would "draw out" the Irish peasants who came to the Engineers' station . . . He saw – he studied – and, with his genial sympathy, he felt the Irish character and nature.'

After the triumph of Divis Mountain, Drummond spent three more years with the Irish Survey, climbing many of the other summits that were scattered across the country in a mission that was often as much a test of physical endurance as scientific ingenuity. A dogged persistence drove him on to brave extremes of weather that took a heavy toll on his health. No sacrifice seemed too much in service to an enterprise that was one of the great pioneering adventures of the period. His various inventions helped the Irish

Survey to achieve an unprecedented accuracy of measurement. As well as the limelight, he devised a heliostat that could be used during the day to reflect the sun at an exact, designated angle; and, for the rods used to measure the all-important first line of the Survey, on which the accuracy of the subsequent network of triangulation depended, super-accurate 'compensation bars', which allowed for the expansion that heat caused in the metal. A baseline of verification was marked out along the shore of Lough Foyle. While forty years before, the founder of the Ordnance Survey, Sir William Roy, had been content to take his line on Hounslow Heath to the nearest 7/10th of a foot, the result for the Irish line was to four decimal places: 41,640.8873 feet. Drummond even devised a scheme to verify the verification, subjecting successive points along the line to a series of triangulations that furnished a mathematical calculation of the entire length.

There was an epic quality to all this striving, which was of a piece with Drummond's larger life as well as the time and society of which he was a part. From Slieve Snaght, the Royal Engineers' surveyors were able to extend their triangles down to Slieve League and Cuilcagh, and so on from there until they reached Hungry Hill and Carrigfadda at Ireland's southernmost tip. By a different kind of triangulation – across history rather than mountains – Drummond could be connected to the larger enterprise of Britain in the first half of the nineteenth century. In this kind of triangulation, in this mapping of the past, my mother's voice comes back to me, during her last days giving me a whirlwind tour of Ireland's troubles: *'Nationalism! The minute that started, there was no peace!'*

There is an irony in the fact that Lough Foyle, the site of Drummond's baseline, so perfectly achieved, should a hundred years later become a borderline between two communities who could not resolve their differences. The beauty of science is the incontestable nature of reality, which means you can hope to reach ever greater degrees of truth. Maybe this was what made Drummond so special as he now moved from science into the endlessly contested arena of human society and politics, behaving as though you could get justice to four decimal points, and bringing to the task as much the eye of the engineer as the scientist, determined to overcome practical problems rather than merely speculate in abstract theories.

In 1829, Drummond returned from Ireland to begin a series of experiments with the aim of developing his light for general use in Britain's lighthouses. Although the fame of the invention brought him to the attention of the highest society, he cast a sceptical eye on such privilege. When he was invited to dinner with King William IV and his courtiers at the Royal Pavilion in Brighton, he wrote about the occasion afterwards, in a letter to his mother, with a characteristic detachment: 'The world is the same everywhere, varying only in the scale. Most of these people are of large fortune, and of a station in society to secure them every comfort and happiness; but they are fashion's slaves, and miserable.' Perhaps it was the scientist's compulsion to see truth that predisposed him to note the aesthetic conceits of the place. 'One room, spacious and lofty, contained gorgeous furniture, and splendid paintings; but the paintings represented nothing, I should apprehend, ever seen in this planet. Birds, beasts, and fishes glittered in gold, but were very unlike the beasts of the field, or the fowls of the air, such as we are accustomed to see them.'

Drummond's ability to see what was actually before him was

a simple but rather rare skill that a growing number of important people were able to appreciate. Not least, the Lord Chancellor, Lord Henry Brougham, who in 1831 requested a demonstration of the famous limelight. A dinner was arranged in the house of one of the Chancellor's friends. Drummond set up the light in a greenhouse in the garden, directing it to shine into the drawing room to which the guests retired after the meal. 'The Chancellor seemed greatly afraid of his eye, and could hardly be persuaded to look at it. I spied him, however, peeping at a corner, and immediately turned the reflector full upon him.'

Blinded by the light or not, the Chancellor appreciated Drummond enough to recommend him, with his experience of the Ordnance Survey, to become chairman of the Boundary Commission that was set up to determine the parliamentary constituencies for the Great Reform Bill. It was the beginning of a different career. Putting aside work on an invention whose commercial development might have brought him considerable wealth, the lieutenant in the Royal Engineers chose instead to harness reason in the pursuit of social justice.

Sweeping away the 'rotten boroughs' and enfranchising the large towns that had swelled in population with the Industrial Revolution, the 1832 Reform Act was the first step towards modern mass democracy. By far the greatest challenge for the commission, in Drummond's words, lay 'in obtaining the correct data on which to proceed with certainty and with justice'. The commission had to assess the spread of population and wealth across 379 constituencies. It then had to redraw the boundaries of the boroughs to create constituencies of equal electoral weight in a country of the most varied geography. It was a mammoth task that required Drummond to supervise, coordinate and appraise the work of twenty-four commissioners and thirty surveyors. To determine the constituencies, he had to devise a complex principle of computation that took into account the continuing property qualification for enfranchisement. Anticipating the debate that the chosen method was bound to provoke, he took care to test its correctness with the leading mathematicians of the time.

At the end of December 1831, he published a list of the 'rotten boroughs', arranging them in ascending order of their importance according to the number of houses and assessed taxes paid. Heading the list was Old Sarum. Amounting to little more than a few fields and some ditches near Salisbury, it was long uninhabited land that belonged to an absentee proprietor, yet it was entitled to return two MPs to the House of Commons. The absurdity inspired the following suggestion from the Poet Laureate Robert Southey for an inscription that might be placed on a monument there:

> Reader, if thou canst boast the noble name
> Of Englishman, it is enough to know
> Thou standest in Old Sarum. But, if chance,
> 'Twas thy misfortune in some other land,
> Inheritor of slavery, to be born,
> Read and be envious! Dost thou see yon hut,
> Its old mud mossy walls with many a patch
> Spotted? Know, foreigner! so wisely well
> In England it is order'd, that the laws
> Which bind the people, from themselves should spring;
> Know that the dweller in that little hut,

That wretched hovel, to the senate sends
Two delegates. Think, foreigner, where such
An individual's rights, how happy all!

Yet there was a powerful opposition that was prepared to defend Old Sarum's right to send two MPs to the House of Commons. As chairman of the commission, Drummond became the butt of their ire. When his recommendations were debated in Parliament, the notoriously caustic John Croker, who regarded the reform proposals as a dangerous encroachment upon England's ancient constitution, ridiculed him as the government's 'blind guide'. It was Croker who, in his pride for the old and mistrust of the new, had coined the term 'Conservative' for his fellow Tories.

A truer measure of what Drummond had achieved was to be found in an editorial that *The Times* published after the Reform Act had been passed in June 1832. It celebrated 'the victory of dispassionate opinion over interested prejudice – of universal justice over glaring selfishness – of principles which are eternal over rotten and obsolete institutions'. On the eve of the Act receiving the Royal Assent, Drummond's fellow commissioners wrote a letter to him expressing their appreciation of the skill, intelligence and – not least – good humour with which he had guided their efforts. They asked him to grant them the favour of sitting for a portrait. 'We hope this will be preserved in your family as a memorial of the sense entertained of your merits by a number of gentlemen who have acted with you in the execution of a delicate and arduous duty, intimately connected with an important event in the history of our country.'

Wearing a dark waistcoat and jacket, a young man in his

mid-thirties stands by a table draped in a crimson cloth, resting his hand on a sheath of papers which I imagine must be the Boundary Commission's report. The sobriety of dress complements a plain, simple setting. The overall suggestion is of reason, energy and purpose, although a hint of a smile brings out an accompanying warmth and humanity.

The absence of any ornament or decoration is striking. There is no room for the incidental. Everything depicted seems to have a symbolic purpose. I wonder what the two thin but wide volumes might be that sit on the table next to the report – an inventory maybe of the new borough constituencies that Drummond and his commissioners brought into being? Far from perfect, perhaps, with a franchise that still limited the electorate to the prosperous male population, but still a truer basis for the representation of the people than the oligarchy that had previously existed, there to be improved upon, step by step, in the years and decades ahead.

The way Drummond is dressed in a practical suit, well cut, tidy but without frippery, echoes the same plainness of the surroundings. There is no sign of cufflinks on his sleeves, no watch in his fob pocket. Their absence is less an index of his austerity than the fact that he had the time neither to think about such things nor to acquire them.

When the commissioners had briefed the portrait painter Henry Pickersgill, whose previous subjects had included Lord Nelson, they gave a description of a man who had routinely worked from dawn to beyond dusk. The completion of the report allowed Drummond a few months of leisure in which to savour his achievement and enjoy its fruits in the first reformed election that took place in December 1832. But soon he plunged himself

into the progressive cause again, becoming Private Secretary to the Chancellor of the Exchequer, Viscount Althorn, in the Whig government that had won a substantial majority. In this position, he had an important role in what must have seemed, to its age, an extraordinary engine room of reform. Within the space of three years, Parliament voted for a grant to support education for the poor, which was the first step towards a system of state education; it introduced the Factory Act to address some of the appalling human cost of the Industrial Revolution; it passed an act to abolish slavery in the Empire; and with the Municipal Corporation Act set up the basis for elected town councils.

There was no shortage of pressing causes to feed Drummond's appetite for ceaseless activity, but at least he found time to fall in love. Maria Kinnaird was the ward of Richard 'Conversation' Sharp, a successful merchant and well-known literary and society host, who was a prominent Whig supporter. She had been orphaned as a small child by the eruption of a volcano on the West Indian island of St Vincent, where her parents had been planters. A considerable beauty, she possessed her guardian's talent for conversation but also sang like an angel.

The portrait of Drummond was completed in April 1835. It offers a snapshot of him a few months before his marriage to Maria, which took place in November, but at a turning point in his political career as well. That year a new Whig government was elected under the leadership of Lord Melbourne and in the summer he was offered the post of Irish Under-Secretary at Dublin Castle, the head of the British administration in Ireland.

As they set up their matrimonial home in the Under-Secretary's Lodge in Phoenix Park, Drummond and his bride must have known that they could not expect to enjoy an easy domesticity.

When one of Maria's previous admirers, Lord Macaulay, wrote from India to congratulate her, he expressed his astonishment that they should have chosen such an exile. He found the sweltering heat of Calcutta hard to endure, but the last place on earth he would have chosen was a city 'on fire with factions political and religious, peopled by raving Orangemen and raving repealers, and distracted by a contest between Protestantism as fanatical as that of Knox, and Catholicism as fanatical as that of Bonner'.*

His comments may have been exaggerated on the details, but not on the degree of division and acrimony in Ireland. They offered a fair reflection of the challenge that the Drummonds had taken on. In light of the interminable conflict and bitterness that had defined relations between the two countries over many centuries, the job of Irish Under-Secretary was the kind of appointment that might have been regarded as one of the British government's more obviously poisoned chalices.

A significant difference in Drummond's case was that he had been there before; that, as a Royal Engineer working on the Survey, travelling the length and breadth of the country, he had got to know the land and its people with a degree of closeness that eluded the typical English official who rarely ventured beyond Dublin. His 'partiality for Ireland', as his mother termed it, dictated a return, but so too did his commitment to a new age of reform that was inspiring a sustained effort for the betterment of humanity, whether it was the abolition of slavery in the Empire, addressing the evils of the 'dark Satanic mills' in England, or – now at last – beginning to grapple with the innumerable injustices of Ireland.

* A bishop who had persecuted Protestants as heretics during the reign of Queen Mary.

As Under-Secretary, Drummond was head of the Civil Service in Ireland. He formulated policy in consultation with the Chief Secretary for Ireland, who was a member of the British Cabinet, and made decisions in the name of the Lord Lieutenant, who was the sovereign's representative. The new Chief Secretary was Lord Morpeth, and the Lord Lieutenant, Constantine Henry Phipps, the Earl of Mulgrave. Both were young men of about Drummond's age who shared his determination that Catholics and Protestants in Ireland should be treated as equals. They belonged to a new generation who, in an unprecedented departure from the past, had the energy and idealism but also the courage to take on the Ascendancy.

In 1835 the reformers were still at the beginning of a very long road. Although Catholic Emancipation had been introduced six years before, the inequity between Catholic and Protestant was manifest. The country was an overwhelmingly rural society in which the mass of the population consisted of Catholic tenant farmers eking out a subsistence on small plots that were rented from a handful of mostly absent and usually Protestant landlords. If through sickness or other misfortune a peasant failed to pay the rent, then he faced eviction and, for the want of any work, destitution and starvation. No matter how long he and his family might have lived in their home, the law offered no protection.

Another form of oppression lay in the obligation on Catholic tenant farmers to pay tithes to support the Anglican Church of Ireland. With Emancipation, a campaign of organised resistance began. As the government sent in the police and army to enforce the law, violent struggle followed.

When the peasantry resisted the efforts to seize cattle in lieu of unpaid tithes, the army resorted to firearms to quell the unrest.

In confrontations across Ireland, many peasants were shot down but the tax remained unpaid. In 1833 the government passed a Coercion Act, which gave the authorities the power to proclaim martial law and to suspend habeas corpus, but the population remained as determined to withhold the tithe as the authorities were zealous in their efforts to collect it. The disturbances reached a bloody climax at the end of December 1834 with the Rathcormac massacre in County Cork. A crowd of peasants began to throw stones at troops who had been summoned to help enforce a tithe collection. When the crowd refused to disperse after the Riot Act had been read, the troops advanced but were beaten back by spades, sticks and stones. A fierce fight ensued in which the soldiers thrust out with their bayonets but to no purpose. Even after the commanding officer gave the order to fire, the peasants refused to yield. Only under sustained fire did they eventually give ground. More than twelve protesters were killed and many more wounded.

Drummond's arrival in Dublin Castle during the summer of 1835 coincided with the shocked lull that followed this latest episode in Ireland's powder-keg history. He found a country in which the overt bias of the judicial system fuelled the resentment. More than five years after Emancipation, all Ireland's judges, magistrates, high sheriffs and senior police officials were still, almost without exception, Protestant. Any conciliation was rendered only more difficult by the Orangemen, whose very existence was an affront to the Catholic community. When the Orange Order was formed in 1795, members were required to swear an oath of allegiance to the British monarch that included a pledge to maintain the Protestant Ascendancy. A secret article of association excluded the membership of a Catholic on any account. Since the mindset of the organisation was to magnify rather than resolve any differences, Emancipation was a red rag that, in effect, set an orange bull on the rampage, marching across Ireland.

A year into his new job, Drummond had to face his first Orange Day, when he had to combat the provocation of sectarian parades that the government had banned. 'I am very busy with the arrangements for the 12th of July,' he wrote to his mother, 'the day on which the Orange demons walk. It is very difficult to allay their fiendish spirit; but we are improving. There will be so large a force of military and police, with nearly thirty stipendiary magistrates, stationed at the different points at which processions are apprehended, that no great mischief can be done by them, and we shall be enabled to lay hold of and prosecute a pretty considerable number of them.'

But for all the expressed confidence, during his early months as Under-Secretary Drummond must have often felt like a general going into battle with a mutinous army, for he had to manage the bias of the justice system he had inherited. He used stipendiary magistrates because the local magistrates were nearly all Orangemen. Similar care had to be taken in managing his own police force. When on one occasion an Orange procession paraded with fife, flag and drum close by a police station, Drummond asked for the names of the marchers. The chief constable reported, 'Sub-constables Ker and Keenan, who were in charge of the station at this time, could not recognise any of the party, although they walked very close to the barrack.' Where a previous Under-Secretary would not even have taken up the issue in the first place, and would probably have let it drop, Drummond replied: 'As the party walked very close to the barrack, sub-constables Ker and Keenan must be very inefficient persons if they were not able to recognise any of them. His Excellency desires that these sub-constables be forthwith removed to another station.'

Even by the standards of Irish history, it would have been hard to find a more volatile situation in which to begin a new job. The true nature of Drummond's task was less to administer a country than to defuse a dangerously unstable bomb. All the more remarkable then that, with the support of the Lord Lieutenant and the Chief Secretary, he should have been prepared to risk even greater Protestant anger as he made a systematic effort to redress centuries of Catholic grievance.

The first sign of a radical new dispensation was Drummond's decision not to permit military force to be used to collect tithes or rents. The abrupt end to the usual government acquiescence soon provoked a challenge from one of the Ascendancy's most notoriously outspoken agitators. Talbot Glascock was an attorney to the dean of St Patrick's Cathedral in Dublin, who had made a second career fighting each and every incursion into Protestant privilege. Wherever the champion of Catholic Emancipation Daniel O'Connell turned up for an election, Glascock would be there to oppose him. When O'Connell stood for re-election in County Clare, Glascock had to be held in custody after wagering one thousand guineas that he would shoot O'Connell 'through the white liver, without touching his black heart'. Now he used his position as the dean's solicitor to make a test case of the tithes with the following letter:

Sir, The state of the country, and particularly the county of Kilkenny, touching the recovery of tithe rents, renders it absolutely necessary to have the aid of the civil and military powers to effect the service of the process of the Court of Exchequer for the recovery of the tithe composition rent due to the Dean of St Patrick's there. In confirmation of the obvious fact, we beg leave to enclose you the joint affidavits of two authorised bailiffs in the parish of Castlecomer. We therefore have to request that directions may be given for that end.

Drummond answered:

As the proceedings have been taken in the superior courts, through which Messrs Glascock & Cradock may either obtain an order to substitute service of process, or may procure the assistance of the sheriff in serving the processes in question, and as the sheriff, the recognised and responsible officer of the law, is invested with full power to call upon the military and police to protect him in the execution of his duty, His Excellency cannot consent to any direct interference on the part of the Government, when the object may be obtained through the ordinary tribunals in a manner provided for by law.

When Glascock demanded that the case be reconsidered, Drummond stood his ground, reiterating the principle that any legal redress would have to be sought through the due process of the courts. In the face of an overwhelmingly Protestant judiciary, he skilfully deployed the executive authority of the Under-Secretary as a counterweight, ordering the police and military to refuse requests from court officials for assistance unless there was a genuine danger to public order.

He reviewed each case with a rigour that often rattled the nerves of the more emollient politicians he served. It was Morpeth and Mulgrave, after all, who, as the highly visible figureheads of British policy, had to bear the brunt of the Protestant outrage. To their credit, they invested their complete confidence in Drummond, allowing him to be their tutor in a strategy that, in its radical departure from the previous status quo, created battles that they would then have to fight in Westminster.

The following note from Morpeth suggests the degree of reliance they placed in their often exacting Under-Secretary:

My Dear Drummond, I arrived in Babylon this afternoon. Let me have all my tithe cramming as soon as possible. What am I to say when it is objected thus: 'You tell applicants that the sheriff or the court may order out assistance for them, but you tell the police never to budge, without a reference to, and the direction of Government.' You will never quarrel with my letters for being laconic.

Babylon was Dublin, where the great challenge for Morpeth and Drummond, in a city of confused tongues, was to get its long-divided factions to talk the same language. The absence of the word 'But' before the words 'What am I to say . . .' indicated a Chief Secretary who was prepared to embrace even the more controversial aspects of Drummond's strategy.

The alliance of Drummond, Morpeth and Mulgrave possessed an underlying strength which led to measures that, in the context of Ireland, were revolutionary, albeit without the blood that Ireland's revolutions usually demanded. The Constabulary Bill was introduced to transfer the power to appoint constables from local magistrates to the Lord Lieutenant in Dublin Castle. When Morpeth first introduced the bill in the summer of 1835, it was rejected by the House of Lords, but with its successful passing into law the following year Drummond used the new powers under the Act to build a police force that would win the confidence of the Irish people as a whole.

When members of the government in London questioned his insistence on recruiting Catholics, he threatened to resign if they were excluded. It was the key to enabling the police to perform its duties more effectively, he argued. Three years later, a parliamentary committee cross-examined him on a policy that might seem self-evident in its wisdom today but was not then:

'Where the greater preponderance of the population was on the side of the Roman Catholic religion, you would in general appoint Roman Catholic policemen?'

'I would leave the service completely open to applicants of either creed; but I think it would be desirable that a large proportion of both officers and men, should be Roman Catholics. The proportion of Roman Catholics among the officers is at present decidedly much smaller than of Protestants.'

'You think it would be better to correct that?'

'I think it would be advisable to correct that.'

'Supposing these principles carried out, do you think that persons of property would have the same reliance on the police that they have now, they being generally Protestants?'

'I feel persuaded that in the course of six months, from the manner in which the police would do their duty, they would have that confidence. A prejudice would have to be overcome; but the more considerate, seeing how the police discharged their duty, would soon be satisfied.'

It was another obvious grievance in Ireland that, since the confiscations of land under Cromwell, 'persons of property' generally were Protestants. They also composed the local magistracy who defended the landowning class with a partisanship that was a significant cause of rural unrest. Drummond hoped, as with the constabulary, to achieve a better balance over time through the gradual appointment of Catholic judges, but in the interim he did the best he could to challenge the failings of the magistracy that already existed.

In his memoirs, the nationalist politician Charles Gavan Duffy, who was a young journalist during Drummond's administration, gave this example. In Duffy's home town of Monaghan, the high sheriff had given the job of sub-sheriff, which involved the selection of juries, to a notorious Orange leader who had been tried for murdering a Catholic but acquitted by a jury that had been composed of Orangemen. 'Any time between the Union and the Irish administration of Mulgrave and Drummond such an appointment might have been made with perfect impunity. It was said, indeed, that if Judas Iscariot was selected for such an office the remonstrance of Catholics would be treated as an impertinence.' But on this occasion Drummond wrote to the high sheriff requesting that he find a substitute. When he refused, Drummond had the sheriff himself dismissed. The Protestant gentry retaliated by refusing to take up the vacant office, intending to paralyse the administration. 'It was like a cordial to the heart of Ulster Catholics, who had never before had a taste of fair play in such contests, to see how Drummond and his colleagues dealt with this impediment. A Catholic gentleman of insignificant estate, but of good sense and good education, was immediately appointed High Sheriff, and for the first time since a M'Mahon held the office under James II, a Catholic framed grand and petty panels, controlled prisons, and received the circuit judges.'

In using the robust exercise of executive power to correct a biased and corrupt system, Drummond went to extraordinary lengths to uncover the underlying reality of a situation.

When a landowner in Tipperary was shot dead, the local magistrates used the occasion to make a general complaint about the state of lawlessness in the county. They asserted that juries were often intimidated and appealed to the Lord Lieutenant for the right to impose tougher penalties on people who possessed unregistered arms.

Drummond replied that the government would spare no effort to bring to justice whoever was responsible for the killing. But concerning the magistrates' comments, he expressed doubt that the alleged jury intimidation could exist without court officials bringing it to the attention of the executive. The allegation was so serious that, before deciding what action to take, he would make an immediate inquiry into the evils that the magistrates complained of and their causes.

Over the next month, he then oversaw an inquiry that analysed all the relevant statistical information relating to crime in Tipperary and questioned the judicial officials who ran the court circuits of the county. With 'a desire that a matter so serious should not rest in vague conjecture, or on opinion not sustained by facts', he brought to the task the same regard for precision and accuracy that had, in an earlier career, distinguished his invention of the limelight, or the measurement of the baseline of verification along the shore of Lough Foyle, or the determination of the new constituencies for the Great Reform Bill of 1832. He wanted the truth, as much as it was possible to obtain.

The inquiry completed, he then sent a second letter to the Tipperary magistrates, only five weeks after the first, in which he set out his findings in the most exhaustive detail. Going through every allegation the magistrates had made, he set out his understanding of the true state of affairs. He backed up each assertion with the relevant evidence, quoting and naming the court officials who had provided testimony: the Crown solicitor of the Munster circuit, Mr Barrington; the stipendiary magistrates, Major Carter, Mr Willocks, Mr Vokes, Mr Singleton, Mr Tabuteau, Captain Duff, Captain Nangle . . . There was a table that set out the homicide cases that had been prosecuted and tried at the assizes over the last five years, with the number of convictions and acquittals as well as the number of cases in which the jury disagreed.

All the detail may have lacked the drama of a battle, but of course it was a battle of a kind, a battle for reason over speculation and partiality, a battle for reason but inspired by a passion for justice, a feat of individual will and conscience that was exceptional enough to justify the name of Drummond being mentioned in the company of such civil rights heroes as O'Connell and Gandhi even though today he is scarcely mentioned at all.

Strictly speaking, Drummond was a public servant rather than a politician. If he often seemed to stray over the dividing line, he did so effectively because, putting aside emotion, he used his command of the facts to bring out what ought to have been undeniable truths. The letter to the Tipperary magistrates was a perfect example of the method. On the basis of all the evidence, he explained, he could not find the intimidation that the Tipperary magistrates had alleged, nor the widespread lawlessness, yet to the extent that crime did exist in the county, he went on, it was important to consider its causes. The character of the great majority of incidents was such that he could not doubt that they were mainly connected with 'the tenure and occupation of land'.

While he did not consider it the occasion for any detailed examination of the issue, he did go on to mention 'the lamentably destitute condition of a cottier tenantry, possessing no adequate means of continuous support'. Might this not in some way be a contributing factor to the lawlessness that the magistrates had observed? 'The deficiency of a demand for labour, and the want, as yet, of any legal provision against utter destitution, leave this humble class, when ejected, without any certain protection against actual starvation. Hence the wholesale expulsion of cottier tenants is unfortunately found with the great body of the people to enlist the strongest feelings.' While crime could never be excused, neither could the lack of social responsibility that led to it:

> Property has its duties as well as its rights; to the neglect of those duties in times past is mainly to be ascribed that diseased state of society in which such crimes take their rise; and it is not in the enactment or enforcement of statutes of extraordinary severity, but chiefly in the better and more faithful performance of those duties, and the more enlightened and humane exercise of those rights, that a permanent remedy for such disorders is to be sought.

The response of the Tipperary magistrates was to suppress the letter. But eventually it emerged in a parliamentary inquiry into 'the state of Ireland' that took place a year later.

Drummond, who had much to say about the state of Ireland, received the unstinting support of Morpeth and Mulgrave in his efforts to improve it, but found that the further away British politicians were from Ireland's shores the more inclined they were to disregard the country's problems. When he urged the Chancellor of the Exchequer in 1837 to introduce a landlord tax to relieve famine in Donegal, the Chancellor dismissed his claims as exaggerated and offered only the most minimal assistance.

To avoid encouraging dependence, the government sought to provide relief in Ireland by creating employment through public works. It had introduced rules that gave local magistrates and landowners the power to call for such works when there was distress in their area, but Drummond did not believe that the landowners would take any significant action if it were left to their own discretion. As Under-Secretary, he had witnessed the 'monstrous state of things' where the government had imported food to relieve tenants whose landlords continued to export their produce. He argued therefore that the only way such public works schemes could provide effective relief was through a compulsory assessment of the landlords of the districts where famine prevailed.

Although he had made the plea many times, the government continued to ignore him. Even when the Chancellor did agree to give £500 to help relieve the famine in Donegal, there were strings attached. The money was to be used 'in sales at a reduced price, restricting all gratuitous assistance to the sick, the old and the infirm'. No underclass in Ireland should be allowed to undermine the effective working of the free market.

But money was not enough. In accepting the assistance, Drummond wrote a note reminding the Chancellor that his warning about the folly of expecting landlords to protect their tenantry had come true in the case of Donegal. Although he must have hoped to persuade the government to dwell at last upon the wider implications, his words contained the despairing tone of a Cassandra.

I foretold . . . that they would as heretofore suffer the people to perish without extending the smallest particle of relief; that they would witness unmoved a degree of suffering and privation which the Government of a civilised country would not be justified in refusing to relieve; and hence that we would again be compelled to import food for the sustenance of those whose labour, in the shape of provisions, is exported without deduction by rapacious and unfeeling landlords.

It was of this that I earnestly, but ineffectually, complained. I urged that when it was proved that a district was in a state of extreme distress, that there should be a compulsory assessment put in force; but I ventured to foretell, that if the proprietors were to be the judges of that state, nothing could be done; and that, as heretofore . . . the Government would be compelled to pay the poor-rates of the west coast of Donegal.

I am really sorry to trouble you with this; but I am anxious to exonerate myself from advocating a principle or a remedy against which I have uniformly protested, and which we are only compelled most reluctantly to resort to, because the Government will not heed our appeal, or give us the means of putting an end to a state of things which is a disgrace to a civilized community.

Even at this point, having deployed every possible argument to no avail, Drummond did not give in to despondency, or turn away to fight some easier battle, as another Under-Secretary might have done. Instead, he continued to struggle for a change of policy.

While the government pursued its romance with laissez-faire, he argued that Ireland was a special case that required urgent state intervention. Of a population that had grown fourfold over only a hundred years, the vast majority was entirely dependent upon the land. Farming ever smaller plots, the peasantry were victim to a series of food shortages that boded far worse unless some other means of support could be found.

A possible solution lay in creating the kind of industrial infrastructure that England already had. The railway, which was then in its infancy, seemed to offer a special opportunity. Ireland's first line, between Kingstown and Dublin, had opened only a year before Drummond had begun as Under-Secretary. The six-mile stretch had provided employment for two thousand workers. What if a network could be extended across the whole country?

Drummond canvassed for a commission to explore the idea, and when it was set up, in spite of the heavy burden of work he already had, volunteered to preside over it. The resulting report, which offered as exhaustive an examination of the social and political factors as the economic ones, was inspired by the belief that, through discarding historical prejudice, the two countries could work together to huge mutual benefit. 'Ireland, though for years past a subject of anxious attention and discussion in public, is really very little known to the British people,' observed Drummond, 'and the disadvantage to both countries, arising from that circumstance, is much greater than generally supposed.'

Recognising the difficulties of attracting private investment, the report recommended that the British government fund the construction of a railway network clustering around a main line from Dublin to Cork, and another up to Navan, which would then split in two directions, with one side of the fork going up to Belfast, and the other to Enniskillen. He argued that such a scheme, through creating mass employment, would be the swiftest way to combat the threat of starvation among the rural poor, but would also help to bring prosperity in the longer term. Simply from narrow self-interest, there were sound economic and political reasons why the United Kingdom should undertake such a project, but there were other considerations, he concluded in his report,

> which it is more pleasing to dwell upon, as being more worthy of a great and enlightened nation – considerations of justice, of generosity – of a liberal concern for the improvement and civilisation of our countrymen. In attending to such considerations, no nation was ever faithless or blind to its own best and dearest interests; and were there no commercial advantages for England in the projects which we submit for adoption, nor any promise of actual benefit to the public treasury, or of relief from the heavy contributions which the unsettled state of society in Ireland annually extracts from it, yet the certainty of rendering this country prosperous, and diffusing the blessings of peace and industry, with their attendant fruits of knowledge and moral culture amongst its people, ought, as we have no doubt it would, be considered an ample recompense.

The Whig government proposed a motion to implement the recommendations of the report but was eventually defeated by a combination of the Conservative opposition and private business interests. In the year that the Great Famine began in 1845, only seventy miles of railway had been built in Ireland, compared to 1,700 miles in Great Britain.

In our age of twenty-first-century scepticism, I am uncomfortable not to be able to find some fault with Drummond. But the poor man never really had a chance to live his life. Had he done so, then perhaps the faults would have begun to tumble out. Is it possible to work yourself to death? It seemed so in the nineteenth century. Drummond's routine was punishing. When he arrived in Dublin Castle in that summer of 1835, he stepped onto a fast-spinning treadmill. If he must have wanted from time to time to step off, the consciousness of his immense responsibilities kept him labouring away in a position that was at one of history's most difficult fault lines. As Irish Under-Secretary, he had to navigate crisis after crisis. There was no escape. Even returning home from Dublin Castle in the evening was to come back to the official residence of the Under-Secretary. His private life was subsumed totally into his public one. Living with him in the Under-Secretary's Lodge at Phoenix Park was his young family, but he had no leisure to spend any significant time with them.

Family letters expressed fears that his health would buckle under the strain. 'The mere bodily fag of this situation is tremendous,' wrote his wife Maria to Drummond's mother in June 1837. A year later, when the railway report had turned the ratchet a notch further, she wrote, '[E]ven his every-day official business occupies him from nine in the morning till a quarter to eight (our dinner hour) so that any extra work brought on by any investigation must either be done before nine in the morning, or in the evening after dinner. I often say that I might as well have no husband.' Here was the Achilles heel of the sapper, who was encouraged to believe that he could be everywhere and do everything.

To spare his eyes, but also, I suppose, just so that she could spend some time with him, she used to read out the correspondence and official documents to him in his study. Of their baby daughter, she commented that he managed to get a peep of her for about five minutes every day, 'but he is on thorns even for these five minutes'.

She begged him to take time off, to listen to the advice of his doctor who told him the same, but to no avail. The 'railroadising', as she called the time he poured into the work of the commission, had been much more than a straw to break a camel's back, but after that he laboured on for another year before he was struck down by a fatal illness that seemed somehow inevitable.

The day before he was taken ill with peritonitis he had worked nine solid hours in his office at Dublin Castle although it was a Saturday. When he complained of severe stomach pains the next morning, a doctor was summoned, but his condition became progressively worse. On Tuesday evening the doctor told him that he had not much longer to live. 'Doctor, all is peace,' he answered. Maria then came into the room. 'Dearest beloved Maria, you have been an angel wife to me. Your admonitions have blessed me.' Many of those admonitions, presumably, had been not to work so hard, but it was too late now.

Drummond lingered on into the next day, in great pain but calm and conscious. When the doctor asked him where he would like to be buried, he answered, 'I wish to be buried in Ireland, the country of my adoption – a country which I loved, which I have faithfully served, and for which I believe I have sacrificed my life.' Those were his last words. He died at about seven in the evening on Wednesday 15 April 1840.

The next day Ireland's leading nationalist newspaper, the *Freeman's Journal*, wrote, 'We have not often, as public journalists, had so painful a task imposed on us as that of recording the demise of Mr Secretary Drummond. At the present time his premature and unlooked-for death will be deemed a national calamity by the people of this country.' Reflecting on the immense obstacles that Drummond had tackled with such persistence and energy, the article could not help make a contrast with the more usual English neglect. 'Ireland would be in a far different position from that which she now occupies had the majority of the English people and their representatives been actuated by the same spirit that regulated the conduct of Mr Drummond towards our long-misgoverned country.' Kipling had yet to be born to coin the phrase 'Lest we forget', but in the case of Thomas Drummond in Ireland in 1840, such a fear did not even exist. 'What Irishman is there who is not familiar with the cutting, and, at the same time, instructive severity of his reproof to those heartless and inhuman landlords who had totally forgotten "the duties of property" and far outstepped its "rights"? To government, which at present needs all the strength it can receive, his loss is, we fear, irreparable.'

In England, the *Morning Chronicle* was one of many papers to echo the verdict: 'The death of Mr Drummond, an irreparable blow to his family and private friends, is scarcely less calamitous to that country to which he was attached, not merely by official ties, but by the sympathies of an ardent and generous spirit. His undivided energies were devoted to the good of Ireland, and his valuable life shortened by unwearied and incessant labours for her improvement . . . he is bewailed, even by those who knew him not in private life, as men grieve for a personal friend. No individual within our recollection has been more generally esteemed and sincerely lamented.'

Drummond had lived up to an age that believed in heroes. As both Ireland and England mourned his passing, fellow Scot Thomas Carlyle was by one of those timely coincidences putting the finishing touches to a series of six lectures on 'Heroes, Hero

Worship and the Heroic in History', which he delivered in London during the month that followed Drummond's death. 'The history of the world is but the biography of great men,' Carlyle famously declared: in Dublin, on the day of Drummond's funeral, Tuesday 21 April 1840, very few people would have disagreed.

All politics stopped for the occasion. A mass demonstration in O'Connell's campaign for the repeal of the union had been scheduled to take place the day before, but, expressing the grief that so many Irish nationalists felt 'for the loss of this truly great and good man', O'Connell argued that it would be better to postpone it until due respect had been paid.

The funeral cortège set off from Phoenix Park at eleven o'clock in the morning. A mounted escort and mutes, who carried the coffin lid covered with a pall and black ostrich feathers, preceded the six black horses that pulled the hearse. More than 150 carriages made up a procession that passed slowly through densely crowded streets, taking more than two hours to reach Mount Jerome Cemetery in the south of the city. Although it was a weekday, most of the shops along the route were closed, in the words of the *Freeman's Journal*, as 'a tribute of respect to departed worth'.

A few days later there was a large gathering in Morrison's Hotel on Dawson Street to discuss the best way of remembering Drummond. Colonel Sir John Burgoyne was asked to chair the meeting. He was a Royal Engineer who had worked with Drummond on the Railway Commission. He told the assembly that he had first met Drummond in 1817 when, as a young Royal Engineers officer, Drummond had visited the British army of occupation in France, with which Burgoyne was serving. Even then he had shown such a spirit of enquiry, observed the colonel, that it was impossible not to see that, given the chance, he would one day become a great man. A committee was formed for the purpose of erecting a tribute to his memory. Subscriptions were then pledged, including £100 from the Lord Lieutenant and £80 from Lord Morpeth.

O'Connell, as ever the great populist, proposed that an account of the day should be published in the newspapers. To cheers he declared, 'It is right that the tribute of a nation's gratitude to a nation's benefactor should be circulated as wide as possible.'

Maria Drummond found some comfort in the extraordinary testimonials of respect and affection for her husband that the newspaper reports offered. She intended to paste them into a book so that one day, when her three small children were old enough, they might know what a father they had. During the first weeks after her husband's death the business of organising tributes to his memory, whether public or private, became a way of coping with her loss.

She was pleased to participate in the memorial committee's plans to erect a public statue, although the only model for such a statue was the portrait of Drummond by Henry Pickersgill:

> It is fortunate that the picture is almost a whole length, as the statue will have to be chiefly copied from that. The cast taken after the sweet spirit had fled would not do, unless they had a good portrait to guide them. Probably Chantrey will be employed. Dear beloved husband! How little did he think of the honours which awaited his memory!

In the event, Drummond's statue was carved not by the distinguished English portrait sculptor Francis Chantrey, but the Irish Catholic sculptor John Hogan, who then lived in Rome, where he occupied a workshop that had once belonged to Canova. Whether or not Pickersgill's portrait of Drummond made the journey to the Eternal City, as Maria Drummond had anticipated might be necessary, the sculptor returned to his native land to oversee the elevation of the colossal statue on a pedestal in Dublin's Royal Exchange.

The varied nature of what Drummond had achieved in his short career required a special degree of symbolism. So Hogan styled him wearing a military uniform, but over the tunic was draped a Roman magistrate's toga, which in classical times had been a sign of both peace and civic duty. In his left hand, he held a scroll that bore the words 'Survey of Ireland', and in his right a mathematical compass. A miniature lighthouse tower stood to one side at the back of the pedestal to represent his invention of the limelight. Some time later Drummond's famous words would be chiselled onto a face of the pedestal: PROPERTY HAS ITS DUTIES AS WELL AS ITS RIGHTS.

Maria offered to add to the public subscription her own contribution of £1,000 if the committee of subscribers would allow the statue to be put up in the Dublin training college of teachers for the National Schools. Her husband had considered the new system of non-denominational public education to be one of the great hopes for healing Ireland's divisions. She must have thought that it was here, among the trainee teachers, that his example could have the most powerful effect, but the committee considered 'a more public situation desirable', so Maria gave the money directly to the training college instead.

The Royal Engineers swiftly fulfilled Maria Drummond's wish that her husband's life should serve as an active example. Their first act of commemoration was to invite a fellow officer of Drummond's to write a short memoir of him, which — with the sort of work ethic that was so typical of Drummond himself – they published at the end of the year in an annual collection of professional papers 'on subjects connected with the duties of the Corps of Royal Engineers'. Captain Thomas Larcom had served with Drummond in the Irish Ordnance Survey. 'For the example and imitation of his brother officers this Notice is submitted,' began the final paragraph of his tribute. 'In death we claim our brother, and step forward to support his bier.' Some years later, in 1853, he lived up to the tribute when, now a major, he became, in the aftermath of the Great Famine, the second Royal Engineer to become Under-Secretary of Ireland. With the highest possible accolade it could give to show its approval, the nationalist *Freeman's Journal* welcomed an appointment that seemed 'to savour of the spirit in which the late lamented Captain Drummond was appointed'. Larcom went on to become the longest-serving Under-Secretary, holding the post with distinction for fifteen years.

As a second act of commemoration, although I don't know exactly when, the corps had a replica of Hogan's statue of Drummond made for the headquarters' mess at Brompton Barracks – out of sight of the public maybe, but in a place where the five Lynch brothers would have been able to find him.

I wondered whether the statue was still there, so that I could pay my respects too. I remembered the words in Ward's history of the School of Military Engineering: *We may well question whether an officer of greater or even equal promise ever wore the uniform of the Royal Engineers.*

When I enquired, the mess secretary found a record which stated that the statue had been 'Transferred to Museum M/2001-208'. I hadn't seen it in the museum, so I wondered whether poor Drummond had been relegated to some storage room. I wrote to the museum curator to ask whether, if so, I might be allowed to photograph him, but was told that the statue could not be found. 'I am hoping that it wasn't disposed of,' he wrote. 'What may have happened is that the mess wanted to dispose of it and the museum didn't have the capacity to display/store it.'

I couldn't help thinking that if the museum had the capacity to display a V-2 rocket and a Harrier jump jet, then why not a statue of possibly the greatest Royal Engineer of them all? And even if the statue could not be displayed or stored, surely a good home could be found for it. But when I asked if there was anything that could be done to track it down, I soon realised that my persistence was not welcome. 'I am wondering whether it was disposed of,' repeated the curator. 'I will keep an eye out for it but am not sure what the answer is at the moment.'

The last line of the curator's reply was a generic invitation from the museum to meet 'Snob the Dog, our new family-friendly character', who had been inspired by a dog that the sappers had befriended during the Crimean War, and whose stuffed skin was still on display.

If Drummond had lost his place of honour among the Royal Engineers, how lucky, I thought, that the statue was only a replica, that I could go to Dublin, where the original still stood beneath the great rotunda of City Hall, as the Royal Exchange became, alongside Hogan's later statue of Daniel O'Connell the Great Liberator. *Property has its duties as well as its rights.* Only in Ireland had the custodians of Drummond's statue remained true to those words. It was why finally Ireland had to break from Britain.

PART THREE

UBIQUE QUO FAS ET GLORIA DUCUNT

10

Home

For to admire an' for to see,
  For to be'old this world so wide—
It never done no good to me,
  But I can't drop it if I tried!

Kipling, 'For to Admire', 1894

On the clock face of the Empire it could be said to be about eleven o'clock, I suppose, when my grandfather Patrick and his older brother Jack finished their training at Chatham. It was 1895, and the Empire was approaching its zenith. That same year, the third of the five brothers, James, who had been working as a chain surveyor in Ennis, followed Jack and Patrick into the British army, taking his oath of loyalty to the Queen on 30 September 1895. He was twenty years old.

'For what Corps are you willing to be enlisted?' asked question 15 of the attestation form. There was now only one answer. 'The Royal Engineers.'

As the clock of Empire ticked on past midnight, the next brother, Michael, only eighteen years old, gave the same answer on 20 January 1899, and it was well after midnight when the youngest brother, Thomas, joined the Royal Engineers on 15 January 1904. Britain was no longer pre-eminent, the great Queen had been dead almost three years, and Thomas swore his oath to a monarch of much shorter reign.

With a kind of vestigial longing for the certainty of the Victorian nursery, I wondered how the world might have seemed if the clock had been stopped when the splendour and self-confidence of Empire were still intact. The first three brothers, who had enlisted before Queen Victoria's Diamond Jubilee of 1897, had experienced the nineteenth-century Empire at its height, before the challenges of the new century began to erode its glory.

Although their military history sheets catalogued journeys that lived up to the corps motto of *ubique* . . . ('everywhere . . .'), they spent their first few years in service to the Queen at 'Home' – an Empire word for England, Wales, Scotland and Ireland. Indeed, James served at 'Home' for more than twenty years until he was posted to France in 1916.

Patrick was at 'Home' from 1 September 1894 to 29 October 1899 – to be exact, as the military service history always was, 5 years and 59 days; and Jack from 1 September 1894 to 6 March 1902, 7 years and 187 days. For a Royal Engineers surveyor, 'Home' in practice meant the Ordnance Survey. After Jack and Patrick had completed their sapper's training, they embarked on the six-month specialised course that included instruction in all the aspects of practical surveying – using the surveyor's chain, observing trigonometrical angles, levelling (determining the relative height of different points), calculating areas, contouring. On

18 October 1895 they were sent to divisional offices to begin work as topographers in the field, Patrick being posted to Chester, and Jack to York on the other side of the Pennines. In practice both brothers were on the move across the surrounding counties, every few days in a different lodging, as they spent morning to night trudging across fields, jumping ditches, climbing over walls.

The magazine for the rank and file of the corps, *The Sapper*, gives a taste of their work in this account of a sapper's life 'on the ordnance survey', which was published in May 1896:

To my mind this is one of the most pleasant and intelligent duties that falls to the lot of the ubiquitous Sapper. Armed with his field book or sketching case, and the multitudinous surveying accessories, 'Thomas Atkins, Sapper, RE', is, in the words of Kipling, 'a thing to behold and to admire'.

What delightful tales he has to spin of his adventures and misadventures whilst at work (and other times), of the interesting spots he is privileged to visit, of the glorious landscape and seascape at times spread before him, and of the many phases of character he comes in contact with . . . Nor is the more serious side of the picture to be overlooked. Whilst many of our comrades are taking it easy we are having many a weary tramp over hill and through moss – now drenched to the skin by Jupiter Pluvius, and then parboiled by our old friend Sol.

We are nearly always a source of anxious wonder to the inhabitants amongst whom we sojourn. We are generally dubbed 'Sappers and Miners', but we have at various times been taken, or rather mistaken, for artists, fire brigade men, and (ye gods!) walking advertisements for patent soaps or medicines . . .

We are as a rule kindly treated wherever we go, and we try to keep up the credit of our beloved corps, though now and again one or another of us oversteps the line between prudence and folly – for we are intensely human.

THE LUNCHEON HOUR.
WHO WOULDN'T BE ON THE SURVEY?

The surviving possessions of my grandfather are so few and scattered as to have the status of relics, which could all easily fit inside his suitcase. From these objects, his grandchildren, who never knew him, can only struggle to construct the character of someone who died so long ago. One of those relics is a Welsh dictionary. Once I thought it was a sign of his fascination with Celtic culture, of his wish to add another Celtic language to the one he already spoke. But the real reason was much more prosaic and practical. The Chester office, to which he had been posted, was responsible for the revision of the Ordnance Survey maps of West Cheshire but also North Wales, so he must have used the dictionary to help him get around, and to cope with some of the most tongue-twisting names to be found in the British Isles.

Coming from Ireland, he would have been well aware of the extent to which names were a political issue. In the time of Drummond and Larcom, the Ordnance Survey had conceived an extraordinarily ambitious project not only to map the landscape of Ireland but also to publish accompanying 'memoirs' that would explain its history. The project was abandoned after the publication in 1837 of the first volume, *County of Londonderry: Parish of Templemore*, which was already controversial under such a name – Londonderry, not Derry? – without anyone even opening the book.* The government refused to continue to fund a costly initiative that, in the words of the Chancellor, would 'open all the debatable questions in Irish party division'.

In Wales, the Ordnance Survey submitted proofs of the maps for correction to Welsh scholars and local authorities, but there were calls in Parliament for a native Welsh officer to accompany each of the Survey parties. History, like the corps itself, was of course everywhere. When the Royal Engineers surveyors were working along the River Ely, north of Cardiff, their arrival prompted a discussion among local historians over the Battle of Rhiwsaeson, which had taken place between the Welsh and Saxons in the early ninth century. Although the objective of the battle had been a hillfort that stood above the modern hamlet of Rhiwsaeson, 'the slope of the Saxons', the thick of the fighting had actually taken place a mile and a quarter further to the

---

* Although it was impossible to escape entirely the institutional prejudice of what was after all a government publication, the project represented a rare effort to provide an objective view of Ireland that was above the historical divide, rather than on one or other side of it.

south-east at a place called Cae-yr-Arfau, 'the field of the arms'. There was a cromlech there, believed to be the tomb of the Welsh chief who had been killed close to the spot, but hardly anyone knew of its existence because it had not been marked on any map. The curator of the Cardiff Museum, John Storrie (a Scotsman who had settled in Wales), sent a report to the Ordnance Survey, which accordingly included the antiquity in its revision of the area.

These first years of Home on the Lynch brothers' military history sheets were years in which Britain swayed between democratic accountability and imperial swagger. If you liked pomp and circumstance, then there was no better place to be. For to be 'Home' meant to be at the heart of a great Empire that, however haphazard it may have been in its growth, had become now the largest the world had ever known. When the Diamond Jubilee of Queen Victoria was celebrated in June 1897, the Royal Engineers as usual played their part. On Sunday 20 June, braving a night of heavy rain and wind, their band performed at a military tattoo in Windsor Castle, while the Queen looked on from the dry fastness of the royal apartments above the quadrangle.* In a 'Reminiscences of All Nations' that acknowledged the other great powers – albeit a rung or two below – the programme included the Russian and Turkish national anthems, the Marseillaise and 'Yankee Doodle'. The next evening the band was at Buckingham Palace, where it played a selection of music to accompany a state banquet. On Jubilee Day itself, Tuesday 22 June, six hundred

---

* If Queen Victoria had been able to attend her great-great-granddaughter's Diamond Jubilee in 2012, she would have had a tremendous sense of déjà vu to see her royal barge make its way up the Thames through squalls of driving rain.

sappers took part in the procession from the palace to St Paul's Cathedral.

The total force comprised more than 40,000 men and 6,000 horses. After dusk, powerful electric searchlights lit up the dome of the cathedral, while bulbs of yellow, red and green lined the route of the procession. Almost every building in central London sparkled with light, whether gas or the newfangled electric light. The day offered an astonishing expression of national pride all the more remarkable for its global reach. 'The illuminations that filled the streets of London yesterday evening with a festive crowd have their counterpart not only in the other cities of the British Islands, but in all the great cities of the Empire,' wrote the *Morning Post.* 'The bonfires that glowed last night upon British hills were links in a chain of torchlight that ran round the world. The 22nd of June, 1897, has thus been in a special sense the festival of the British Empire, and while all British subjects were singing with heart and voice, "God Save the Queen", they were not merely renewing the old covenant of loyalty and unity, but pledging themselves to carry on through the unknown future their common duty of raising higher and higher still that Throne of which the proudest boast is to be "broad-based upon the people's will".'

But from the perspective of that unknown future, 22 June was the highest point, the witching hour of the British Empire.

The one discordant note was Ireland. In the House of Commons, the Irish nationalist leaders John Dillon and John Redmond voiced their protest at the House's Motion of Congratulations to the Queen. 'Why should we rejoice?' asked Dillon. 'I speak here for the Irish race when I say that we have no share in your festival!' Queen Victoria's reign, he declared, had brought to

Ireland neither peace nor freedom nor any of the blessings that Britain enjoyed. Redmond tabled an amendment to the effect that during the sixty years of the Queen's reign, Ireland had suffered from famine, depopulation and the continued suspension of her civil liberties, with the result that the Irish people were too discontented to join in the jubilee celebrations. The amendment was, of course, rejected by a large majority, but it set the tone of division that characterised the jubilee celebrations across Ireland, where the black flags of the nationalists, unfurled to mark a day of mourning, competed with the Union Jack flags and bunting of the loyalists.

In Dublin, a nationalist crowd marched into the centre of the city, tearing down decorations and singing the revolutionary song 'The Boys of Wexford'. When the Irish Socialist Republican Party held an anti-jubilee protest meeting on College Green, students from Trinity College, armed with sticks, marched into the crowd, singing 'God Save the Queen'. The police had to intervene to break up the fight that ensued, driving the students back into the college. When the meeting resumed, the protesters displayed a black flag that bore the following inscription:

> The Record Reign '37–97
> Starved to death, 1,225,000
> Evicted, 3,668,000
> Forced to emigrate, 4,168,000

After a resolution was passed to fight against the British Empire 'until the Republican faith of our forefathers is finally realised', the nationalist campaigner Maude Gonne addressed the meeting. She declared that it was the duty of Irishmen and Irishwomen to protest against the jubilee, because sixty years of the Queen's reign had brought more ruin, misery and death to their land than any previous period of their sad history.

Where would the Lynch brothers have stood on that day? I think they would have understood the sentiments of the young recruit to the Connaught Rangers who, in 1898, expressed his wish 'to be a true, brave and faithful soldier of Victoria', but then declared that if Victoria or her leaders ever turned with cruelty on the Irish race he would be the first to raise his sword to fight against her, with 'plenty of Irishmen at my side, for they are known to be the bravest race in the world'.

When it came to anniversaries, the year 1898 would have meant just as much to them as the Queen's jubilee of the year before. My aunt Joan once found in a book that had belonged to her father a newspaper cutting from the Dublin *Saturday Herald* about the United Irishmen who had planned the rebellion of 1798, which the British put down with murderous ferocity. It told the story of the meetings of the rebel leaders that were held in a merchant's house on Bridge Street, Dublin, which ran down to the Whitworth Bridge over the Liffey. When their meeting place was betrayed, the revolutionaries moved a few yards along the street into the Brazen Head Inn. This was where my grandfather stayed when he was working for the Irish Land Commission after the Great War, and where he would have been able to sit at a writing table that had been used by a later Irish martyr Robert Emmet, whom the British executed in 1803. 'Probably that's why our father called our house Bridge House,' Joan told me.

In the Queen's last years, when there was still the hope that democratic politics would eventually deliver Home Rule to Ireland, she could count on the Lynch brothers' support, but should she ever turn with cruelty on the Irish . . .

II

Kitchener's Revenge

If the attitude of the Lynch brothers to the Diamond Jubilee celebration of Empire was necessarily ambivalent, there was no such reserve about the pride they were able to take in the corps of Royal Engineers. In Ireland, there had been Drummond, but also his comrade in the Survey, Thomas Larcom. Elsewhere, the Engineers were engaged in every significant enterprise of Empire. If sappers often joked that they should be allowed to run the country, in many ways they already did.

During the brothers' first years in the corps, the Royal Engineers were heavily engaged in what was perhaps the greatest adventure of all in this *Boy's Own* age – to avenge General Gordon's death. The leadership of the campaign to reconquer the Sudan, announced in March 1896, had been entrusted to an officer of the corps, Colonel Sir Horatio Herbert Kitchener, then sirdar of the British-controlled Egyptian army.

While Jack and Patrick were working on the revisions to the Ordnance Survey maps of England and Wales, 'tramping over hill and through moss', their comrades in the Sudan were surveying a desert furnace. The logistical challenge was how to keep an army of 25,000 men fed in a wilderness. The corps built one railway along the river and, to relieve a bottleneck, a second one across a salient of desert to a point where the Nile became more navigable. Alongside both, they built a telegraph line. Among the first cargos for the newly built railway were the dismantled sections of a gunboat flotilla that had a shallow enough draught to navigate the Nile cataracts. The sections were then reassembled and launched on the Nile under the supervision of Gordon's nephew, Major W. S. 'Monkey' Gordon, RE.

Kitchener made a slow, but remorseless advance along the length of the river, each cataract a hard-won notch on the long, difficult journey to Khartoum. In September 1896, he took the Dervish stronghold of Dongola beyond the third cataract, but it took more than a year to reach Abu Hamed beyond the fourth.

Back in England, the corps reminded the public of the personal nature of all this activity by holding an exhibition of General Gordon's relics at the Royal United Service Institution in Whitehall. Visitors could see the full-dress pasha's coat that he wore as governor general of Sudan; a Chinese map on which he had marked the positions of the various battles in blood from his finger; and another map on which, excellent surveyor that he was, he had located the Garden of Eden.

Gordon had become the great saint of Victoria's age, offering a benchmark for the extraordinary outpouring of evangelical fervour with which so many influential people of the period justified Empire in terms of the fruits of civilisation that it brought to 'benighted' peoples. The cynical French might think that this trek into the desert was merely Britain's bid to extend her hold over Africa, but the

British had become used to the idea that, actually, what they were doing – in that evocative, terrible phrase that Kipling would soon coin – was shouldering the 'White Man's burden'.

The newspaper accounts of the Sudan campaign reflect the imperialist mindset at its most doubt-free time. Before Khartoum had fallen to the Mahdists, explained the *Star*, 'the mischievous power of the slave-dealers was so broken that their terrible trade was practically at an end. They have had their revenge since in streams of blood, and the work of humanity and civilisation has been thrown miserably backward. Let us trust that this fresh departure may prove to be the dawn of a brighter era, and that the awful crimes perpetrated in Darkest Africa may become things of the past.'

The entrenched racism, so shocking to our time, was a quotidian theme in the reports of the desert railway's construction. '[T]he gentlemen who are constructing and conducting the military railways of the Sudan,' wrote the correspondent for the *Daily News*, 'are dependent on the labours of hard-working but totally irresponsible natives, as a result of which there is probably no accident, mistake, or disaster conceivable by the human brain that could come as a surprise to them.' And a little later, 'The stokers, of course, are natives, and naturally inept.'

A young Winston Churchill wrote a bestselling account of the campaign, *The River War*, which offers perhaps an even more striking example of the racial prejudices of the imperial age. In an introduction to the Sudan, Churchill distinguished two main races: 'the aboriginal natives, and the Arab settlers. The indigenous inhabitants of the country were negroes as black as coal. Strong, virile, and simple-minded savages, they lived as we may imagine prehistoric men.' According to Churchill, the Arab settlers dominated the black savages, through their superior intelligence and force of character, imposing over time their customs, language and blood. 'The qualities of mongrels are rarely admirable,' he wrote of the interbreeding between the two. '[T]he mixture of the Arab and negro types had produced a debased and cruel breed, more shocking because they are more intelligent than the primitive savages.'

Here was the future inspirational leader of Britain's fight against the evil of Nazism writing the kind of nonsense that the Nazis themselves spouted. For all its immense achievement, it was in the nature of Empire to foster such attitudes, a part of the hubris that brought about its own downfall.

So 'ere's *to* you, Fuzzy-Wuzzy, at your 'ome in the Soudan;
You're a pore benighted 'eathen but a first-class fightin' man;
We gives you your certificate, an' if you want it signed
We'll come an' 'ave a romp with you whenever you're inclined.

We took our chanst among the Khyber 'ills,
The Boers knocked us silly at a mile,
The Burman give us Irriwaddy chills,
An' a Zulu *impi* dished us up in style:
But all we ever got from such as they
Was pop to what the Fuzzy made us swaller;
We 'eld our bloomin' own, the papers say,
But man for man the Fuzzy knocked us 'oller.

Then 'ere's *to* you, Fuzzy-Wuzzy, an' the missis and the kid;
Our orders was to break you, an' of course we went an' did.
We sloshed you with Martinis, an' it wasn't 'ardly fair;
But for all the odds agin' you, Fuzzy-Wuz, you broke the square.

That was Kipling in 1890. Now it was time to face the fuzzy-wuzzy again and to reassert the authority of the British square. In September 1898, Kitchener repaid the nation's trust with an overwhelming victory over the Mahdist forces at Omdurman outside Khartoum. Of course the outcome was never in doubt. Kitchener commanded a force of 8,000 regular British troops, and 17,000 Sudanese and Egyptian soldiers. On the other side, the Khalifa had an army of 52,000 men. But the modern firepower of Kitchener's army gave it the overwhelming advantage. During Gordon's time the Hadendoa warriors of Kipling's poem had faced Martini-Henry rifles; now they faced Maxim machine guns. The casualty figures reflected the inequality of the struggle. By the end of the battle 9,600 men in the Khalifa's army had been killed, and another 13,000 wounded. On the British side, 47 men were killed and 382 men wounded. Young Winston, who was present at the battle as a cavalry officer riding with the 21st Lancers, described the crushing advantage that the British forces had:

By 6.45 more than 12,000 infantry were engaged in that mechanical scattering of death which the polite nations of the earth have brought to such monstrous perfection . . . The Maxim guns exhausted all the water in their jackets, and several had to be refreshed from the water-bottles of the Cameron Highlanders before they could go on with their deadly work. The empty cartridge-cases, tinkling to the ground, formed small but growing heaps beside each man. And all the time out on the plain on the other side bullets were shearing through flesh, smashing and splintering bone; blood spouted from terrible wounds; valiant men were struggling on through a hell of whistling metal, exploding shells, and spurting dust – suffering, despairing, dying.

Two days later, a flotilla of gunboats steamed into Khartoum for a memorial service. The flagship vessel the *Melik* was moored opposite Government House where Gordon had made his last stand, while Kitchener stood on the shore with his staff. At ten o'clock the first boom of a twenty-one-gun salute rang out and the band of the 11th Sudanese Regiment began to play 'God Save the Queen'. To the sound of gunfire and the national anthem, the Union Jack was hoisted above the palace to be followed – as form required – by the crescent flag of the Khedive of Egypt, in whose name Kitchener had fought this battle.

There's a photograph of Kitchener that Churchill used as a frontispiece to *The River War*. In the 1902 edition that I read someone had scribbled beneath the picture the words 'God Save the King'. From the perspective of posterity, I find it a chilling

image of a man who fills me with as much ambivalence and fore-boding as Drummond inspired admiration.

On 8 November 1898, the Hero of Omdurman received a welcome in Chatham that recalled the extraordinary day of celebration that had marked the unveiling of Gordon's statue eight years before. Once again, the whole town turned out as Kitchener – Lord Kitchener now – rode in procession with the mayor along a route lined with soldiers. At Brompton Barracks, the officers of the corps were on parade at Gordon's monument.

Flanking the statue itself were 250 boys from the Gordon School, which had been set up in the general's memory. They received Lord Kitchener's special attention. After he had made a brief inspection of the line, he said to them, 'My boys, I am very glad to have had the opportunity of greeting you on my return from the Sudan. I trust many of you will grow up to be brave soldiers whom at some future day I may have the pleasure of seeing under my command.' It must have sounded like an appealing promise of another *Boy's Own* adventure. But by the time they were grown up, Kitchener was pointing his finger at a generation about to fight in a war that put an end to such adventures for good.

The high point of hubris was reached with a dinner that was put on in the officers' mess. The Duke of Cambridge, who had been at the unveiling of Gordon's statue, proposed the toast to the health of the sirdar of Egypt. There was a symbolic connection between the two events, the second answering the first in a tick-tock motion of vengeance. The programme card, which had been designed by two Royal Engineers officers, was a sheet of three triangles that was designed to be folded into the shape of a pyramid. The middle triangle, which gave the details of time and place, depicted the battlefield. Top left, the portrait of Gordon

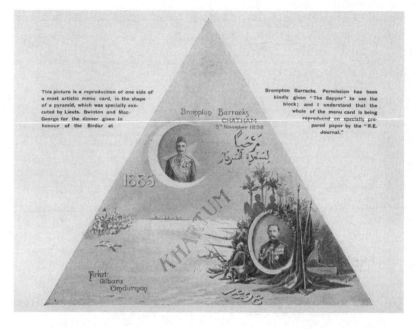

wearing his pasha's uniform was cradled in a crescent; and bottom right, shaded by the trees of a desert oasis, looking as solid as the Rock of Gibraltar, was Kitchener in an oval frame – turned into a circle through Britain's imperial might – while his soldiers' rifles dispensed death to the Mahdi army. Between them, rising like smoke from a fire, were capital letters that spelt out the word KHARTUM. On the left-hand triangle, a Dervish bearing a long spear sat on the ground looking up longingly at a menu board. Had he been allowed into the mess, he would have been able to enjoy an hors d'oeuvre of oysters, an entrée of sweetbreads in *financière* sauce or mutton cutlets in aspic, and a main course of roast beef, stuffed turkey or ham. Dessert included trifle, charlotte russe and fruit vols-au-vent. On the right-hand triangle, the evening's programme of music (to be played by the band of the Royal

Engineers) stood against the background of the Sudanese desert. As if expressing a favourite out of a varied repertoire with an Eastern theme (including a selection from *The Mikado* and Strauss's 'Rosen aus dem Süden' waltz), Gordon's camel nuzzled 'I'll Sing Thee Songs of Araby' by Frederic Clay.

The three Lynch brothers then serving with the corps, Jack, Patrick and James, were scattered around the country, 'on the Survey'. Even if they had still been in Chatham, as lowly sappers they would have had no more chance of gaining entry to the dinner than the Dervish with his spear, but I can imagine them reading all about it in the corps magazine, *The Sapper*, which reproduced the menu card in its Christmas issue.

If this revenge dinner seems with hindsight to express the pride that goes before a fall, the fall itself was less than a year away.

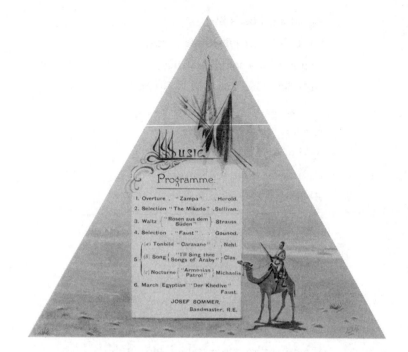

Meanwhile, the gulf between propaganda and reality had become a chasm that only the occasional dissident voice managed to bridge. In the early summer of 1899, the horde of Kipling imitators that dominated the poetry pages of *The Sapper* (not to mention English literature more generally) was joined by one Leo E. H. Koch, of the Royal Army Medical Corps, whose critical view of military life, 'Atkins on Kipling', unprecedented for its tone of disaffection, somehow slipped past the editor.

> They talk of 'Tommy Atkins',
> Said a soldier once to me,
> And Kiplin' writes a lot of rot
> About our grand Arm-ee;
> But Kiplin' don't know everythin'

About a soldier's life,
For he's never joined the Army,
And known a soldier's strife;
He's never been to Ord'ly Room,
And stood and 'eard his 'bloke'
A-tellin' of sich orful lies
As'd make the devil choke;
He's never done no 'jankers',
He don't know what it is;
He's never had no 'Pack Drill',
Nor done six months in 'Pris'.
A coal fatigue, I do believe,
Would kill him on the spot.
If he wants to know what life is,
I can recommend the 'Shot',
Where you're whitewashin' and scrubbin'
From mornin' until night,
Where everythin' you do is wrong,
And nothing's ever right.
To understand poor 'Tommy',
Which Kiplin' claims to do,
He must live the life amongst 'em,
And be a soldier too.

But it needed more than one unknown poet to dispel the rose-tinted view. Going into the Boer War, which began on 11 October 1899, everyone expected another quick victory, as the mighty Empire rolled over yet one more foe much weaker than itself. On 9 October 1899, an army of over 50,000 men was mobilised to join the British forces that were already in South Africa. Day after day, through the remainder of that October, troopships set off from Britain's ports, every departure accompanied by a patriotic send-off. On Saturday 28 October it was the turn of the Union Castle steamship SS *German*, which was bound for Cape Town with the 1st Battalion of the Rifle Brigade. The colonel-in-chief of the regiment, the Duke of Connaught, came down to Southampton for the occasion. 'As the Duke of Connaught watched the vessel, now slowly parting from her moorings,' the *Morning Post* reported, 'a thousand voices on the *German* sang the National Anthem, and a thousand more on the shore joined warmly in the refrain.' The band then played a medley of farewell songs – 'Soldiers of the Queen', 'Say Au Revoir not Goodbye', 'Rule Britannia' and of course 'Auld Lang Syne'.

The next day, the *Lloyd's Weekly Newspaper* published a poem from the famous children's author E. Nesbit, 'Song of Old Wars and New':

> Our troopships take the sea,
> White men again must face white men
> To keep the white man free.
> The sword we hold
> Is strong as of old,
> For our men are heroes' kin.
> We've learned the way to fight, my boys,
> We've learned the way to win!

Sure of further glory, the Empire was gaily tripping off to yet another far-flung war. But once again a jarring note was struck in Ireland. Here the soldiers setting off for South Africa faced as much hostility as support. When the Royal Irish Fusiliers passed nationalist areas of Belfast on their march to the railway station, they were pelted with stones. Nationalists everywhere were united in condemning an imperialist venture that offered so many parallels with their own experience of English rule. In Dublin a mass meeting was called to express sympathy with the Boers.

The crowd cheered Maude Gonne when she told them that a regiment of Irishmen had been formed in the Transvaal, but it was a 'sorrow and humiliation', she said, to know that there were regiments of Irish name that had gone out to fight the Boers. 'It is to be hoped that when they see the green flag of Ireland waving side by side with the banner of the Transvaal, they will, even at the eleventh hour, remember that they are Irishmen and cast off the hideous English uniform and fight on the side of right and justice with the rest of their countrymen.' The idea blossomed over the coming months into an anti-recruitment campaign in Ireland.

Whether it much entered the minds of the Irish soldiers, or indeed the dissenting English soldiers – of which there must have been a few – perhaps a saving grace of imperial Britain, for all her hubris, lay in a long history of parliamentary democracy, which allowed dissenting voices to have their say.

In the new year, the leader of the Irish Parliamentary Party, John Redmond, proposed an amendment to the Queen's Speech, that the war should be brought to a close 'on the basis of recognising the independence of the Transvaal and the Orange Free State'. The vote was defeated by a large majority. But at least there was a vote, after a long debate in which Redmond explained eloquently why so many Irish people considered the war to be 'immoral and unjust'.

At every turn of the war the dissident voices continued to have

MICK: "Sure, that was a close shave for yer heart, Pat."
PAT (who has received a bullet in the left arm): "Bedad, but it wasn't, now, for I had me heart in me mouth all the toime."

their say. When the British began to pursue a scorched earth policy, herding Boer families into concentration camps, Redmond's deputy, John Dillon, made sure to mark its significance in Parliament. 'I assert without fear of contradiction that this policy of shutting up women and children in prison camps is entirely without precedent in modern times, and that therefore the Government which indulges in it is disgracing and dragging in the mire the good name of this country.' Liberal politicians joined in the chorus of criticism. The future prime minister Lloyd George accused the War Office of 'a policy of extermination against children in South Africa'. In some countries such a comment might have landed you in a prison camp yourself. What a strange spectacle this ancient kingdom must have offered the outside world – a fiercely proud society of aristocratic privilege and deep inequality, yet diverse, free-spoken and tolerant (at home, if certainly not on the veld) even in moments of the greatest crisis.

Queen Victoria's death at the beginning of 1901 brought to an end a long reign that had suddenly turned sad and inglorious. The switch from the confidence of the Sudan to the quagmire of the Boer War had been so fast. It seemed as if overnight, with the passing into a new century, all the previous assumptions about Britain's position of pre-eminence in the world had to be re-evaluated.

The last of the Lynch brothers to take an oath of allegiance to the old Queen was Michael, who joined the corps in January 1899. And Edward VII was already well used to his throne when the youngest, Thomas, enlisted five years later. It was not such a long period of time in between really, but the huge upheaval of the intervening war must have made the feel of passing into a different age all the more profound. Michael had a taste of the old mood of confidence, while Thomas joined an army undergoing rapid reform amid widespread anxiety about Britain's ability to remain a Great Power.

When the Boer War began, Michael was still living in barracks at Chatham, where the combination of parade ground and mess room forged an *esprit de corps* for a new imperial adventure that I suppose even a sapper from the west of Ireland would have found difficult to resist. His older brothers, Jack, Patrick and James, by contrast, continued to move from lodging to lodging in different parts of the country, far removed from military life as they charted map revisions for the Ordnance Survey, although they could still follow the fortunes of their comrades overseas in the corps magazine.

When the war failed to be 'over by Christmas', *The Sapper* began to publish letters from serving soldiers from about the time the siege of Ladysmith was lifted in February 1900 – albeit many weeks after those letters were written. The sense of shocked but dawning reality about the true nature of the war that the country had so gleefully rushed into was expressed well in a letter written by a military surveyor called Corporal Comb. Sent out to South Africa as part of a four-man mapping team, he might easily have been my grandfather, who was very shortly to set out on his own first foreign posting:

Knowing how eagerly any news, however brief, would be hailed from this part of the globe by our comrades at home, I send herewith a short account of the doings of the Mapping Section, Field Intelligence Division, Natal.

We left England on the 23rd September 1899, as everyone is aware, just before war was declared. I cannot help thinking of the many and varied opinions we possessed at that time concerning the war. Some said it simply meant a pleasant trip to the Cape and back, and that not a shot would be fired. Others, that if the Boers did go to war it would result in a pure 'walk over' for us. Alas! such has not been the case. But to continue. We had no sooner put foot on the shore of South Africa than war was declared. Our party was at once ordered to proceed to Ladysmith, and arrived there at 6.30 a.m. on the 20th October 1899, just in time for the first engagement.

As regards our work, we have not had an idle moment during the siege. You will naturally wonder what there was to do to keep us so busy during the whole of the 119 days. Well, among other things, we produced hundreds of maps of Natal, and during the last month of the siege were engaged in producing plans and sections of the whole of the Ladysmith defences.

The house we used as an office was in the line of fire of Bulwana Long Tom, so we received rather more than our share of shells, 46 falling within a radius of 100 yards, and two within 1 and 3 yards respectively of the front of the building, smashing the windows and filling the rooms with débris; but in time we became accustomed to the whiz and bang, and paid little heed to them.

Towards the end of the siege we existed on horses, mules and ground Indian corn mixed with starch in the place of bread. These loaves might, I think, have been advantageously substituted for the ordinary shells; I am sure they would have done equally as much, if not more, damage. We began to think we were having rather a painful as well as novel experience.

But thank goodness this terrible siege has come to an end, and I cannot express to you our feelings of joy and thankfulness when it became an absolute fact that we were free men again.

Another letter was from an unidentified sapper serving with 17th Field Company, RE. He was writing in the aftermath of a Boer ambush of an armoured train near his camp at Chieveley:

By the time you receive this letter you will have read all about the dreadful battle we had here yesterday. I'm sure you will believe me when I tell you I have seen enough active service to last me all my life. The losses on our side were very heavy. We started shelling the Boer position at 4 a.m., and the fight lasted until one o'clock, and during the whole of those nine hours the rattle of gun and rifle fire never ceased. Their gun fire was not very effective but they made up deficiencies by their rifle fire. The position the Boers held was as strong as a position could possibly be, and they even had the range of their guns marked out beforehand by large stones.

One gun the enemy used did not smoke, and fired seven shells in rapid succession. Our gunners tried to put it out of action, but owing to it not smoking, failed to locate it. The Irish Brigade suffered very badly; the Dublin Regiment alone lost 200 out of 600, and those who came back were hysterical with rage at the way their poor chums had been so cut to pieces.

The elusive Boer guns were a much remarked-upon feature of the early stage of the war. 'These Boers are stickers,' commented another sapper in the 17th Field Company. 'It isn't so much their grit as the splendid artillery they possess. Their guns have disappearing mountings – a sort of "jack-in-the-box" action – consequently our gunners cannot get them.'

On board the train that had been ambushed near Chieveley were not only six hundred Dublin Fusiliers but also Winston Churchill, war correspondent of the *Morning Post*, who was among those taken prisoner by the Boers. *Ubique* would have been a good motto for him, such was his knack for turning up at the hotspots of British history.

Many British newspapers published eyewitness accounts of his bravery. When the trucks were overturned, he rallied the soldiers, exposing himself to heavy gunfire. The soldiers cut loose the disabled trucks from a still-working engine, onto which they then carried the wounded. The engine continued on its way, while Churchill, according to the *Post*, 'took a rifle and waited on with the retiring party, so as to cover the others' escape'. After the letters from the living, *The Sapper* would publish long lists of the dead, which brought out how the great killer of the war was neither bullets nor shells but disease:

27118, 2nd Corpl. E. O'Leary, 20th Co., died May 2nd, enteric, Modder River.

28279, Lance-Corpl. G. Fitzpatrick, 8th Co., died May 5th, enteric, Orange River.

2740, Sapper J. Keefe, 37th Co., died May 3rd, enteric, Ladysmith.

26558, Driver C. Clayton, 47th Co., died May 7th, enteric, Dewetsdorp.

22792, Sapper A. Harris, 45th Co., died May 5th, enteric, Kimberley.

24985, Sapper W. Huntingdon, died May 7th, dysentery, Kimberley.

And so on for page after page.

After the military setbacks of the first two months of the war, the morale of the corps received a boost from the appointment of Kitchener as chief of staff in South Africa at the end of 1899. Soon after Kitchener's appointment *The Sapper* reprinted a story that had appeared in the *Daily Telegraph* which reflected the heroic reputation Kitchener then had among the nation as a whole:

A lady missionary was passing through one of the lowest slums of Liverpool, when she came upon a trio of three ragged little urchins excitedly discussing the present war.

'I tell yer, they've sent Kitchener,' the youngest was insisting lustily. 'Who is Kitchener?' asked the lady. 'Kitchener? Don't yer knows Kitchener?' (in withering contempt.) 'Why, he's the champion of the whole world, he is; and they've sent 'im to lick the Boers. They should 'a sent 'im long ago.' 'But what do you know about Kitchener?' 'What do I know? They should 'a sent 'im to the Boers at fust.'

And 'at fust', Kitchener did go on to lick the Boers. By June 1900, Pretoria had fallen. All that remained was a routine mopping-up operation, and the Transvaal was annexed into the British Empire in September.

Briefly, the old tone of triumphalism returned to the magazine. For example, this joke in the August 1900 issue:

Teacher: 'Why, Tommy, you have spelt "Kruger" without a capital K.'

Tommy: 'That's correct, teacher. Kruger hasn't a capital now!'

But Tommy still had a lot to learn. The Boers switched to an immensely effective guerrilla war. Kitchener, the meticulous planner, who had spent two and a half years in the Sudan building a railway to keep his army supplied for a battle that would last only one day, carried out a ruthless strategy of denying supply to the Boers. Over eight thousand blockhouses were built to restrict the freedom of movement of the Boer fighters; British troops then swept the countryside destroying farms and any source of possible sustenance. The displaced women and children were herded into camps, where approximately 30,000, about one in four, died of starvation or disease.

As a son of a daughter of a Royal Engineer, I had been pleased to find so many reasons to feel proud of the corps, but pride quickly crumbled as I read the details of Kitchener's 'cruel system', which in the words of Emily Hobhouse, the British peace campaigner who wrote the report that exposed what had been going on, fell 'with crushing effect upon the old, the weak, and the children'. Here was the madness of a military mind unable to imagine the human dimension. When Kitchener had her deported from South Africa under martial law, she wrote to him, 'I feel ashamed to own you as a fellow-countryman.'

'When the Children of Israel made bricks without straw, / They were learnin' the regular work of our Corps . . .'

In 1901, the regular work of the corps included building the concentration camps and blockhouses of Kitchener's system. Yet Kitchener remained Britain's great hero, the toast of the Engineers, the frontispiece photograph of countless celebrations of Empire. One reason why Emily Hobhouse had been able to expose the inhuman conditions of the camps was because, as a woman, she was outside the power structure of the establishment, although with enough connections within it to have a voice that could at least make itself heard. If she had been a scullery maid no one would have taken any notice of her. The establishment had become too self-confident in the years of glory to question one of their own. As Gordon's death led to Kitchener's revenge, so too did the triumph of Omdurman lead to the shame of the Boer concentration camps.

Not that anyone expressed too much shame at the time. There may not have been any more revenge dinners held in the officers' mess at Chatham, but to the very last of his days Kitchener carried on unchallenged as Britain's ultimate soldier.

12

From Gibraltar to St Helena

When the Boer War began in 1899, the Lynch brothers had up to that point spent their careers entirely at 'Home'. In the case of James, who had been permanently attached to the Ordnance Survey, this remained so until he was sent to France in 1916. But now, one by one, the other three – first Patrick, then Michael, then Jack – were posted abroad.

On 30 October 1899 Patrick set off for Gibraltar, although for a sapper, Gibraltar was really a home from home. It was here that the non-commissioned ranks of the Royal Engineers had first come into being in the eighteenth century as the 'Soldier Artificers Company', which had the task of fortifying a town that was seized from Spain in 1704 during the War of the Spanish Succession. The phrase 'as solid as the Rock of Gibraltar' was a testament to their handiwork, which helped the garrison to endure the 'Great Siege' of 1779–83.

After suffering four sieges during the eighteenth century, the Rock faced none in the nineteenth. It had become so famously impregnable that I was puzzled at first why a topographical surveyor like my grandfather had to be sent there. Barely three square miles in total, the Rock must surely have been not only the most heavily defended but also the most heavily mapped territory in the entire British Empire.

It required only a brief acquaintance with the period's technological revolution in weaponry to discover the answer. As the twentieth century approached, the increased range of modern artillery posed a new threat to the possession, which came sharply into focus when, during the Spanish–American war of 1898, the Spanish erected gun batteries to prevent the Americans from landing troops in the Bay of Gibraltar. For the first time, the Rock came within range of the guns from the mainland.

After her eventual defeat in the 1898 war, Spain was not considered herself to be a serious military threat to the fortress, but in this time before the *entente cordiale*, when Britain still pursued a policy of 'Splendid Isolation', the Colonial Office feared the possibility of a French army moving through Spain as far as the Bay of Gibraltar. In the National Archives I was able to look through its review of the defence plans for Gibraltar in May 1899, when it asked that a map be made to include the Spanish defence works, a new railway that had been extended as far as Algeciras, and the topographical features of Gibraltar itself. When Patrick arrived six months later, it must surely have been to contribute to this map.

Marked 'Secret', the completed map was printed by the War Office. It included a table that listed the location and type of the twenty-eight heavy guns that then defended the fortress and harbour. The discovery that there was even more powerful artillery on the Spanish coastline caused the territory to remain a focus of military concern long after Patrick had returned from his

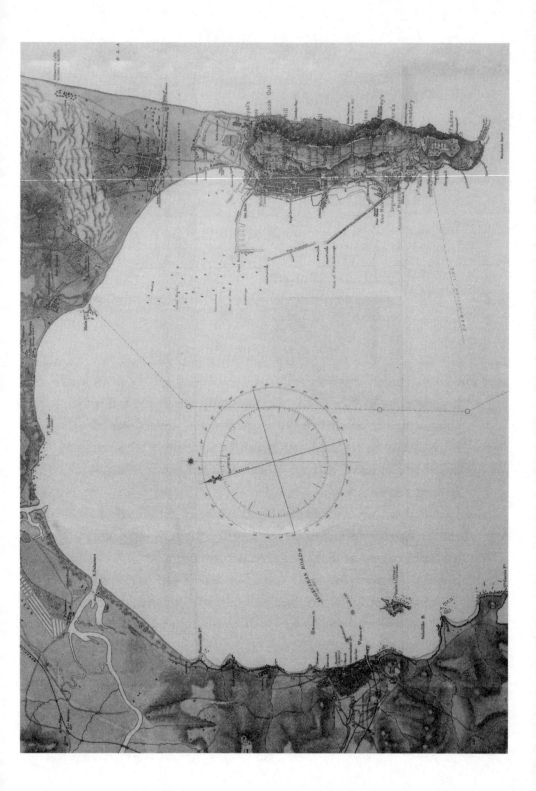

EXISTING ARMAMENT
Corrected to Feb: 1903

NAME OF WORK	B.L 9.2	B.L 6	Q.F 12pr	Q.F 6pr	R.M.L 17/2	R.M.L 10in	R.M.L 10	R.M.L 64	Machine	REMARKS
Waterport Casemates										2cm
Montague Cavalier										2cm
South Bastion										1cm
Ragged Staff Flank										2cm
Cumberland Flank Batt.y										2cm
New Mole Batt.y										2cm
Engineer "				3						
Napier "					1					
Devils Gap "		2		2						
Prince Ferdinands Batt.y				2						
11th Rosia Batt.y									1cm	
Buena Vista "				2						
Edward VII "	2									
West "	2									
South "			4							
Buffadero "	1									
Jews Cemetery Batt.y	1									
O'Hara's Batt.y	1									
Lord Aireys "	1									
Spyglass "					6					
Signal Hill	2									
Signal Station				2						
Rock Batt.y	2									
Middle Hill Batt.y					6					
Farringdons "						2				
Governors Lookout Batt.y	1									
Calpe Batt.y						3				
Princess Caroline Batt.y							2			
Upper Galleries				2				11		
Lower "								7	10	Under reconstruction
Princess Royals Batt.y										" "
Genista Batt.y										
General Defence		8						27		
TOTALS	9	6	8	4	13	1	12	5	20	48

Defence Electric Lights _____ † E.L.

posting there in June 1900. An Admiralty report the following year recommended that all British guns on the western side of the Rock should be replaced with ones that were 'superior in range, accuracy and power to guns which the enemy may be expected to bring against them'.

But it was not enough to alter the state of profound anxiety about the future defence of the territory. The concern was that more powerful enemy artillery might make redundant work that had been in progress since 1895 to update and enlarge the harbour. There was a proposal that instead a new harbour should be built on the east side of the Rock, which, sea-facing, would be out of sight of the Spanish coastline.

The prevailing tone was one of extreme uncertainty. The artillery arms race that had followed the Franco-Prussian War of 1871, in which Krupp and Schneider-Creusot vied with each other to produce ever more powerful and innovative guns, had changed the landscape of military technology out of all recognition. 'The past history of Gibraltar is of little value as to the form of attack that might be developed against it now,' wrote the governor of the territory in August 1901. He pointed out that fourteen miles of Spanish coastline formed an 'enfolding front' that offered exceptional advantages to enemy artillery. 'It is evident that the best, indeed the only, measure open to us now is to have a careful and accurate survey made of this country. This I am having done, but it is necessary to proceed cautiously and deliberately with so secret a service.' With help from the Intelligence Division of the War Office, he had arranged for an undercover agent to make detailed observations on the military installations in the region.

Now that the Empire was long over I was able to read – neatly filed away in foolscap folders tied with pink ribbon – the private fears that lay behind the *fin-de-siècle* facade of invincibility. The mandarins were keeping calm but, in their scrawled notes appended to this or that report, there was growing apprehension.

The concerns over Gibraltar were only part of a much bigger picture, which the director of Military Intelligence, W. G. Nicholson, sketched out in comments he made for the war minister on the various plans for Gibraltar's defence:

> The growth of continental navies, especially those of France and Russia, renders it more and more difficult for us to retain the command of the Sea, and it seems not improbable that before long we shall be compelled to consider the question of alliances as the only means of upholding British interests abroad without incurring serious expenditure at home. It can hardly be disputed that, if we possessed powerful allies, our position at

Gibraltar and Malta and in Egypt would be much more secure than it is at present.

And so the scene was set for the bloody twentieth century. Before long, Britain had signed the *entente cordiale* of 1904 with France, and the Anglo-Russian Convention of 1907. Splendid isolation made way for the Triple Entente, and it was no longer the French or Russian navies that Britain worried about but Germany's. Suddenly the world was on the high road to the Great War.

The next brother to serve abroad was Michael, who, on 18 September 1901, arrived in Canada. Of the five brothers, Michael was the only one not to have worked as a surveyor. Instead, he trained to become a submarine miner.

In 1900, the Royal Engineers devoted nearly a quarter of its manpower to the defence of British ports. Thirteen regular submarine mining companies comprised about two thousand men, and there were as many volunteers. Their role was to install and maintain – and, if necessary, detonate – mines in the waters around strategically important harbours. In a complex system of integrated defence, they operated a network of underwater mines that were connected by electric cables to an observation station on the shore, and powerful carbon arc searchlights that were carefully sited to detect any hostile vessels. They possessed their own fleet of specialised, 'Gordon-class' mine-layers, each vessel about eighty feet long and over a hundred tons in weight, and a team of divers to provide underwater maintenance. The submarine miners boasted that they could lay down a minefield defence in any port of the Empire with three days' notice.

After qualifying as an 'Electrician Superior' at the end of 1900,

Michael spent most of 1901 with the 30th Company of Submarine Miners, which was based at Fisher's Nose Wharf underneath the citadel that commanded the entrance to Plymouth Sound. When he went to Canada in September, it was to serve with the 40th Company of Submarine Miners in Halifax, Nova Scotia, which was responsible for defending one of Canada's two Royal Navy bases.

As a sapper on the ground Michael was of course not in the best place to see the big picture, but if he had thought to count the Royal Navy ships that came into harbour over the next four years of his posting, he would have noticed an ever dwindling number, as the Admiralty switched ships from the western hemisphere to face the growing threat in home waters. Soon the submarine miners themselves would join the retreat. When he was posted back to Britain in 1906, it was not only Michael who left Nova Scotia, but the entire garrison. As the high tide of the British Empire receded, no longer would the Royal Navy serve as its sole protector. The naval stations at Halifax and Esquimalt on the Pacific coast were transferred into the ownership of the Canadian government, which established its own navy in 1910.

Old empires fall, new ones rise. Nothing is ever still. The same was true of Michael's trade. While he was away in Nova Scotia, the Royal Navy introduced a revolutionary new 'A-class' submarine boat, the first of which, the HMS *A1*, was launched in July 1902. The trials were so successful that in 1905 the War Office decided that the 'Senior Service' should henceforward assume responsibility for harbour defence. In an emasculating reduction that took away not only their boats and high-explosive mines but also their operations buildings and wharf-side sheds (ideal for maintaining the navy's new submarines), the Royal Engineers' submarine miner companies were left with only their searchlights. The sappers were either transferred to other units or re-formed into 'Electric Light' companies to man coastal defence observation stations.*

Michael arrived back in Britain immediately after the shake-up, joining a searchlight battery at Nothe Fort, Weymouth, in March 1906. He was a recently promoted lance corporal, with a 1st Class Army Certificate of Education, who had excellent prospects for further promotion, but it seems his career had passed into a backwater. Like the redundant minefields of the submarine miners no longer wired to the operations room overlooking the harbour, he had been disconnected from the nodes of history. To use an analogy from his surveyor brothers' trade, he had ceased to provide a baseline from which I could triangulate to the map of Empire. He travelled but did not travel. Over the coming years, his military history sheet logged an impressive list of foreign postings, but in each case, whether it was Ceylon (30 September 1909 to 26 October 1911), Singapore (27 October 1911 to 21 December 1912) or Sierra Leone (10 October 1915 to 4 December 1916), he was tied to the fixed searchlight emplacements by the harbour, seeing the sea, but never finding out about the islands that lay beyond the horizon.

The oldest of the five brothers, Jack Lynch, had his opportunity to travel abroad in March 1902, after more than seven years' service. In his case there was no lack of scope for significant triangulation.

---

* The human cost of the War Office decision proved catastrophic. The thirteen new A-class submarines turned out to be deathtraps. When the HMS *A1* was struck by the liner *Berwick Castle* in 1904 and sank with the loss of all on board, it was the first in a series of similar fatal accidents that most of the boats suffered.

The baseline lay in the Boer War, which was only just coming to an end. The disastrous conflict, which had dragged on for three years and required 450,000 troops to defeat a force a fraction of the size, added to the Empire's sense of its waning power. If it had taken so long to win against the Boers, how might a British force fare against a modern, well-equipped European power?

One of the most conspicuous failings of the war was the lack of any maps of South Africa that were adequate for military operations. During the Battle of Modder River, the commanding general, Lord Methuen, was surprised to discover that his troops were unable to ford the river and had no idea where to go to find a crossing point. When the British attacked Spion Kop, they captured a low-lying hill without realising that it was exposed to fire from a Boer force that occupied a yet higher summit. In both cases, heavy casualties were the result.

In 1902, the Intelligence Division of the War Office created a small 'Colonial Survey Section' to address a failure of military planning that would be made public, along with the many other military shortcomings of the conflict, when a Royal Commission of Inquiry published a report on the war the following year. Comprising two officers and four NCOs, the purpose of the section was to carry out topographical surveys in the immediate vicinity of British bases abroad that were considered to be of 'special military importance'.

This was Jack's first foreign posting. He was originally to have gone out with a field survey team to South Africa, but as it became clear that a peace treaty was only months away, the team was reconfigured to become the nucleus of the new Colonial Survey Section, the CSS, which the War Office sent to Mauritius and then St Helena.

The Sapper recorded the details of the smoker that the

Ordnance Survey office in Southampton organised as a farewell to Jack and his two comrades, Sappers Weston and Evans. Sergeant Fincher took the chair, while Corporal Lucas acted as master of ceremonies. 'The King having been proposed by the Chairman and duly honoured, Sapper H. H. Evans opened the programme by singing in fine style "Young Jack Crawford".' After a long evening of more songs and comic routines, the chairman proposed a toast to 'our departing comrades', wishing them God-speed and a safe return. On behalf of the mess, he then presented each of the men with a bottle of whisky, a pound of tobacco and a briar pipe. Jack, who as a lance corporal was the senior member of the departing group, responded by thanking the chairman for such a wonderful send-off. *The Sapper* did not report his exact words, but I have no doubt they were full of the warmth and wit for which he would later be remembered. And although again *The Sapper* does not report it, I can see him clasping his comrades' hands and loudly singing 'Auld Lang Syne' as the smoker finally came to a close.

Lying in the southern Indian Ocean halfway between South Africa and India, Mauritius had been captured from the French during the Napoleonic Wars. It had been an important port with a large garrison until the opening of the Suez Canal in 1869 diverted the trade. At about the same time the outbreak of an unusually virulent form of malaria, which killed about one in ten of the population, led to the evacuation of most of the garrison, but towards the end of the nineteenth century it assumed renewed importance when the capital, Port Louis, was fortified as a coaling station for the Royal Navy. The same logic lay behind the continuing strategic importance of St Helena.

Of the two islands, Mauritius, the land of the dodo, seemed as lacking in British associations as St Helena was full of them. In the British Library, I pored over the six sheets that made up the Colonial Survey Section's map of an island that covered an area of nearly eight hundred square miles. The predominance of French names brought out its status as a colony snatched from another empire.

On the island the men were joined by the commanding officers of the section, Major W. A. Harrison and Lieutenant F. B. Legh. In April 1902 they started out by measuring a baseline for triangulation along a straight section of railway near Providence eastwards towards Camp de Masque station. The peaks that they used as triangulation points included Monts Blanche, Couve, Barbe and Bailleduc, while the towns had such names as Beau Bassin, Quatre Bornes and Bon Accueil. Not far away was the forest of Nouvelle Découverte.

The pretty French names did nothing to make up for the gruelling, often dangerous nature of a military topographer's work. It was Jack's job to get to know every nook and cranny of the island. Travelling across the terrain on foot and camping out in the open, he had to venture into disease-ridden swamps and marshes that any sane person would avoid. When he was hospitalised for ten days in August 1902 with malaria, it was really too much of an occupational hazard even to be considered bad luck.

What a world of difference modern medicine can make, I thought as I looked through a contemporary tourist brochure. 'Beyond Mauritius's sun-kissed beaches, this exotic island offers a wealth of opportunities for you to be chilled and thrilled.' If there was any truth to such words during Jack's time on the island, chills and thrills meant fits of shivering and sweating, along with severe headaches and nausea. After he returned to work again, I wondered whether he continued to suffer from attacks, which he would have had to keep at bay as best he could through a combination of quinine 'tabloids', plenty of tonic water and, not least, a very tough constitution.

In 1902 the world had only just discovered that the cause of malaria was the mosquito. While Jack was still struggling to recover his health, the physician Sir Ronald Ross became in December of that year the first Briton to win a Nobel Prize for – to quote the citation – 'his work on malaria, by which he has shown how it enters the organism and thereby has laid the foundation for successful research on this disease and methods of combating it'. Although it wasn't soon enough to help Jack, Ross travelled to Mauritius in 1906 to write a study that offers some measure of the prevalence of the disease. In an island population of less than 400,000, over the period 1900 to 1906 malaria accounted for an annual average of 4,384 admissions to hospital, with a death rate of 84.

When the CSS finished its work on the island in April 1903, a reduced section of three men travelled on to St Helena: Lieutenant Frank Legh, 2nd Corporal Jack Lynch (he had been promoted during his year in Mauritius), and Sapper H. H. Evans.

If Mauritius, with its French-speaking population, was one of the least British corners of the Empire, St Helena, by contrast, a fraction of its size, corresponded exactly to Shakespeare's description of the 'scepter'd isle'. Less than ten miles from side to side, it was one of those islands where you can never forget you are on an island, surrounded by the sheer cliffs of a 'fortress built by Nature for herself', so far away from anywhere else necessarily to become a 'little world'. While Mauritius, with its incongruous

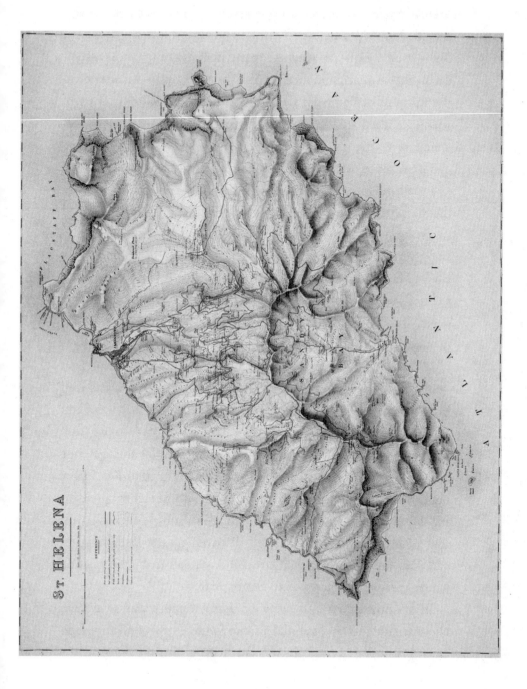

St. HELENA

French names, straggled formlessly over six sheets, St Helena appealed to me for the way I felt I could almost take it in my hand like a paperweight, as well as for the richness of imperial associations that had accumulated since Cromwell granted a charter to the East India Company to colonise the island in 1657. If there was just one map I could take with me to a desert island, this would surely be it.

The essence of an island fortress, St Helena was certainly of a size well judged to remind its most famous resident, Napoleon, that he, who had once ruled an entire continent, was now confined to an island – and had also been defeated by one. The only way Napoleon could possibly forget this painful truth was to confine his walks to St Helena's valleys, for as soon as he took to his horse and ventured over the brow of a hill, then suddenly the ocean was before him, and very soon a cliff edge forced him to turn back.

If Britain's second-oldest remaining colony had been best known as a place remote enough to contain Napoleon, it flickered back into life as somewhere more important than just a coaling station when the War Office needed to find a safe place to put Boer prisoners of war. In June 1901, its name appeared for the first time in the list of foreign stations of the Royal Engineers that *The Sapper* published every month. 'Dear Editor,' wrote the new correspondent for the St Helena station, 'When you see the above heading, you may well exclaim, "Has someone discovered us at last?" Apparently, no one has thought fit to send any news from this historic natural prison, so allow me to recapitulate.'

In late March 1900, a party of thirty sappers was sent from Chatham to the island to build a camp for more than four thousand Boer prisoners of war. It was an urgent mission because the conditions of the soldiers' captivity were terrible, the War Office having made no detailed plan for how to cope with so many prisoners. After the Battle of Paardeberg, the men had been transported on freight trains to the British naval station of Simonstown, where they were confined aboard prison ships. The overcrowding caused an epidemic of typhoid fever in which several of them died. Sending the prisoners to St Helena seemed the most expeditious and secure way of remedying a situation that risked an international outcry. The pity was that the British did not learn sufficiently from what had happened to prevent later on the scandal of Kitchener's concentration camps.

The sappers arrived at the island to find the first transport of prisoners, the SS *Milwaukee*, already waiting for them in the waters by the island's principal settlement, Jamestown, under the guard of a Royal Navy cruiser, HMS *Niobe*. The prisoners included the commander of the Boer forces at Paardeberg, General Piet Cronje.

He and his wife, with only a Bible to amuse themselves during the 2,000-mile journey to the island, had spent most of their time sitting together in silence holding hands. Anxious to cheer them up, the ship's officers invited the couple to join them in the mess, where they set up a gramophone. After the general listened in amazement to a Sousa march and the American gospel composer Ira Sankey singing his hymn 'The Ninety and Nine', he asked whether the trick had been achieved through ventriloquism. Taking the gramophone to pieces, the ship's captain explained how the machine worked and then, reassembling it, presented it to the general for his entertainment during his stay on St Helena.

When Napoleon made the journey to the island after his defeat at Waterloo, he had his own Field Library to consult and the company of a sizeable staff – as well as a Royal Navy admiral and an entire squadron of ships; but the view that awaited everyone, whether Boney, General Kronje or my great-uncle Jack, was the same volcanic rock, rising, in the words of another visitor, Charles Darwin, 'abruptly like a huge black castle from the ocean'. Napoleon's secretary, the Comte de Las Casas, was with him when, on the morning of 15 October 1815, he took in the first sight of the island. 'We beheld a kind of village surrounded by numerous barren and naked hills towering to the clouds. Every platform, every aperture, the brow of every hill, was planted with cannon. The Emperor viewed the prospect through his glass. I stood behind him. My eyes were constantly fixed on his countenance, in which I could perceive no change; and yet he saw before him perhaps his perpetual prison.'

Everything about St Helena suggested the purpose for which it

became most celebrated. In a ravine between two steep hills was Jamestown, so locked away from the rest of the island that a huge feat of engineering was required to compensate for its isolation. To the left of the town was Ladder Hill, named after a steep stairway that led up to the fort that perched on its summit. Some years after Napoleon died, the 'ladder' was replaced by a funicular railway that took supplies up to the barracks. But after the opening of the Suez Canal, the island became even more of an out-of-the-way spot than it had been in Napoleon's day. So the Royal Engineers dismantled the pulley system and tracks, leaving behind a central flight of 699 wooden steps that, rising at a forty-degree angle, formed the longest straight staircase in the world.

'On viewing the island from an eminence,' commented Charles Darwin, who visited during the voyage of the *Beagle* in 1836, 'the first circumstance which strikes one, is the number of the roads and forts: the labour bestowed on the public works, if one forgets its character as a prison, seems out of all proportion to its extent

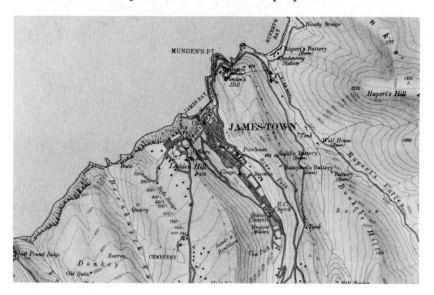

JACOB'S LADDER, JAMESTOWN, ST. HELENA (699 STEPS)

or value.' The island was as much a botanist's paradise as it was an engineer's. Darwin noted its 746 species of plants, all but fifty-two of which had been mostly imported from England and seemed to thrive far better than they did in their native country, so that it was only on the highest and steepest ridges that the indigenous species were still predominant. 'The English, or rather Welsh character of the scenery, is kept up by the numerous cottages and small white houses; some buried at the bottom of the deepest valleys, and others mounted on the crests of the lofty hills.'

Napoleon's residence at Longwood reminded him of a 'respectable gentleman's country-seat', but the only direct reference he made to the island's most famous guest was to mention that, during his own much more brief stay of a few days, he found lodgings close to the Emperor's tomb. 'After the volumes of eloquence which have poured forth on this subject,' he added, in a footnote, 'it is dangerous even to mention the tomb. A modern traveller, in twelve lines, burdens the poor little island with the following titles – it is a grave, tomb, pyramid, cemetery, sepulchre, catacomb, sarcophagus, minaret and mausoleum!'

It was a great scientist's lament for the tendency of *Homo sapiens* to gild the lily to the point that it became difficult to determine its genus. But it was only natural that the average sapper should have taken pride in the fact that it was the Royal Engineers who had built the tomb – or 'vault' as *The Sapper* magazine called it – of the greatest general of modern times.* It was a simple vault that did not even bear his name, because the British and French could not agree on the words for the inscription, but Napoleon

---

* The two stonemasons who did the work were Sappers John Warren and James Andrews.

himself would surely have appreciated the fact that it had been built by soldiers. A company of sappers was present at the Emperor's funeral, which took place on 9 May 1821. Two of their number lowered the body into its resting place, while other sappers refilled the grave and sealed it with plain Yorkshire slabs.

The event was a farewell to a great general but also a salute to the common soldier, in whom he inspired a legendary devotion. During the Second Empire, Napoleon III ordered a commemorative 'St Helena Medal' to be issued to all the surviving veterans, 'the grognards', of the Grande Armée. While the face shows the head of Napoleon, the reverse is inscribed:

A

SES

COMPAGNONS

DE GLOIRE

SA DERNIÈRE PENSÉE

STE HÉLÈNE

5 MAI 1821

Boney thought of his soldiers to his dying day, 5 May 1821, just as he had thought of all too many of them to their dying day. Yet they continued to revere him. In 1840 his remains were returned to France, where they were placed in a red porphyry sarcophagus beneath the dome of the 'Soldiers' Church', the Invalides. France could now pay honour to him in her own capital. But for the first twenty years after his death that role had been left to a handful of British soldiers and colonial officials, stopping off at St Helena on the long journey between India and Britain.

The task of looking after his grave had been entrusted to an old corporal from the 2nd Battalion of the 53rd Regiment, which had guarded Napoleon while he was alive. *The Sapper* published the following anonymous account, which describes the veteran showing some officers around the memorial garden:

A pretty geranium hedge in full blossom bordered the path which led to the sacred spot; on either side rose steep hills, which, uniting behind the tomb, formed a deep dell open only to the southward, where it looked down a valley; a neat green railing encircled a space of brilliant sward about ten yards in diameter, and in the middle of this, under the appropriate shade of venerable weeping willows, stood the square iron railing which guarded the last home of Napoleon . . .

'But perhaps, gentlemen, you would like to enter the railing; here is one of the bars which takes out, and as none of you are very stout you may slip through. I recollect not long ago an old fat general from Bombay, who, rather than not go inside, took off his coat, waistcoat, and almost everything he wore.'

We followed the old man's advice, and, entering the aperture in the railing, stood over the remains of l'Empereur des Français. I know not why it was, but we simultaneously took off our hats; we all felt that respect and reverence which we should have expressed had he been alive, and seemed to be hurt at the idea of a group of British officers thus unceremoniously invading the last resting-place of the 'vanquished victor'. It was not romance that occasioned this sensation (one of my companions having served in the navy since Trafalgar, and been two years a prisoner in France, whilst another from his earliest youth had been fighting in the Peninsula against the armies of the man whose dust now lay below us), but that deference which is always due to the memory of those whose superior talents and strength of mind have made them rise above the rest of their contemporaries. No inscription, not even the name 'Napoleon' had been engraven on the slabs; fame such as his requires no other or more splendid memorial than that which it will ever retain – the regrets of the French, and their recollections of the glorious deeds performed by their armies which led on to glory and victory by celui qui n'est plus.

As I read of the Emperor's two tombs and 'the regrets of the French' that guaranteed his immortality – passing French frigates still stop off at the island to express their sorrow – I thought of the rain and the lichen in Quin graveyard, every day carrying off yet another Clune or Lynch or McInerney beyond memory.

During the Boer War the island's character as a prison expressed itself in two large camps. I found them both on Jack's map – Deadwood Plain to the west of Jamestown, and Broad Bottom to the south-east. The more privileged prisoners were allowed to rent houses across the island. So many took advantage of the concession that there was scarcely a spare room to be found. Even the island's only hotel was being run by prisoners.

The Royal Engineers were quartered in Jamestown, which at sea level had the disadvantage of being five degrees hotter than the high plateau that formed most of the island. Napoleon's grave, to judge from *The Sapper* – which had, anyway, been empty for sixty years – was not enough to compensate for one of the duller postings. 'The town offers no attractions, and there is absolutely no place of entertainment where bachelors can spend their evenings. Pleasant walks are out of the question, because, to leave the town, means a laborious walk up steep, rough, rocky roads.' Although regular football and cricket matches against Boer teams or other regiments on the island offered some respite from the boredom, *The Sapper*'s correspondent on St Helena still passed this final verdict: 'After a few months one is, as a rule, what is termed "fed up" with the island, not without reason, and the "top note" is "roll on".'

The efforts to achieve the 'top note' had led to some spectacular Boer attempts to escape. One prisoner, Andries Smorenburg, had tried to post himself to a false address in London. He put himself in a wooden crate marked 'HANDLE WITH CARE' along with enough food and water for a three-week voyage to Southampton. In spite of the warning label, the crate was tossed about so much in the hold of the mail ship that Smorenburg was knocked out and lost most of his water. He was discovered soon after the ship had left St Helena and handed back to the authorities when it stopped off at Ascension Island nearly a thousand miles further north.

The very first effort to escape took place before the prisoners had even disembarked from the SS *Milwaukee*. Colonel Adolph Schiel was a famous German mercenary who had once been military adviser to the King of the Zulus. After the defeat of Zululand in 1887, he switched his allegiance to the Transvaal, where he formed a German brigade at the beginning of the Boer War. A photograph that appeared in the *Sketch* newspaper soon after his capture at Elandslaagte depicts a tall, imposing man in his forties with a moustache that outdid even Kitchener's.

'For some reason or other,' commented the *Sketch*, 'he, like so many other Continentals, has an intense hatred of England and Englishmen, and has never missed an opportunity of doing us a bad turn.'

What better way of embarrassing the English than by slipping away while the *Milwaukee* was still anchored off Jamestown in quarantine. Schiel bribed a boatman to take a letter to a Dutch cruiser that he had noticed in the roadstead, but the letter was mistakenly taken to a British ship instead. When the colonel was arrested, he was found to be carrying a large knife. As he was led from the landing stage through Jamestown up to High Knoll Citadel, a fortress that overlooked Ladder Hill, the soldiers and sailors who passed him sang 'Rule Britannia' and 'Soldiers of the Queen'. Some days later there were questions in Parliament about their lack of etiquette.

When Napoleon was on St Helena, he was guarded by a garrison of three thousand soldiers and a squadron of eleven Royal Navy ships, which constantly patrolled the waters around the island. An Act of Parliament was passed making it a capital offence to do anything that might assist his escape. Napoleon found the measures absurd, expressing his pity for the 'poor soldiers fatigued to death with pickets and guards, or harassed carrying loads up those rocks'. The governor had only to guard the sea borders of the island to make escape impossible, he told his Irish doctor, Barry O'Meara. In such a remote island surrounded by cliffs, the general-turned-armchair-gaoler explained, the only extra precaution that the British needed to take was not to allow any ship to depart from the island without first ascertaining his whereabouts. He expressed the hope that he would be allowed to return to Europe once he was no longer considered to be a danger. He refused to acknowledge that he was a prisoner and claimed to consider any attempt to escape to be beneath his dignity.

Yet that did not prevent his followers from devising endless schemes to rescue him. For, as Napoleon himself observed, so long as he was alive, escape was still theoretically possible. One of the most spectacular involved a famous smuggler, Thomas Johnson, who had broken out of several British prisons. He planned to arrive off the coast of St Helena in a submarine. Making contact with the Emperor, he would help him at nightfall to slip out of Longwood House disguised as a footman. Reaching the cliffs, the Emperor would then be lowered down to the waiting submarine in a mechanical chair. But Napoleon died before the plot could be carried out.

While most of the previous efforts of the British army had been spent in turning St Helena into an impregnable fortress and prison, the three Royal Engineers who belonged to the Colonial Survey Section were among the very few who appreciated the island for itself. Their job was, after all, to map and record its topography. In this respect, they were following in the footsteps of Darwin, who nearly seventy years before had come to examine the geological history of the island, and proceeded in a methodical manner that was very similar to their own. When he obtained lodgings within a stone's throw of Napoleon's tomb, it was not through any esteem for the great general but because it was in a 'capital central situation' from which to explore the island.

'The best position for his camps must be carefully thought out,' advises a Royal Engineers surveyor's manual. The more I read, the more I realised that Jack's work was at the very heart of the map. The practice was for the officer to undertake the triangulation and supervise the fieldwork, while the NCO – on St Helena, Jack was the NCO – with the help of a sapper, recorded the topography, using a plane table. A board fixed horizontally to a tripod, the plane table was equipped with a special telescopic sight – an alidade – that measured the angle of distant points. Once the NCO had plotted the position of the triangulation points on a sheet attached to the board, he would sketch in the details of the land by eye. When he left one observation point for a new one, he built a cairn so that he would be able to sight the old position. Within the framework of the measured distances, he would then add the contours of the hills, calculating the gradient with a clinometer.

All the sketches in the field were made with a pencil, HH for the rays that the surveyor drew and then erased after having calculated the exact position of the trig points, and H for the detail. At the end of the day, he then inked in the completed work, using sticks of India ink that allowed a much finer finish than their liquid equivalents. In the pursuit of the highest possible accuracy, the practice was to record everything that could be seen no matter how vague. Even the most distant detail was drawn as carefully as possible, rather than simply roughed in with loose sweeps of the pencil, because the information would later help to locate some valley or spur that might otherwise have been overlooked.

In terms of the look of a topographical map, it was the NCO surveyor who, on the plane table, drew all the detail of what we actually see. He was likely to be far more accomplished in the sheer knowledge and skill of surveying than the officer, whose all-round training did not afford the same opportunity to accumulate specialist experience. Yet the work of a non-commissioned soldier was veiled in anonymity, the officer taking the credit for the final achievement.

In June 1903, the mapping of St Helena began to fall behind when the rains set in, but at least the turn in the weather allowed me a brief glimpse of my great-uncle in the National Archives, since Lieutenant Legh had to write to the director of Military Intelligence at the War Office to explain the delay. 'As the winter has only just begun, worse weather may be expected. At present about ten square miles of country have been "plane-tabled", 5 ½ weeks having been expended on that work, by the NCO and man.'

The 'NCO and man' were my great-uncle Jack and Sapper Evans, but as they were from the uncommissioned ranks, they were of little account. When the director of the observatory at the Cape of Good Hope, Sir David Gill, contacted the War Office about a year after the map had been completed to seek some of the calculations that had been used in the survey, the head of the Geographical Section, Colonel Close, wrote back to him, 'The man who carried out the St Helena survey was Lt. F. B. Legh R.E., now serving at Chatham.' But Legh measured only the triangulation points. My great-uncle Jack drew the physical features and detail that you actually see on the map that the

Ordnance Survey office in Southampton made up and printed from his plane-table field sheets.

Although the Colonial Survey Section finished their work on the island in early September 1903, it took another year for the finished map to reach the War Office. Along the bottom edge was stamped: 'INTELL. DIV., W.O. MAP ROOM', 'Recd. 5 OCT 1904' and 'UNIQUE COPY'. And scribbled in pencil, from a time when presumably the work of the CSS was still an official secret: 'Not allowed out of the building without Mr. Mumford's permission.'

On a scale of two and a half inches to a mile, the map was about eighteen inches high and twenty-four wide: it contained in a single sheet an island whose total area was only forty-seven square miles, about a third of the area of the Isle of Wight. Leaning far over the table in the British Library Map Room, I noticed that the baseline for triangulation – the start of all creation in the map-makers' world – had been indicated on Deadwood Plain in the north of the island, near the old Boer camp outside Jamestown. Next to each of the two tiny triangle symbols that marked the terminals their respective heights were given – 1,757ft for the north terminal, and 1,743ft for the south. Over the length of a little more than a mile, there was a drop of just 14ft on this most rocky and undulating of islands – a place where there seemed scarcely a feature that wasn't ringed with contours.

The south terminal, close to a wood called Mulberry Gut, was about a quarter of a mile's walk from Napoleon's residence at Longwood. I could trace the roundabout path that Darwin would have had to take from his lodgings near Napoleon's Tomb if he were to reach Diana's Peak, the highest point of the island, which was only a mile away as the crow flies (although Darwin noted how few birds there were of any kind on the island). And there was enough detail to attempt a guess at where those lodgings might have been. Prospect House, perhaps? Or Hutt's Gate? Darwin relied on the assistance of an old goatherd 'who knew every step amongst the rocks', but the Survey Section's map, with its topographical precision, would have helped him to plot a path through a maze of contours that made short distances a long journey.

Napoleon could also have done with a map like this, I thought, as I tried to figure out the best escape route from Longwood House to the coast. I imagined the smuggler Tom Johnson's submarine waiting for him, submerged in Prosperous Bay, marked on the map as the 'landing place of the English in 1672'. All the Emperor had to do was get there.

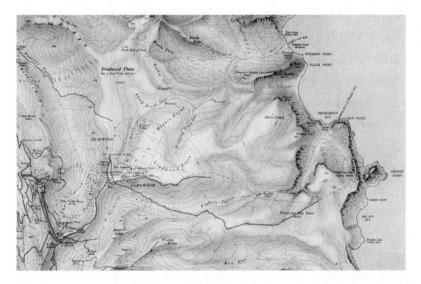

One day, he goes out for his ride, as he does most mornings, cantering eastwards across Longwood Plain. Instead of turning back when he reaches Horse Point, where the ground begins to get rough, he gets off his horse and scrambles down a ravine to a little river. He knows the quickest way to reach it from the map that he studied the night before. He plunges in, making himself as indistinct as possible. The sentinels would have to know where to look to spot him from the two batteries that, facing out to sea, dominate the rocky ridge on the north side of the river. And even if they did see him, everything happens so quickly. It takes only five minutes for the Emperor to reach the shoreline by Bryan's Rock, where a skiff is waiting. In another five, he is safely aboard the submarine, which quickly submerges beyond detection. Six months later he is ready to menace Europe again.

South-east of Longwood Plain can be found a stretch of level land, called Prosperous Bay Plain, that the map of the Survey Section reveals to be about the only spot on the entire island that is truly free of contours. It is where, two hundred years after Napoleon arrived on the island in 1815, the construction of a runway and airport now offers a new means of escape, ending St Helena's fabled isolation for ever.

It was at this point in my daydreaming that I became aware of a library security guard standing over me. I wondered what breach of library rules I could possibly be guilty of.

'Do you come from that island?' he asked.

'No,' I answered, 'but I'd very much like to go there.' I explained that my great-uncle Jack had been a member of the Colonial Survey Section that had mapped the island in 1903, and that my grandfather had joined the section, too, when it went on immediately afterwards to map Freetown in Sierra Leone.

'I'm from Freetown,' he said. 'I grew up in a village called Regent, near Sugar Loaf Mountain.'

'The Colonial Survey Section mapped it,' I said. 'On the mountain you can still find the stone they used to mark its summit. My grandfather was there.'

'I wish you all the best,' he said, resuming his round of the Reading Room.

I was sorry the rules of the library seemed to prevent any further conversation. I would have liked him to see the map of Freetown that my grandfather had helped to make. It lay on the table beneath the map of St Helena. I would have liked to ask him about his memories of the place. Slipping it out from underneath, I soon found the village of Regent, close to Sugar Loaf, where the guard said he had grown up.

In Sierra Leone, Lieutenant Legh reported to Captain Hugh Drummond Pearson, who took command of an enlarged Colonial Survey Section in Freetown in November 1903. I read about this third mission of the section in one of the five volumes of the official *Corps History*. It was only a short paragraph which of course did not give the names of the four NCOs and sappers. But I know from the service records that one of them was my grandfather; and that my great-uncle left the CSS at this point to return home. The military history sheets as usual give the exact dates of their departure and arrival: Jack got back to England on 12 September 1903, and Patrick arrived in Freetown on 10 November 1903.

After nearly two years overseas, Jack was able to spend the Christmas of 1903 in County Clare. I imagine him buying drinks for himself and his kid brother, Thomas. I imagine him telling Thomas of his adventures in the Colonial Survey Section – how he had followed in the footsteps of Darwin and Napoleon.

If Thomas had even been in any doubt about following in the footsteps of his brothers, Jack's return surely helped to settle the issue. In the new year – on 15 January 1904, to be precise – Thomas, aged nineteen, took his oath of attestation, completing a straight flush of Lynches to enlist in the corps, with the small, puzzling anomaly that he was the only one of the five to join at Fermoy in County Cork rather than Ennis. But otherwise there was nothing to undermine the sense I had of family destiny at work, with some pleasing synchronicity to be found in the patterns of chance and circumstance.

Ten days after his recruitment, Thomas took a dictation test at the Fermoy Garrison School. In a loopy, copperplate hand – legible in a way that so often the handwriting of the clerks filling in the service records was not legible – he wrote:

> While looking for marine animals, with my head about two feet above the rock shore, I was more than once saluted by a jet of water, accompanied by a slight grating noise. At first I could not think what it was, but afterwards I found out that it was this cuttle-fish, which, though concealed in a hole, thus often led me to its discovery. That it possesses the power of ejecting water there is no doubt, and it appeared to me that it could certainly take good aim by directing the tube or syphon on the other side of its body.

No reference was given in the test to identify the passage. It was only when I discovered that Darwin had visited St Helena that I came across the same words in the first chapter of *The Voyage of the Beagle*. Thomas had got them down word-perfect.

If this description of the great naturalist crawling over the rocks was a good one to suggest the kind of passion for detail that a future surveyor needed, Thomas was less successful in the arithmetic test that he took at the same time. Scribbling a large X or R across his workings, the orderly room sergeant who had marked the exam gave him only four right answers out of seven. Not really a good enough basis for a trade that would require Thomas to demonstrate a perfect command of complex trigonometrical calculations. It surely accounted for why, once he had completed his training, Thomas was posted to the Ordnance Survey companies only as a clerk, not a surveyor.

'Find by Practice, the cost of 3856 articles of £12. 16s. 5d. each . . .'

As I went over the miscalculations that caused my great-uncle, not quite in command of the imperial system, to give the wrong answers, suddenly this person from another generation whom I had never known but who shared my weakness at figures, seemed very close – just by virtue of a very ordinary failing.

In his eleven years with the Royal Engineers, Thomas passed only the first of the three classes of the Army Certificate of Education and remained a sapper to his dying day. It was his two eldest brothers, Jack and Patrick, who were the obvious high-flyers. The Colonel Survey Section, in which they both served, reported directly to the Intelligence Division of the War Office, and drew on the very best of the Royal Engineers' military surveyors.

13

Africa

After my mother died, my father struggled on for four years without her. The order of her funeral service stood like a tombstone on the worktop of the kitchen where he ate his meals alone. It was only when he died himself, in May 2014, that I became aware of the other significant things that my mother had salvaged from her past life in Ireland. Among her jewellery, which my father had locked away in the safe under the stairs, was a gold locket I had never seen before. Inside were two photographs of her father in his Royal Engineers uniform, one of them faded to the slightest ghost of an image.

When I removed the faded picture from its mount, I found hidden behind it, no bigger than a penny, the tiny oval of a St Benedict Medal, which, had my mother ever discovered this hiding place, might have helped her to settle the doubts over whether her father's name was Bernard or Bennett.

On one side was the saint holding up a cross in his right hand; on the other, the design of the cross on which two sets of intersecting initials offered a prayer. On the vertical bar, CSSML: *Crux*

sacra sit mihi lux (Let the Holy Cross be my light); and on the horizontal, NDSMD: *Nunquam draco sit mihi dux* (Never let the dragon be my guide). Around the rim of the medal were the letters VRSNSMV and SMQLIVB: *Vade retro satana! Nunquam suade mihi vana! Sunt mala quae libas. Ipse venena bias!* (Get behind me, Satan! Never tempt me with your vanities! What you offer me is evil. Drink the poison yourself!)

The combative, feisty words reminded me of my mother, but I was impressed too by how much information the Order of St Benedict had managed to squeeze into such a small space. The fact that I had never known of the medal's existence before seemed to me only the latest example of what the last four years had taught me many times, that the most precious things are often hidden away and never told.

I liked the way in which the medal offered a graphic representation of connection, the initials requiring knowledge of the prayer, and the bars of the cross bringing together the two halves through one shared letter: S. S for Serendipity. There is a mysterious, subsisting pattern to all things that shows itself only partially.

I was born in Farnborough on 4 December, the feast day of St Barbara, who is the patron saint of Engineers. My parents' house stood at the end of the runway that belonged to the Royal Aircraft Establishment. The sonic boom of jets caused its windows to crack on several occasions. My father worked there as a research scientist. It was the golden age of the jet, but the history of the place could be traced back to the beginning of the twentieth century when the Royal Engineers established their balloon factory on Farnborough Common. On 10 September 1907, the factory launched Britain's first airship, the *Nulli Secundus*, which flew all the way from Farnborough to St Paul's Cathedral, crash-landing at Crystal

Palace on the return journey; and on 16 October 1908, Sam Cody, the Royal Engineers' Chief Instructor in Kiting, made the first aeroplane flight in Britain.

I doubt that my mother was any more aware of these associations than she was of her father's middle name, but the common history my parents shared before they even knew each other made them all the more striking to me.

My father was little more forthcoming about his past than my mother had been. But he returned to it briefly when he was grappling with the depression that overtook him after my mother's death. As he struggled to find any satisfaction from life, I told him that maybe it would help to keep a journal. When he said he didn't know where to begin, I said why not write about his time at Farnborough, which would at least be fascinating for his family.

I was surprised to receive a few days later this characteristically terse email: 'Hi Charles, I thought you might be interested in this excerpt from my journal. Love, Dad.' What followed was an account of British aviation at the most exciting time in its history by one of the boys from its back room (I'd often noticed on his bookshelf the tatty but colourful dust cover of the novel *The Small Back Room*. It was only then that I realised what personal significance it had for him):

This is about my time as a psychologist at the Admiralty under N.A.B. Wilson, at Queen Anne's Mansions, near St James tube station. It is quite remarkable to think that I have not thought about the office for fifty years. It was antiquated even then. I would suppose that the site has since been recycled at least once.

Dr Wilson had a fearsome reputation. Supposedly, he had a foul temper, but in fact I never saw it. For some reason or other, he treated me as a favourite son. It was always understood that I would join the Institute of Aviation Medicine at Farnborough, as a more or less permanent secondment, and that was the way it happened. I was an Admiralty psychologist at Farnborough, where it was expected that I would assist in naval projects. There were two aircraft in issue: the Buccaneer and the TSR2. The Buccaneer went into service in the Fleet Air Arm and the TSR2 didn't quite make it: it was too complex and expensive. I had very little to do with the Buccaneer. Group Captain Ruffell-Smith flew me up to Brough to see the manufacture of the wings. He just called at the squadron office at the Royal Aircraft Establishment to pick up the keys of the Proctor Trainer we flew in, drew something like a straight line on a chart with a ready-to-hand blue crayon, told someone where we were going, and took off. Group Captain Ruffell-Smith was a force to be reckoned with. A well-known flying doctor, he had built up an enviable reputation: he was reputed to have flown a Canberra round and round in a perfect circle, so he never left its contrail. And, as one might expect, he gave the Proctor's controls to me . . .

Here, my dad switched the story with his usual modesty to the Buccaneer wing factory. I never found out what happened after he took over the controls of the Proctor Trainer. But, sapper-style, he was such a jack of all trades that I like to think that he flew in a perfect circle.

It was the first and last time that he wrote about his days at Farnborough. It was only after he had died that I found the research papers he had written. I put them in my grandfather's old suitcase, where they joined the service records of the five Lynch brothers. One paper, submitted to the Air Ministry in July 1961, was called 'Oscillatory Motion in Flight'. Drawing on experiments conducted in a Gloster Javelin jet, its purpose was to determine the limits of aircrew tolerance. It was full of technical language that I couldn't understand, though I gleaned enough to picture the terrifying scenario of a pilot flying faster than the speed of sound yet hugging the contours of the ground in order to evade enemy radar. The G-forces are tremendous but even worse is the roll, pitch and yaw of the aircraft as the cockpit shakes violently from side to side. The purpose of the paper was to help to devise effective instrumentation for aircrew who were operating at the edge of human endurance. Another paper, called 'The "Hilo" Indicator', described 'an experimental investigation of human factors relevant to the design of a long-range carrier-borne angle of approach indicator'. The research had been prompted by a new generation of naval aircraft that landed on carriers with increased approach speeds. My father was helping to develop the optimum dial to enable pilots to touch down safely – green for too high, red for too low, cyan for just right.

Although Patrick Lynch did not live long enough to meet his daughter's future husband, I couldn't help but think that he had a lot in common with him. After all, to get to wherever he had to go, especially flying so low, the pilot would need to have a decent topographical map. In their different ways, they were part of the same enterprise.

My father's death brought me to the point where two families intersected like the bars of the cross on Patrick Bennett Lynch's St Benedict Medal. If up until then I had explored only one bar, it seemed quite natural now, dipping into my mother's box of photographs, briefly to look at the other.

A year later, I heard the news that an old friend of my father's had died, the neurologist Oliver Sacks. My brother Jonathan sent me a piece Oliver had written in *The New York Times* after discovering he had terminal cancer:

> I have been increasingly conscious, for the last 10 years or so, of deaths among my contemporaries. My generation is on the way out, and each death I have felt as an abruption, a tearing away of part of myself. There will be no one like us when we are gone, but then there is no one like anyone else, ever. When people die, they cannot be replaced. They leave holes that cannot be filled, for it is the fate – the genetic and neural fate – of every human being to be a unique individual, to find his own path, to live his own life, to die his own death.

Among the deaths that made Oliver aware of his disappearing generation were those of my parents. At Oxford, my father and Oliver had been close friends. And they had been at St Paul's School together before that.

In my mother's box of photographs, I was able to go down to a stratum of post-war Oxford pictures to find one that Oliver had taken of my father as a young man attempting to blow the perfect smoke ring. Suddenly I had slipped into the Never-Never Land of my parents' youth among the Dreaming Spires. Just as there were several pictures that Oliver had taken of my dad, there were several pictures that my dad had taken of Oliver, looking Brando-like in a biker's jacket. I was startled to see in one of them a reproduction of Henri Rousseau's *The Snake Charmer*, which I recognised immediately from my own childhood but never imagined could have had this other existence. Reduced by time and familiarity to an inert object whose significance his children did not know, it continued to hang in my father's study until he died. But when the house was sold, this cheap Ryman's reproduction

nearly went in a skip just like my grandfather's old suitcase, until, fighting against my good sense, I decided to take one more item from the past that there wasn't really room for.

Irish charmer Patsy Lynch joined the *enfants terribles* in Oxford

during the Hilary term of 1952. If my mother's arrival was the reason why my father, who had won an open scholarship to New College, graduated with only a second-class degree, he never doubted that it was worth the disruption. 'She keeps me human,' he once said of her. He knew that she had saved him from the tyranny of that metronome on the Oxford mantelpiece.

In another photograph my father took, Oliver holds up a flower to his eye in the Botanical Gardens by Magdalen Bridge, perhaps the closest Oxford could come to recreating Rousseau's landscape. With hindsight the photograph seemed to me to hint at the possibility of a hidden romance, although my mother would have dismissed such an idea as nonsense. In the past that definitely did happen, she remembered that Oliver, who was a powerful swimmer, used to take the mooring rope of a punt between his teeth and pull her and my father along the River Cherwell. But if there was any element of sublimation in this act, it passed over her head. Oliver was a bit weird, she told me, but good fun. Once, she met his mother, a famous obstetric surgeon who had brought my father and his two brothers into the world. 'She's very nice when you get to know her,' my father said, though with the warning, 'Don't forget she's Jewish and you're a Catholic. They clash.' My mother answered, 'Why should there be a clash? Jesus was a Jew.'

In a photograph taken about three years later, Oliver can be seen among the guests at my parents' wedding. But after that point, he left the punt to drift on, ducking beneath the water to swim into a different story.

The wedding took place on 25 June 1956 at St Mary's Catholic Church, Station Road, in Chippenham, where my mother's brother Thomas had settled. Even if Jesus was a Jew, my mother still had to receive a dispensation to marry one, while the bridegroom's parents, who did not approve of their son's marriage to the woman who had stopped him from getting a first, refused to attend.

On the marriage certificate, my mother gave her father's name as 'Patrick *Bernard* Lynch'. Although she would never get to discover the truth of his real name, at least she had found someone to fill the chasm that had opened up when he died.

With the Colonial Survey Section in Sierra Leone, Patrick Bennett Lynch was making a topographical survey of the jungle at about the same time as Henri Julien Rousseau was imagining it. Rousseau, I read, never left France. The pictures he painted were inspired by books and visits to the Natural History Museum or the botanical gardens in Paris.

What did I have to imagine my grandfather's jungle? I wondered, as I returned to the Empire of November 1903 when he saw Africa for the first time: books and museums, now unexpectedly a locket with a photograph of him in his Royal Engineers' uniform, his service record of course, but also the map of the Colonial Survey Section, kept for posterity in the British Library.

The CSS's mission in Sierra Leone was to make a topographical map of the Freetown Peninsula on a scale of one inch to the mile. The unit's arrival there, on 31 October 1903, was calculated to make the most of the coming dry season to establish the necessary network of trigonometrical observations across the peninsula. The 'White Man's Grave' had a climate that was oppressively hot and humid, with malarial fevers especially prevalent at the beginning of the rains, which lasted from May to October. Three times the average annual rainfall of England was squeezed into this six-month period. In next to no time, the rain could reduce a pith helmet to a messy pulp.

For most of its 120-year history, the colony had comprised only the comparatively small area of the Freetown Peninsula itself which the CSS was mapping, but in 1896 the British government declared a protectorate over a hinterland of about 25,000 square miles. Although the immediate historical context was the late-nineteenth-century 'Scramble for Africa' of the European powers, the British were following an already long-familiar pattern of colonial expansion in areas of the 'uncivilised world', by which trading treaties with previously independent kingdoms became the means of their eventual subjection.

The Royal Engineers' own *Corps History* explained the routine that the growth of nearly all Britain's colonies had followed. The first stage was exploration of a newly discovered territory. Then trade began and trading companies were formed with rights of administration over the trading area. And then:

as trade increased trouble arose internally with the inhabitants and externally with other nationals who might be competing for the local trade; complications were also sometimes introduced by missionary enterprise. Trouble with the inhabitants led to military operations, usually conducted by local armed police, but if these were not successful an appeal was made to the Central Government and help given by naval and military forces.

'Trouble' was a simple fact of colonial geography like the mosquitoes or the monsoon. When the 'trouble' reached a certain level, the central government would appoint an official to take charge, first as a consul or commissioner, but then as a governor. The rights of government that had been granted to the trading companies were then limited and finally cancelled.

In the first stages of the occupation of an 'uncivilised country', the most pressing needs were those of survival which the traders provided for themselves – food, clean water, shelter and a fortified compound. 'In this respect they followed the precedent of the Roman armies, of which it has been said that every man was an engineer.' But when it came to the next stage – the stage of building a civilisation – then it was time to call in the Royal Engineers 'for Survey work and Boundary Commissions and then as engineers to construct roads, railways and telegraphs; or as one officer put it, to convert the somewhat bumptious, partly civilized natives of the coast towns into humble and useful members of society'.

When my mother reminisced about her childhood, she often mentioned a beautiful bloodstone ring that her father used to wear on the little finger of his left hand, but which she hadn't seen since he had died. She said that it had been given to him in exchange for some kindness by an African chief, whose name she once knew but could no longer remember. I wondered whether the chief had been able to offer Patrick any insight into the other society that had existed before the white man came, maybe even give voice to the sense of injustice that his people felt towards these intruders from far away who, with so little regard for their customs and way of life, were imposing their rule over them. If so, then Patrick would have been able to tell him that once there had been chiefs in Ireland too. Perhaps it had even provided a basis for a mutual understanding.

Five years before my grandfather's arrival in Sierra Leone, the population of the newly declared protectorate had risen against the British in the Hut Tax wars of 1898, when the governor, Colonel Frederic Cardew, decreed that they should contribute to the cost of the new protectorate's administration. At Westminster, it was the Irish nationalist MPs who were among those most able to sympathise with the natives' plight. Michael Davitt, who had campaigned for land reform in Ireland, raised what he called the 'obnoxious tax' in a Commons debate on the rebellion. The chiefs had protested to the governor, he said, saying that they were poor people, that their houses were not worth more than three or four times the amount of the tax, that there were valuable houses of white men on which not a single penny would be levied. He pointed out that ethnographer Mary Kingsley, who had an intimate knowledge of West Africa, had condemned the tax as oppressive and unjust. 'A more criminal policy could not have been pursued if the Governor had come from Colney Hatch.' (Colney Hatch was a notorious lunatic asylum.) He hoped that the Colonial Secretary would take some steps to try to have this trouble settled without having these unfortunate people mowed down by Maxim guns.

Maxim guns were very much the preferred method of dealing

with such trouble. The rebellion was eventually quelled by a series of military operations in which armed columns marched through the protectorate, burning villages. Most of the British soldiers involved would have belonged to a battalion of the West India regiment, which was the main military presence of the British army in Sierra Leone. As the climate of West Africa was considered dangerous for Europeans, the rank and file were black soldiers recruited in the West Indies, under the command of a few white officers and NCOs. To this force were added small Artillery and Engineers detachments.

I got some idea of what these punitive expeditions were like from the *Corps History*, which described a raid that was made on the native town of Tambi several years earlier in 1892, when the British sphere of influence in the hinterland had yet to be formalised as a protectorate. Rebel chiefs had been gathering in Tambi, about 150 miles to the north of Freetown, and fearful of a native uprising, the British sent a force of about six hundred men.

The commander of the expedition, Colonel Alfred Ellis, had at his disposal one or two Maxim guns, artillery and a Royal Engineers rocket detachment under the command of a Lieutenant G. H. Boileau. Sailing up the coast, the expedition landed at Robat on the Great Skerries River, and marched in single file through fifty miles of thick jungle, Boileau mapping the route with the aid of a prismatic compass. When they reached Tambi after a march of five days, they came upon a defensive entanglement of bamboo, beyond which lay a clearing and then the town itself behind a strong stockade.

As Ellis's men took up position before the bamboo defences, they were joined by a force of 'friendlies' – in the words of the *History*, 'naked savages from neighbouring villages who had suffered from raids and were eager for revenge or loot'. The friendlies tried to cut down the bamboo entanglement but a volley of bullets from the stockade, whose defenders were armed with old guns that they had bought from traders, sent them scattering in confusion.

So the Royal Engineers used their nine-pounder Hales rockets to set the place on fire. The sappers then blew up the front gate and the townspeople suffered the full impact of modern weaponry as Ellis's troops swiftly quelled any opposition. While only nine men of the British force were wounded, five friendlies were killed and thirty-two wounded. Meanwhile the enemy was estimated to have sustained 1,500 casualties, of whom two hundred were killed. 'Tambi taken by assault and destroyed on April 7,' began the telegram that was sent to the War Office on Colonel Ellis's return to Freetown.

Colonel Ellis had a taste of what it felt like to be on the receiving end when, a year and a half later, he led a punitive expedition against the Sofas tribe who were causing 'trouble' in the north-east corner of the Sierra Leone hinterland. Camped in the Konno district close to the poorly defined line between the British and French spheres of influence, he suffered a surprise attack from French troops who were undertaking their own punitive expedition against the Sofas. Nine of the British force were killed, including three white officers.

The French commander, Lieutenant Maritz, was mortally wounded in the return fire from the British troops, but before he died he was brought to the British camp, where he explained that in the bright moonlight his men had mistaken the pale campaigning uniform of the British officers for the white dress of the Arab commanders who led the Sofas warriors. In this time when Britain was still enjoying her splendid isolation, there was a fear that the incident might spark off a confrontation between the two colonial powers, but the British eventually accepted that it had been a regrettable misunderstanding. Renewed urgency was given to the Boundary Commission which had been set up to determine the exact border between the British and French spheres of influence but had yet to complete its work.

It was the kind of incident that Henri Rousseau might have read about in his morning newspaper before setting off to do his research in the Natural History Museum. But if so, it was an aspect of jungle life that, unlike the lions and monkeys and even the occasional tiger, never made it into his pictures. Long after the incident had left the headlines, the routine punitive expeditions continued, killing scores more inhabitants of the interior, who were of no account in the balance of power. To oppose the will of the white man was to court implacable retribution. As British rule consolidated its hold, the best hope for the natives in the long run was to become, as the anonymous Engineer in the *Corps History* had put it, 'humble and useful members of the white man's society'. The missionaries provided a pathway, although it would require the death of colonialism itself before the natives could expect the community they had joined to treat them as anything other than God's rather lowly creatures.

The business of bringing civilisation to 'Darkest Africa' provided plenty of ripping yarns for the Lynch brothers to read about. Their own trade of topographical surveying was of course at the very heart of the enterprise, and presumably part of the purpose of the travelogues that so often appeared in *The Sapper* during these years was to give them some idea of what to expect when they received the inevitable posting.

Although I am aware of no letters that survive from my

grandfather's time in the Colonial Survey Section, Corporal Patrick Lynch's commanding officer left behind not only letters but also a diary, which I found among the Royal Commonwealth Society collections at Cambridge University Library. Captain Hugh Pearson, who I couldn't help notice was an alumnus of St Paul's like my father, had previously been in charge of the Anglo-Liberian Boundary Commission that had earlier in 1903 determined the border between Sierra Leone and Liberia. A few years before, he had served with the Royal Engineers in India, where he had taken part in famine relief operations and seen action on the North-West Frontier. With the outbreak of the Boxer Rebellion in 1900, he joined the China Relief Expedition. Arriving too late to see military action, he was appointed Garrison Engineer to the Eight Nation Alliance Force, which had made its winter quarters in the Temple of Heaven, Peking.

Affable and hard-working, with a passion for sports, Pearson had gone straight into the army from St Paul's. Uncomplicated, practical rather than thoughtful, he did not seem to me to write with any exceptional discernment, but his account, full of adventure and incident, gives a vivid picture of the Empire at its height, his very human impressions serving to capture the attitudes and values of a turn-of-the-century Englishman who believed in Henty heroes even if he sometimes found it difficult to live up to the standard in the field.

'I don't think it's cricket,' he wrote on one occasion during his time in China, complaining of some fellow officers who had improperly accepted gifts of furs and porcelain, only to continue: 'I need not talk about cricket, though, as I went on a fine old looting expedition last week.' Some officers had discovered a silver bell in the Empress's Resting House weighing well over a ton.

They asked Pearson to blow it to bits in return for a share, so once again a jack-of-all-trades sapper proved his worth.

And Pearson was able to record for us the moment of the Great Queen's passing, the news of which he received on 24 January 1901 – two days after she died – outside the city walls at Machiapu terminus, where he had been sent to supervise work on the railway:

> Somehow one never thought the Queen could die, and we had got into the way of thinking she would go on for ever, so that it makes it all the harder now it has come. The whole atmosphere somehow seems to breathe, 'The Queen is dead', and we all seem to feel a family loss. She will be very much missed in the army and Tommy all over the world will feel it dreadfully. She was such a splendid figurehead and was simply adored by every soldier in the service. All her little messages – 'Hope the wounded are doing well, etc' – were appreciated nobody knows how much because one knew she meant them. I wish she could have lived to see South Africa put to rights and I am sure the war must have been largely responsible for her end. Every nation of course has its flags half mast and I should think they would all go into mourning as well as ourselves for the greatest Queen and most tender-hearted woman I suppose that has ever lived.

Of course I was hopeful that Captain Pearson's diary might offer some sketch of my grandfather, Corporal Lynch, who had not left any similar cache of personal papers to his descendants, but in 1903 the segregation between the messes was every bit as thoroughgoing as the one that existed between the races. Even on the journey out to Freetown, aboard the SS *Tarquah*, the captain travelled separately in first class. He may have thought that his men were 'going to turn out excellent', but that didn't mean that he would get close enough to mention any of them by name. The only exception was his fellow officer, Lieutenant Legh (although even then mentioned only by his surname).

On surveying trips into the country beyond Freetown, the four enlisted men stayed in one tent and the two officers in another. To Pearson's chagrin, 'Legh' turned out to be a rather cheerless companion who rarely smiled. 'Nothing makes him pleased,' he complained. 'When I came in rather enthusiastic over erecting my first trig-point and very hungry for tea, I said "Isn't the camp life glorious?" and he simply said, "Oh, I don't know." It is so damping having a man like that.'

But the hierarchy of military life – and the British class system – meant that the unsmiling Legh was the only company Pearson could really hope for. Corporals Sloan and Lynch, and Sappers Miller and Smith, might be enjoying a smoker around the camp-fire, but it wouldn't do for the captain to join in.

Soon after they had fixed a baseline for triangulation, near Kossoh Town, most of the Survey party went sick. '[O]ne of my men, having had fever for two or three days, suddenly took it into his head to go up to 104.5 and was in a state of more or less collapse,' wrote Pearson, 'and now Legh has been in hospital for three or four days, having had fever for a week, and a third man cannot do an honest day's work without collapsing altogether. In fact, the only two of us who are capable of doing much are my drunken corporal and myself.' In light of what I had learned about my grandfather in later times lodging at the Brazen Head Inn in Dublin, I couldn't help but think that the 'drunken corporal' must have been him.

While the two officers chose and calculated the triangulation points that provided the skeleton for the map, Corporals Sloan and Lynch charted the topographical detail of the land by plane table. The thick forest, the absence of roads and the haze from harmattan winds that picked up dust from the Sahara made West Africa one of the most difficult places in the world to conduct a survey.

'No one knows how triangulation is to be carried on when you cannot see a hundred yards,' wrote Pearson.

Whether they would be able to make a sighting depended on the chance of the weather. Often they would spend hours trudging up steep hills, many over two thousand feet high, only to find the summit covered by cloud. Pearson thought the region would be a perfect place to try out one of the new flying machines that were then making the world's headlines; in their absence, he had the idea of improvising observation points in trees. Local carpenters were employed to clear sightlines and to build platforms, which were pulled up eighty feet by rope and pulley. One of the carpenters was struck on the neck by a falling branch and paralysed. 'The doctor tells me that his spine is affected and he will be a goner in a month or two. Bad luck, isn't it?'

Pearson forced himself to climb the trees in spite of the fact that he suffered from vertigo, but after some weeks his fear of heights eventually caught up with him:

I am sorry to say I have quite lost my head over trees and I don't think I can go up another. I hated them before, but I went up one with Legh 128 feet and when I got to the platform I was as white as a sheet and trembling all over. I am quite sure I would have dropped off if there was another ladder to go up. I had a rope round my chest going down, and I don't think I can go up another as I am sure with my head it is dangerous. I am awfully sick about it as of course the trees are my palaver.

One reason why Pearson had forced himself to climb the trees was to impress the black porters who were looking on. Such pretences of invincibility were part of the imperial show. When Pearson's canoe sank one day in the middle of a crocodile-infested river, his hammock boy who was in the canoe with him immediately swam to his assistance. 'I shook him off and stopped to explain to him that the white man could always swim and he eventually allowed that I was able to take care of myself.' But the captain's essentially outgoing, friendly nature meant that he sometimes struggled to maintain the mask: humanity often broke through, especially when it was a question of sport. In one of the villages, he came upon a boy whipping a crude peg top. 'In a weak moment the spirit moved me to present him with one of the old tennis balls I carry around with me. His joy was unbounded like the ball.'

The section raced to complete the survey before the start of the rainy season. Long days of hard physical exertion in swamp and forest began to take their toll. One of the men caught sunstroke and coughed up nearly a pint of blood; another was found to have lost over six stone in weight. 'We get on here in our usual desperate state,' Pearson observed. 'One day I think, "By Jove, ripping! We have done it!" The next the whole of my crew are in hospital.'

By the beginning of June 1904 there were heavy thunderstorms every day, but by then they were putting the finishing touches to the survey and the captain was confident enough to book the passage back to England. Of his men, he wrote, 'they are beginning to smile again, bless their hearts, and we shall leave no bones in Freetown'.

Haunted by the deadly reputation of the place, the members of the Colonial Survey Section were pleased to get out of West Africa alive. They had no desire to be in Freetown one day longer than was absolutely necessary, but the map they made would help me to learn about a place that would become even more dangerous 110 years later. In 2014 the Royal Engineers were back, but this time building Ebola treatment centres.

The name of the town hovers above the shoreline of the coastal city. Its history began on the headland of Falcon Bridge Point, which can be found on the map just where the word 'FREE' elides into 'TOWN'. It was here that a settlement of black poor from London was established in 1787 under the aegis of the anti-slavery movement. Originally called 'Granville Town' after the anti-slavery campaigner Granville Sharp, it was intended to show that a trading community could exist without reliance on slave labour. The land had been bought from a local chief, King Tom, who

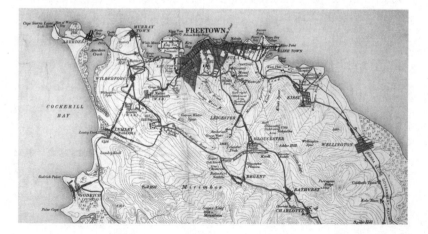

lived across the bay on a headland that is still called 'King Tom Peninsula' today. King Tom's successor, King Jemmy, drove the settlers off, burning their houses, but the Anti-Slavery Society sent out Alexander Falconbridge to re-establish the settlement. Falconbridge was a former slave-ship surgeon, who had joined the abolitionist cause and provided important testimony about the cruelty that the slave trade involved. His name is a small example of how easily the associations of a place can be distorted, from Falconbridge to Falcon Bridge.

'Was this the place where the falcons gathered?' I wondered when I first looked at the map in the British Library reading room. Hunting for titbits tossed to them from steamers on the final approach to the nearby harbour, they would have made a fabulous Rousseau painting.

The stretch of water between Falcon Bridge Point and King Tom Peninsula is called 'Kru Bay' on the map of the Colonial Survey Section, but the first maps of Sierra Leone called it 'St George's Bay'. This was the name that the abolitionists gave to a new company that they formed in 1790 to support the settlers. It was on behalf of the St George's Bay Company that Falconbridge renegotiated the purchase of land from the local chiefs. Under his direction, the few remaining survivors – only forty-six left out of an original number of more than four hundred – then regrouped in a settlement about a mile and a half to the east. They took the name 'Granville Town' with them, although it would be lost in a later return to the first site.

It was no surprise to see that the name of 'Wilberforce' had been given to a village on high ground to the west of the city. Just a short walk away from where I live in south London, there's a blue plaque to him: 'On this site lived WILLIAM WILBERFORCE

Statesman & Emancipator 1759–1833'. The famous campaigner against the slave trade was a director of the St George's Bay Company. When Parliament passed a bill in May 1791 that granted the company a royal charter, the motion was closely connected with an unsuccessful bill that Wilberforce had proposed only a month before, on 18 April, for the abolition of the slave trade. It had been defeated on two principal grounds: that British plantations in the West Indies could not survive without slave labour; and that slaves were the only merchandise that Africa was capable of producing. The incorporation of the new company was presented to Parliament as an experiment to prove that neither supposition was true. The St George's Company would run a successful plantation using the labour of free men and for the first time establish a commercial venture in Africa itself that was not based on slaves.

Under the new name of the Sierra Leone Company, the directors raised capital of £150,000 for a venture that was at the very beginning of an active national conscience. As the correspondent to the *Woodfall's Register* of 2 January 1792 wrote:

What noble ideas does the contemplation of this new establishment furnish us, both with respect to this country and to Africa itself! To the character of this country must certainly be added a considerable portion of lustre, when we consider that this establishment is intended to annihilate those piratical expeditions for flesh and blood known under the name of the slave trade. To its commercial dignity and importance great will be the gain, when it is considered that in five or six years only, a greater market will be opened in Africa by the Sierra Leone Company for the consumption of British manufactures than all the slave-merchants put together have ever opened since the beginning of their trade.

With an ample stock of goods to help secure their cooperation, Falconbridge persuaded the local chiefs to allow the settlement to move back to its original spot, where, in February 1792, it was given the name of 'Free Town' in accordance with the anti-slavery principles of the Sierra Leone Company. In February 1792, the tiny colony swelled in size with the arrival of fifteen company ships from Nova Scotia, bringing nearly 1,200 freed slaves who had been loyal to the British during the War of American Independence. They left the same harbour of Halifax that my great-uncle Michael, still then a submarine miner, was defending when the map of the Colonial Survey Section was being made. The commander of the exodus was John Clarkson, who stayed on as the colony's first governor. It was his brother Thomas who had become one of the most energetic early anti-slavery campaigners after winning a Latin essay competition at Cambridge University: '*Anne Liceat Invitos in Servitutem Dare?*' ('Is it lawful to enslave the unconsenting?')

After a difficult crossing of many weeks, the Nova Scotia settlers rejoiced to reach their promised land, but it turned out to have even more hazards than a sea voyage that had already claimed sixty-five lives. Freedom offered little compensation for the lethal climate. Falconbridge's wife, Anna Maria, wrote of the madness of the attempt to create an instant colony: with insufficient time to build proper accommodation before the onset of the rainy season, the inhabitants were exposed to the elements, most of them succumbing to fever in the wet conditions. 'We seem daily advancing towards destruction,' she wrote in July 1792. '[F]ive, six, and seven are dying daily, and buried with as little ceremony as so many dogs or cats.'

The fledgling colony managed to make it through to the dry

season, when it was able to recover from the crisis and even begin to prosper, but meanwhile the slave trade was going on all around it. A few miles up the Sierra Leone River was the British-owned slave fort of Bunce Island. Here, in exchange for European goods, African traders sold their captives to British slavers, who then transported them in their thousands to America. It was the owners of the fort, John and Alexander Anderson, who had provided the ship that had brought the Falconbridges to Sierra Leone in the first place. They even entertained the couple at Bunce Island upon their arrival.

The dining room looked directly over the slave yard, Anna Falconbridge recalled. 'Involuntarily I strolled to one of the windows a little before dinner, without the smallest suspicion of what I was to see; judge then what my astonishment and feelings were, at the sight of between two and three hundred wretched victims, chained and parcelled out in circles, just satisfying the cravings of nature from a trough of rice placed in the centre of each circle.'

The abolition of the slave trade in 1807 closed down the fort, but many more years were required to stamp out the trade completely. The Royal Navy established a squadron that patrolled the coast of West Africa, intercepting the vessels that continued to trade. Their human cargos were then released in Freetown, which in this way became a mix of different peoples from all over Africa, as few of the liberated slaves – or 'recaptives' as they were known – chose to risk returning to their original countries.

The resettlement of the recaptives was an engine for the nineteenth-century growth of the town. But the first generation of settlers regarded the new arrivals with as much fear as sympathy. After the abolition of the slave trade in 1807, Sierra Leone became a Crown colony and the Sierra Leone Company was reorganised as the 'African Institution'. When the new governor, Captain Thomas Thompson, arrived in 1808, he found that a shipload of African captives – Bambana people from Mali – had been freed by the Royal Navy but then immediately imprisoned again because the settlers in Freetown were afraid that they would kill them and take over the colony.

So he broke their fetters, armed them with muskets, and led them out to a mountain about three miles inland, which on the map of the Colonial Survey Section is called 'Leicester Peak'. He gave them food, clothes, tools, seed and plants. He told them that the British government would continue to supply them for a year, but after that they would be expected to support themselves by their own industry.

The following year, he built a public road to a river about two miles further inland. Here he laid a foundation stone for another settlement, which he called Kingston, after his own native town of Kingston upon Hull. The humanity Captain Thompson showed during his brief time in the colony deserved to be remembered, but such has been the sway of royalty in all times that, unsurprisingly, a few years later, the name of Kingston was changed to Regent's Town, in honour of the new Prince Regent.

The name 'Leicester' pre-dated the existence of the colony. The highest point on the approach to the Freetown Peninsula from the sea had been called Leicester Mountain after the Earl of Leicester, who had sponsored a voyage of exploration and trade to the African coast in 1582. When my grandfather and his comrades in the Colonial Survey Section arrived three hundred years later, they discovered that it was too small to be a mountain and the name was changed to Leicester Peak.

Captain Thompson was recalled from Sierra Leone after

attempting to stop abuses to an apprenticeship system that required the freed slaves to work a number of years for settlers in the colony. As put into practice by the colonial officials, it had amounted to slavery by another name. Although the abuses resumed under Thompson's successor Captain Columbine, the Chief Justice of the Colony, Robert Thorpe, exposed the scandal in a series of pamphlets that he wrote upon his return to England in 1813. He accused the new governor of conniving with the super-intendent of recaptives, Kenneth Macaulay, in the mistreatment of the liberated slaves. He alleged that, to feed them, Macaulay had purchased rotten flour from the captured slave ships under the governor's control. '[I]t was served to them for food even when sour until they were almost famished; they were obliged, for the preservation of life, to devour morbid offals wherever they could find them, and became so covered with a wretched disease called the Craw-Craws, that existence was protracted misery.'

Captain Columbine died from fever after little more than a year in office, but the man who replaced him seems to have been scarcely an improvement. According to Thorpe, Governor Maxwell ran the colony as though it were his own fiefdom: he impressed able-bodied men into the army, took mistresses from among the freed women, made others work on his farms without payment, and exploited his official position to monopolise the trade in the colony. When they were released from the slave ships in Freetown, each recaptive was given two complete sets of English clothes. 'Since Governor Maxwell turned trader, he has supplied them from his own store, and charged as high a price to Government as any merchant on the coast would have done.'

Rather than continue to endure the kind of treatment from

which the Royal Navy was supposed to have rescued them, many of the recaptives fled into the surrounding hills. The settlement of Wilberforce was founded by recaptives who had originally been sold for transport to America at the slave mart of Cabenda, near the mouth of the Congo River. At first it was called the Cabenda Settlement, and for a few years the recaptives were left on the hill to look after themselves.

Until 1815 Britain had been too preoccupied with her struggle to defeat Napoleon to pay much attention to such a small, distant colony. But after the Battle of Waterloo, she was able to play a more energetic part in shaping its future, which naturally she did in the image of herself. With the Royal Navy providing a constant supply of recaptives, freed from the slave ships, more new settlements sprang up around Freetown. The road that Governor Thompson had taken as far as Leicester and Regent was pushed on further into the hills. A new cluster of settlements was named in honour of the younger and more popular members of British royalty. Gloucester was founded in 1816, after Prince William, the Duke of Gloucester, who was the nephew of the King and first president of the African Institution. In 1817, Charlotte and Leopold were founded in honour of the marriage between the Regent's only daughter and her husband. When at the end of that year the Princess died in childbirth, Leopold was renamed Bathurst, after Lord Bathurst, who was Secretary of State for War and the Colonies. War and the colonies then provided the themes for the next cluster of settlements that were founded in 1819: Wellington, Waterloo and Hastings, the last after the then governor general of India, Lord Hastings.

Over the next century the presiding colonial power continued to provide the lion's share of the names, but looking at the Colonial

Survey Section's map, I found myself fascinated by the multicultural variety of names that, even at this high point of Empire, had nothing to do with Britain at all. A profile of Sierra Leone published in 1863 wrote of the 'perfect Babel of confusion' in a colony where, among the liberated Africans alone, fifty different languages were spoken. Nearly every tribe in West Africa had its representation. The more prominent groups gave their names to the areas of Freetown where they had settled. Kissi, Fula, Kongo Town, Kru Town can all be found on the Colonial Survey Section's map. Each name offered a different road through African history and culture, a different set of traditions, customs and beliefs.

The Kru were of two kinds: the Fish Kru who lived along the Grain Coast, roughly coextensive with modern-day Liberia; and the Krumen, who came from the interior. The Fish Kru were famed for their prowess in the water. The 'Blind Traveller' James Holman, who in the 1820s embarked upon a celebrated voyage around the world, was on the Royal Navy frigate HMS *Eden*, passing Cape Palmas on the Grain Coast, when several Kru canoes paddled out with goods to trade. As they left, one of the Fish Kru leapt from the frigate, swam to his canoe and rolled aboard, his companions who were already in the canoe leaning to the other side to compensate. 'These men may truly be called Fishmen, for they appear almost as independent in the water as the fish who inhabit it.'

It was the custom of the Fishmen and Krumen to leave home to seek their fortunes. They paddled up the coast in their canoes to Freetown, where they worked as migrant labour. With the money they earned, they returned to their native villages long enough to buy wives and to establish a household but then went back to Freetown, working until they could afford finally to retire to their villages. They worked as servants, porters and warehousemen, but especially as sailors. When attached to any of the cruisers of the West Africa Squadron, a Kru headman was rated as a petty officer and had up to twenty Kru sailors serving under him. Possessing a fierce sense of independence, the Kru were one of the few tribes in Africa that did not practise slavery (although their womenfolk might have argued with that).

Aboard the Royal Navy ships, rather than use their original African names, the Kru sailors chose chance English words as nicknames that would be easier for the other sailors to remember: Johnny Soda Water, Charlie Rum, Bottle O'Beer, but the most popular name of all was Freeman.

In the few months that the Colonial Survey Section spent on the Freetown Peninsula there was neither the time nor the desire to do any more than record the existing names of places. But the idea that the history behind those names would be an important feature of an ideal map went back to the time of Drummond and Larcom in Ireland, when the Ordnance Survey undertook the ambitious scheme to publish accompanying 'memoirs' to its maps of the country. That project had foundered as much on practical reality as political controversy, for the names on a map beg endless questions.

If I choose to dwell on the Kru rather than the Kissi or the Fula or the Kongo people, it is because those Kru sailors remind me of my grandfather and great-uncles, as well as the Irish Wild Geese, who went far away in search of their livelihoods, but always considered Ireland to be their true home, who fought in other countries' armies, but kept their spirit of independence. It's impossible to know, but I like to imagine that the African chief who gave the bloodstone ring to my grandfather was a Kru.

Free Irishmen. Free Krumen. In both cases, religion offered a notable expression of their independence. Just as the Irish held on to Catholicism in spite of the best efforts of the English to knock it out of them, so the Kru resisted the efforts of the missionaries who flocked to Freetown in wave after wave during the nineteenth century to convert them to Christianity.

It was a curious fact that exercised the minds of a parliamentary committee when it prepared a report on the West Coast of Africa in 1842. 'The Krumen are a very peculiar race, distinct in their habits, customs, and language from all the surrounding tribes,' observed an appendix to the report. 'They are all pagans; they make no wars, carry off no slaves, and are altogether averse to the trade in men; they are generally men of great muscular power and activity, enterprising and industrious.'

Among the evidence that was put before the committee was an interview with a Kru called George Coffee, which had taken place aboard the HMS *May*.

'You never heard of Christian religion?' asked the ship's captain.

'Oh yes, America juju men came to Kru country from Cape Palmas,* tell him all that, but Krumen no savy that palaver.'

'That was a good palaver; it was good for you to savy that palaver.'

'No, don't savy that palaver.'

When the captain asked whether Krumen believed that there was 'only one God, or two or three Gods up above', George answered, 'How Krumen savy that? Krumen no go up alive to savy that.'

There was a robust common sense about his replies, even if the evangelical cast of the times predisposed his British hosts to dismiss them as heathen ignorance. There was much common

---

* Cape Palmas, in Liberia, was the site of an American settlement for freed slaves that had foundered in the early 1830s.

sense, too, about the framework of the juju religion, which George and a fellow Kru with him called Tom tried to explain. There were many devils, both good and bad, who had to be propitiated with sacrifices in acknowledgement of their power either to heal or hurt. The fetish symbols they made were intended to represent this idea to their minds.

But what chance could such practices have against the power of Christian Belief? As much a driving force behind colonial expansionism as trade, the fiercely evangelical Christianity of the Victorians rested on tenets whose observance could only incline them to consider Africa to be a dark place into which they must bring the light. You must not worship false gods, said the First Commandment. Nor make any graven image, said the Second. The very sincerity of their religious convictions fed both their assumption of a cultural superiority and the zeal with which they laboured to spread the word of God against what must at first have seemed overwhelming odds.

Many of the first missionaries who travelled out to Sierra Leone died from disease, but Christian faith sustained the endeavour. When the assistant secretary of the Church Missionary Society, the Reverend Edward Bickersteth, sailed to West Africa in 1816 to report on the state of its settlements and schools, he found that many of the natives 'appeared hardly to have ideas of any good to be obtained from white men, but rum and tobacco for themselves, and guns for defence against their enemies', but he believed that their very ignorance justified the work of the mission. 'Could our friends have entered into that darkness which may be almost felt, in which I have been; could they have seen the houses dedicated to evil spirits, the figures of them which the natives honour, how would they persevere in their endeavours to rescue these deluded and benighted Heathens from their wretched condition, and impart them the knowledge of the true Mediator between God and man!'

He visited the society's institution at the new settlement near Leicester Mountain, where he found the schoolmaster Mr Butscher struggling on his own – after his wife had died from fever – to cope with the religious instruction and education of 150 children. Every week the release of more Africans from the captured slave ships swelled the numbers yet further. 'Many of them, alas! soon fall victims to the hard treatment which they had received aboard the slave ships; and many, if not most of the others, remain, for want of European assistance, in a deplorable state of ignorance, indolence, licentiousness, and sin.' The only solution, he concluded, was without delay 'to communicate that religious instruction, which, when truly received, will effectually arrest the progress of evil, and furnish a stimulus amply adequate to excite these poor fellow-creatures to industry'. He estimated that for a colony which then numbered about 10,000 inhabitants such a task would require twelve schoolmasters and twelve schoolmistresses. The practice of the time, whereby such missionary teachers usually turned up in husband-and-wife pairs, lent a suitably biblical character to the enterprise. Twenty-five years later, the teachers in the colony had multiplied to the extent that they were teaching 6,500 children in more than twenty schools. Through the remainder of the nineteenth century, missionaries continued to flock to Freetown, which was the principal gateway to the hinterland beyond.

In Freetown, almost every Christian denomination had its representation. The missionaries came from England but also Ireland, Europe and America. By the time the Colonial Survey Section was mapping the Freetown Peninsula in 1903, the 'Heathen' was much more likely to be a European visitor. Captain Pearson described a Sunday when some villagers came into his camp to take him to task for not going to church. When he told them that he was much too busy, they answered that his soul ought to be his first consideration. 'I pointed out how selfish that would be to think of my own soul and I expected them to do that for me and [they] said that they had been praying for me in church.'

The Scramble for Africa had been preceded by a scramble for souls. Opening up Africa to the blessings of Christianity and civilisation was perceived as a moral duty, although in practice it meant that over time the native tribes lost their previous independence. When the Sierra Leone colony had first been established in 1787, it was no more than a tiny toehold on the coast, whose existence depended on the goodwill and toleration of the surrounding tribes. Over the years that followed, it grew first to encompass the Freetown Peninsula, and then, as the missionaries and traders pushed deeper into the hinterland, the sphere of influence was further extended through treaties of 'peace, unity and commerce', in which the local rulers agreed not to cede their territory 'except through and with the consent of the Government of Her Majesty'. The declaration of the protectorate in 1896 was the final act in what had been a long process of creeping imperialisation.

In its early stages there was much that was enlightened and well meaning about the project, a genuine humanitarian impulse seeking to bring the benefits of European civilisation to societies that had previously suffered terribly from the ravages of slavery, superstition and inter-tribal warfare.

Writing of West Africa in 1853, after a stint of five years as Colonial Secretary, Earl Grey wrote that British policy had been:

to keep constantly in sight the formation of a regular government on the European model, and the establishment of a civilised polity, as the goal ultimately to be attained; but, in the endeavour to arrive at it, taking care that each successive step shall appear to the people themselves as nothing more than the natural mode of providing for some want, or remedying some evil, which they practically feel at the moment. It is thus in fact that our own institutions and laws have grown up, as well as those that have been most permanent and most successful among other nations.

The pity is how quickly British confidence in the European model assumed a racist cast. When the colony's first black governor, William Fergusson, was appointed in 1844, it was a mark of the kind of progress that Grey approved of, but soon afterwards he was chiding Fergusson's white successor, Governor Macdonald, for recommending a separate ward for European sailors in Freetown's Kissy hospital. '[T]he aim of the Government in all its measures,' he wrote, 'ought to be to break down the unhappy distinctions made between persons of different colour.'

The very belief in the superiority of European values served only to encourage the spread of such unhappy distinctions. The hut tax in Sierra Leone had been conceived out of the conviction that native Africans would benefit from contributing to the cost of a colonial administration that worked for their improvement, yet the implementation of a measure that symbolised the African chiefs' loss of independence, departed so far from Earl Grey's principle of incremental improvement as to provoke a war. The ethnographer Mary Kingsley, who was one of the very few British visitors to seek to understand African values rather than impose European ones, attributed the hut tax rebellion to the natives' 'reasonable dislike to being dispossessed alike of power and property in what they regard as their own country'. But it was too much to expect a similar respect for the native viewpoint among the largely upper-class, public-school-educated colonial officials who ran the Empire at the turn of the century.

The hut tax remained in force in spite of the rebellion, although much modified to be more palatable to the native population. A former district commissioner of Sierra Leone, T. J. Alldridge, commented of the tax that 'the people have by now grown to understand that they are getting back more than they pay'. He considered it to be an unfairly maligned measure that in reality was helping the inhabitants to enjoy the security and prosperity of the modern world. Through ending the lawlessness that had previously blighted the place, through replacing superstition and fetish with science, the establishment of the protectorate had made it possible for the people 'to be free from that shocking terrorism which was the perpetual condition of their existence'.

Travelling across Sierra Leone, Alldridge had spent much of his career as a commissioner negotiating the treaties through which the tribes ceded authority to the British Crown. In 1910, after he had returned to West Africa to write about a place he had first visited nearly forty years before, he published a book that was a kind of colonial administrator's *res gestae*. With its uncomplicated view of progress *A Transformed Colony* celebrated a catalogue of 'improvements that would have been inconceivable to me had I not witnessed them'. In this last year of Edward VII's short reign, the familiar voice of Victorian confidence and certainty still prevailed.

On the Colonial Survey Section map it was easy to trace some of the 'improvements' that Alldridge noticed. There were the wide roads that linked the capital city to the surrounding settlements, but also the new 'Sierra Leone Government Railway' that went inland to Baiima nearly two hundred miles away. Alldridge had been in West Africa long enough to be able to imagine the novelty of a journey that had previously taken many days. '[W]hen, on the morning I start on my trip up-country, I hear myself say, "Baiima" as I ask for my ticket, I can hardly believe the report of my senses.'

A local branch line, looping its way back and forth in the surrounding hills, through steep cuttings and across high, precipitous bridges, offered a spectacular example of engineering that took colonial administrators from Freetown up to a hill station that had been built eight hundred feet above sea level a few miles to the west near Wilberforce. The opening ceremony had taken place only a few weeks after the Survey Section had arrived in Freetown to map the area. Captain Pearson took the line when he had to measure a trig point on the hilltop. He would have boarded

the train at Cotton Tree Station. An easy walk from the Survey office in the government quarter of Tower Hill, it was the first stop after the railway left its terminus near the harbour. The tiny wooden shack of a ticket office stood by the massive trunk of a cotton tree, whose giant branches spread out over a single, narrow-gauge track that passed down the dusty red road of Westmoreland Street.

In recreating this colonial vision of the city, some care was needed to unravel the strands of different times. The railway no longer runs down Westmoreland Street, it no longer runs at all, and the name of the road has changed too. Today it is called Siaka Stevens Street, in honour of the country's first president who, after ten years of independence from Britain, turned Sierra Leone into a republic in 1971.

Much older than Sierra Leone itself, the cotton tree still stands, a survivor of Freetown's history of slavery, colonialism and

Congo Town Bridge (Sierra Leone Mountain Railway)

civil war. According to legend, it was here that, on a Sunday in March 1792, the black loyalists from Nova Scotia gathered to celebrate their safe arrival in Africa. Back again in the land from which their ancestors had been taken.

'Wake! Every heart and every tongue,' they sang, 'to praise the Saviour's name. The year of jubilee has come. Return, ye ransomed singers, home.'

A preacher gave a sermon that was inspired by Psalm 127, 'Except the Lord build the house, they labour in vain that build it.' The first task of the settlers was to clear about eighty acres of land, which was then divided into town lots for the population. Three broad avenues were marked out between the two bays that flanked the headland, intersecting at right angles nine streets that ran from the coast towards the mountains. As instructed, the colony's first governor, John Clarkson, named the roads after the directors of the Sierra Leone Company. Maybe there was something about its sheer beauty that caused him to call the eastern of the two bays after his fiancée, Susan, who was waiting for him back home in England. Whatever the reason, while St George's Bay would eventually give up its name to the Kru, the name Susan stuck – although any beauty to be found in today's Susan's Bay must contend with the fact that it has since become an over-crowded slum with poor sanitation that, even before the Ebola crisis of 2014 made everything many times worse, led to frequent outbreaks of cholera.

Today the first of those three avenues, as the traveller approaches the town from the sea, is called Wallace-Johnson Street, after the twentieth-century Sierra Leonean nationalist and trade union leader Isaac Wallace-Johnson. But in 1903, when Captain Pearson and the Colonial Survey Section disembarked from the SS

Tarquah, its name was Water Street. Liverpool was just ten days away on the fast new steamships of the Elder–Dempster line. Running parallel to the harbour, it was the busiest road in the city. This was where the bustling fruit and vegetable market was located.

The origin of the name was not the sea – as one might have thought from just looking at the map – but a spring. Close by the market was the outlet of a channel that brought down pure water from the mountains. 'Once you drink of King Jimmy water,' wrote the old commissioner, 'however far you wander from it you must always return to it.' King Jimmy was in fact 'King Jemmy' who had burnt the original English settlement to the ground in 1789 after succeeding King Tom, the chief who had first granted the land.

Water Street was also where you would find St George's Cathedral and the Wilberforce Memorial Hall. The latter was destroyed by a fire in the 1960s, but I am looking at them both on a picture postcard with an Edward VII stamp, of the kind that my grandfather might have sent home.* With its crenellated tower and Gothic windows, the cathedral has the look of one of those imposing parish churches that the Victorians, onward Christian soldiers, built across the towns and suburbs of England. At first sight, it could easily be England. The black passers-by dressed in white dashikis and the corrugated-iron roof of the hall are the only signs that it isn't. The head of one of the passers-by is hidden beneath an open umbrella, as likely a

---

* T. J. Alldridge thought that the availability of such postcards on the steamers moored in Freetown's harbour was a significant example of the colony's trans-formation: '[I]t marks a great advance as it is now recognised in civilised countries as being one of the most up-to-date and necessary requirements of all travellers in whatever part of the world they may be.'

Wilberforce Memorial Hall, and St. George's Cathedral, Freetown, Sierra Leone.

SIERRA LEONE

protection from the sun as the rain, which in Sierra Leone battle to outdo each other in their severity.

At one end of Water Street loomed the Colonial Hospital, overlooking the waterside market at King Jimmy's Wharf. Known as the Connaught today, it is still Freetown's main hospital. I have seen it quite often while writing this book, as the backdrop to TV news reports on the Ebola crisis. It is a place of primordial suffering but also relief that stands on the site of the Old King's Yard, a compound where two hundred years ago the men and women who had been freed from slavery were housed and treated before resettlement. Above a gate, an inscription from 1817 still reads 'Royal Hospital and Asylum for Africans rescued from slavery by British valour and philanthropy'.

If my grandfather ever got to see it when he was in Freetown in 1904, I think he would have been interested in the story of the man who put up the sign. In 1817, the governor of the colony was

Brigadier General Sir Charles MacCarthy. Of Jacobite descent, MacCarthy had many years before, as a young Irishman from Cork, been one of the Wild Geese who had fought in the Irish Brigade of the French royal army. After the Revolution of 1789, he was among the first Irish Roman Catholics to join the British army when William Pitt the Younger allowed the Irish Brigade to switch its allegiance to the English Crown.

Taking office as governor of Sierra Leone before full Catholic Emancipation, he was required to swear an oath against popery and transubstantiation, but he did not allow the small print to become an obstacle to his common sense, preferring to overlook this absurd remnant from the religious division of the past. Deeply sympathetic to the plight of enslaved Africans, he worked hard to win their freedom, and also sought to clamp down on racial discrimination within the colony, appointing many black people to senior administrative posts. A man of his age, MacCarthy believed that Britain was bringing to Africa the gifts of a more advanced civilisation, whether it was order, freedom or a Christian god. Among the more notable gifts that he brought to Freetown in his time as governor were bricks and mortar. He constructed hospitals, churches, barracks and courthouses, giving a European concept of construction to a town that would one day be dubbed the 'Athens of West Africa'. Even the flight of stone steps that led up to Water Street from the landing stage had been built under MacCarthy's direction. Every visitor from Britain would have climbed them upon their arrival in Freetown. Steeped in the Jacobean traditions of his family, MacCarthy must have been pleased to be able to follow a British sovereign again, which he did with an Irishman's passion. On one occasion, when two German missionaries walked out of a Christian Mission Society meeting while the national anthem was still being sung, he declared angrily, 'Christianity without loyalty is a mere name!' His loyalty would cost him his life when he became British commander-in-chief during the first Ashanti War of 1823. Leading six hundred men against an army of 10,000 (the Maxim machine gun had not yet been invented to make up for the disadvantageous odds), he ordered his band to play 'God Save the King', thinking the sound of the national anthem would terrify the enemy. After he had been captured and beheaded, his skull was hung up in the Ashanti King's fetish house, while a gold cast of it was used as a drinking cup.

Whatever games history might subsequently play, a significant part of British valour was Irish ferocity. The rebel soul that so often defied the Empire played an indispensable role in extending – and mapping – its frontiers. The five Lynch brothers belonged to a rich military tradition that brought with it a bitter logic, as Irishmen like my grandfather, who had once sung 'Soldiers of the Queen', began to sing 'The Soldier's Song' instead.

Ireland's priests were no less engaged in the imperial enterprise than her soldiers. While my grandfather was still serving with the Colonial Survey Section in Freetown, Father John O'Gorman, from County Carlow, was appointed to be the first Roman Catholic Bishop of Sierra Leone. Between the long, dangerous journeys that he made to open mission stations in the interior, he looked after a growing congregation in Freetown that attended the Sacred Heart of Jesus Cathedral in Howe Street. Among them, I imagine, was my grandfather. A little further up the road was St Joseph's School, which had been founded in 1866 by the Irish Sisters of Mercy, the same order of nuns who ran my mother's school in Tulla.

This kind of connection was not uncommon in a British Empire that, for all its far-flung nature, was threaded through with endless home associations. One day Captain Pearson was in thick forest near the village of Tombo, about thirty miles south of Freetown, when a white man in a clerical collar came out of a native hut and invited him in for tea. He turned out to be the acting Anglican Bishop of Freetown, Canon Smith, who knew Pearson's family from the time he had been a curate at St Mary Abbott's Church in Kensington. 'Of course I immediately rose to the occasion and talked Sunday schools etc and they all thought what a godly young man.'

The only time the captain went willingly to church was when the bishop allowed him to use the tower of St George's Cathedral as a trig point. From the top, there was a clear sightline up to Leicester Peak – the mountain that turned out not to be a mountain. The ground between the two provides the basis for a day trip that would have given, say, an Elder–Dempster passenger a good taste of the town, taking him from Water Street, close by the harbour, to the summit that he would have seen before his actual arrival, as the steamer made its way towards the lighthouse on Cape Sierra Leone. With the aid of one of the maps that the trig points furnished, I can follow him at a safe distance through the streets of the colonial town, stopping off at the notable landmarks along the way.

Once I have climbed down in my mind's eye from St George's tower, I cross the road to Wilberforce Hall, just opposite the cathedral on the corner of Gloucester Street, which was opened in 1887 to celebrate both the centenary of the town and the Queen's Golden Jubilee. A stroll to the far end of Gloucester Street brings me to Victoria Park, which was laid out on land that had previously belonged to a colonial fort to commemorate the Diamond Jubilee of ten years later. The Survey headquarters is close by, but I want to press on upwards. At the park I take a left turn into Garrison Street and then, reaching St Joseph's, a right into Howe Street. Soon it becomes the Regent Road, as I pass the long line of barracks that occupy an open, grassy slope, notably free of trees, on Tower Hill. Upon this esplanade stands an old Martello tower that gives the neighbourhood its name, although since 1870, when the Engineers put an iron tank on top, it has served the city as a water supply. The road becomes steep now as I approach the green curtain of densely wooded hills that is the town's backdrop. Continuing on up the mountain road, I reach a secluded lane that leads to the government sanatorium of Heddle's Farm. It had once been the country residence of the governor, but in my grandfather's day it was used as a convalescent home for colonial administrators. A greyish-white bungalow, standing on wooden pillars, it looks from a distance like some fruit sprouting out of the luxuriant foliage of the thickly wooded mountainside. Jalousie windows allowed the recuperating patients to look out over the town to Susan's Bay and the harbour below.

Anyone homesick for 'dear old England' could, every fortnight or so, trace the course of the Elder–Dempster liner disappearing over the far horizon with one final wisp of smoke. The coming-and-going of these ships, as regular as clockwork, were the Empire's beating heart, a reassurance of the peace and order that justified its existence. Although it would have been scant comfort for the malaria-stricken residents of 1903, some years after my grandfather's posting, the owner of the Elder–Dempster line, Sir Alfred

Lewis Jones, left a large bequest for a research laboratory in Freetown to develop better medicines with which to fight tropical diseases.

Resuming my journey beyond Heddle's Farm, I return to a road that is now no more than a rusty-red track. As I approach the village of Leicester, about 1,500 feet high, the flanking vegetation breaks out into a profusion of lantana bushes covered in pink flowers, yellow mimosa and locust trees with dangling clusters of long green pods.

Beyond the village, the climb up to Leicester Peak itself requires a scramble over steep, rocky boulders. Along the way I pass a few isolated bungalows, the last of which is Bethany Cottage, a sanatorium that belonged to the mission of the American United Brethen. I try to imagine the scene that Alldridge described when he stopped off here in 1908. '[R]ed hibiscus, frangipane and white spider lilies were in full bloom. Lounging in my most comfortable rokhee chair, chatting with pleasant companions while taking in the beauty of the scenery, it was really quite delightful; so that for the time we felt contented and at peace with all mankind, and affectionately inclined even to the West Coast of Africa, which with all its faults is able to provide us with enchantingly beautiful scenery, pure air and most needful repose.'

A few hundred more feet brings me to the summit, which flattens out into a narrow plateau. The explorer Richard Burton, who visited Freetown in 1882, suggested that a traveller might find in its outline the form of the 'maneless lion' that accounted for the colony's name, Sierra Leone, a confusion of two languages that seems apt for a colony that embraced such a confusion of peoples, whether the liberated black slaves of the original settlement, the natives of the hinterland or the British colonial officials.

Here, on top of lioness hill, I take in the splendid view and, making out St George's tower, trace the way I have come. Looking in the other direction, inland, I recall the guard in the maps reading room of the British Library, as I see ahead of me, less than a mile further on, the village of Regent where he grew up, and beyond, the highest peak on the Freetown Peninsula, Sugar Loaf Mountain. I press on, determined to reach its summit. After a difficult hike through dense forest and a scramble up some steep slopes, I achieve my goal at last. And waiting for me at the top is a rectangular stone pillar, erected by the Colonial Survey Section, which bears the inscription:

K
2496
C.S.S.
1904

Like Ozymandias' stone in the desert, a relic of yet another fallen empire.

14

The All Red Line

S oon after my grandfather arrived home from Sierra Leone,
he was sent to the Isle of Wight on a training exercise. As
recently as the 1860s, when the government had built several forts
both at the mouth of the Solent and on the south-east side facing
the Channel, the island had been regarded as a place of high military importance, its long wide beach between Sandown and
Shanklin providing a perfect place for a French invasion. After
the Franco-Prussian war of 1870 the forts became known as
'Palmerston's follies', but although the threat of an invasion had
receded in the last decades of the nineteenth century, the island
continued to be an excellent practice ground for the War Office's
military surveyors. With its forts, guns, beaches, towns and even
railways, it offered in miniature all the challenges that they might
be expected to encounter around the world.

Patrick arrived on the island on 28 July 1904, to find that his
brother Jack had already been there a week. Perhaps they spent
an evening or two in the NCOs' mess swapping tales of their
adventures over the previous two years, catching up on scraps

of information about what the other three brothers were up to, only to be very soon sent off again in different directions around the world, not knowing when or where they would see each other again.

In my mother's box of photographs I found a postcard that Patrick had sent back to the Isle of Wight from the Federated Malay States ten years later. It was a picture of himself and his comrades in the Colonial Survey Section. Addressed to the 'President, RE NCOs' mess, Victoria Fort, Yarmouth, Isle of Wight, England', it was written in a looping hand that brought back to me my mother's comment about what beautiful writing her father had had. 'Best wishes for a prosperous new year to all. P.B. Lynch, C.S.M., R.E., Col. Sur. Section, Fed. Malay States.' If the postcard

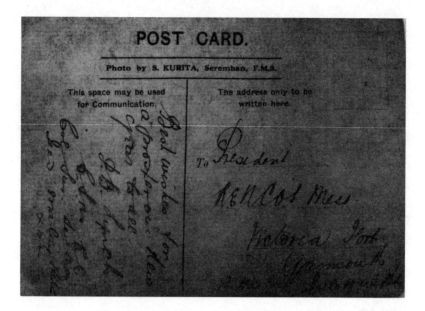

had been sent to the Isle of Wight, I thought, how come it was back in the possession of the family? But when I looked at the address side of the card more closely, I noticed that there was neither stamp nor postmark. So most likely he had never sent it after all. Maybe he had written the card in some remote place in the rainforest, and when he got back to the section's base in Serembam it was too late to post it in time for the new year.

The sepia picture of the section in their khaki drill jackets posed its own puzzle. Was my grandfather the man with a faraway look at the end of the first row? Or was he the man with the dark tie standing in the middle of the row behind? No matter how many times I compared the picture to the other photographs that existed of my grandfather – only two – I couldn't make up my mind.

This postcard that was never sent triggered a memory from fifty years ago of my mother taking me to the Isle of Wight when

I was a small child. The only details I could recall of the trip were the short crossing on the ferry, eating porridge with demerara sugar in a seaside hotel, and a castle. It could have been one of about twenty castles on the island, but I wondered now whether it had been the Victoria Fort. I wondered too whether my mother had known about the connection.

I couldn't help but ponder the irony that, if indeed all those years ago she had been trying to find out about her father, she was a generation closer but had so much less to go on. Just her own childhood memories and some pictures in a box that could be counted on the fingers of one hand – isolated pictures that I was now trying to connect with equally isolated papers retrieved online. Dry, official documents whose existence would nonetheless have amazed her.

There is no photograph showing the brothers together, but there is one of the three youngest, James, Michael and Thomas, although once again I had some doubt over whether I had guessed their faces correctly. Sitting in the foreground, Michael and Thomas each wear an Irish flat cap and Norfolk jacket with stiff collar and tie. Standing behind them with the regulation moustache of the military is James – I think – who is wearing a long overcoat and holds a pair of gloves in his right hand. It must have been a cold winter's day, and my hunch is that this photograph, which obviously marks a special occasion, is a recruitment picture taken when Michael joined the Royal Engineers, in Ennis in January 1899. On his lapel, he wears what could be a Royal Engineers badge, although the picture is so blurred that it looks a little bit like a shamrock too.

I found another picture of Michael taken about three years later when he was serving in Halifax, Nova Scotia, in which the sapper's

badge can be made out more clearly, but I am aware of no other photographs of either James or Thomas. They will appear, perhaps, in some lost photograph of a passing-out parade, of this or that RE section or company, but as I write now, they have yet to be fished from the sea of infinity.

The nature of their work meant that the five brothers had few chances to meet one another during the quarter-century of their service. Comparing their military history sheets, the only shared posting I could find was when the Intelligence Division of the War Office sent both Jack and Patrick on the same survey expedition to Canada in 1907. Otherwise, the closest the brothers ever came to a full reunion occurred when Jack, who was travelling to Australia aboard the RMS *Omrah*, stopped off at Colombo, in April 1910. He dropped by the NCOs' mess to discover that he had only just missed his brother Michael, who was serving on searchlight duty with the 31st Fortress Company but had been posted upcountry for manoeuvres at Diyatalawa. Meanwhile, somewhere else on the island, impossible to say exactly where, was Patrick, who had been sent out there a few months after returning from Canada in 1908. During his three years of work on the first comprehensive topographical survey of Ceylon, he was constantly on the move, charting the land through which he passed, two inches to a mile, on a plane table, remote from the world in a way that the generation of Skype, Twitter and Facebook must struggle to imagine.

Jack was, to quote the dedication of Skeen's 1906 *Guide to Colombo*, which I am sure he must have used during his short stay, one of the 'never-failing stream of travellers which flows through Lanka's isle en route to other climes'. As he made his way back from the mess to the RMS *Omrah*, his last taste of the town would have been the Fort district, laid out according to the familiar colonial pattern. Passing Chatham Street, he would have been able to correct his pocket watch to local time on the Old Clock Tower, which, providing a point of certainty amid the flux, also served as a lighthouse. Beyond the massive Grand Oriental Hotel, keeping an eye on the comings and goings at the passenger jetty, was a white marble statue of Queen Victoria, which the colony had erected on the occasion of her Diamond Jubilee.

Yet if the Empire seemed outwardly to be carrying on much as it had before, the death of Edward VII in May 1910, only a few weeks after Jack's arrival in Australia, woke people up to how fast the times were actually changing. Three years later Jack, who had met and married a local girl called Mary Jane Kennedy in Melbourne, became the first of the brothers to leave the Royal Engineers, requesting his discharge after eighteen years' service.

As I tried to iron these years into a simple succession of events, from the arrival of Jack and Patrick on the Isle of Wight in 1904 to Jack's discharge from the Royal Engineers in 1913, navigating through time with the aid of the military history sheets, it was hard not to notice the storm clouds of history massing ahead of me: war, revolution and even the destruction of the Empire itself.

When Jack was sent to British Somaliland in November 1904, he was working not for the Colonial Survey Section, which operated in dependent territories that were integrated into the economic life of the Empire, but instead for the Foreign Office. He was involved in a very different mission to a notoriously anarchic part of the world where the British aim was less to rule than to maintain some semblance of order. A small but difficult and harassing war 'in an uncivilised and comparatively unknown country' – as the General Staff of the War Office put it – had just come to an end.

A protectorate on the Horn of Africa, British Somaliland was sandwiched between Italian Somaliland to the east and French Somaliland to the west, and stood on the other side of the Red Sea from the small colony of Aden, which commanded the shipping lanes that led into the Arabian Sea and to India beyond. To the south lay Abyssinia. Of chief use to the Empire as a source of fresh meat for the colony across the straits, the protectorate was nicknamed 'Aden's Butcher's Shop'.

The British presence, which had been established after the withdrawal of a previous Egyptian garrison in 1884, was confined to the coastal towns of Berbera, Bulhar and Zeila. Its primary activity was to maintain order among the nomadic tribes who grazed large herds of camel and sheep in the interior. In 1885, a Royal Engineers officer Lieutenant Harald Swayne, who had built a fort for a small garrison at Bulhar, was ordered to map the caravan routes of the interior. Two years later he was asked to prepare a survey that would include the whole territory of about 60,000 square miles. To assist him in the mission, he was joined by his brother, Lieutenant Eric Swayne of the 16th Bengal Infantry. With a party of thirty Somali tribesmen to protect them from the bands of robbers and intertribal feuds that made travel in the interior extremely dangerous, the two brothers compiled over the next five years a complete sketch of the protectorate.

In 1900, there was an uprising of Dervish tribesmen. Because of his knowledge of the region, Eric Swayne, now a lieutenant colonel, was appointed to lead a campaign against the rebel leader Mohammed Abdullah Hassan, whom the British dubbed the 'Mad

Mullah'. As Swayne pursued the Mullah's army of Dervishes across Somaliland, he supplemented the sketch maps that he had made with his brother with more detailed maps that were made by compass. Constantly on the move, he had no choice but to judge the distances by the time and rate of marching.

In 1904, the Mullah, who had survived repeated efforts by the British to defeat him but paid a heavy price in men, retreated into neighbouring Italian Somaliland, where he parleyed for peace. The British authorities took advantage of the lull in hostilities to make the topographical maps that brought Jack and his plane table to the region. I found some of those maps in the first volume ('Geographical, Descriptive and Historical') of the *Military Report on Somaliland* that the General Staff of the War Office published in 1907. They contained all the necessary information to help fight the next battle that was bound to ensue when the Mad Mullah, having gathered together his scattered forces, resumed his

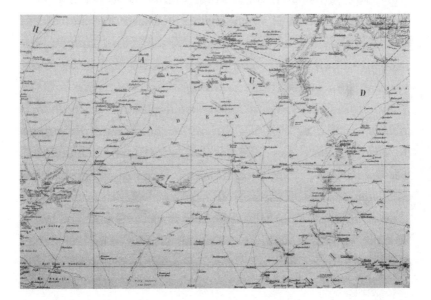

ambition to establish a Dervish state. They charted the mountain ranges and passes; and they charted the tracks, with appraisals of the ease of going – 'very difficult route', 'hilly country', 'open, bare in parts, liable to flood in rainy weather'.

The dominating feature of the region was the Haud, a vast expanse of thorn-bush desert that stretched across the territory in a band 150 to 250 miles wide. A principal consideration in mapping it was the location of water, the letter 'w.' at intervals along the tracks marking its possible presence according to hearsay and travellers' tales, while specific elaborations recorded the observed reality, 'Large tank, water always remains', '2 wells (rain water)', 'dry wells' . . . In the campaign against the Mullah the strategic occupation of the water points had been a means of forcing engagements with the Dervish army, yet at the same time the very scarcity of water made it difficult to capitalise on any military success that resulted from such engagements.

As well as the physical features of the landscape, the map recorded the events of recent history, marking the sites of the battles that had been fought over the last few years, with crossed swords at Courgerod, Ferdiddin and Jidbali, and also the places where the Mullah had made his camps.

The arid, barren nature of a terrain that had no economic importance lent a touch of absurdity to the exercise. Never had the mad British come quite so close to mapping nothingness. But the mistakes of the recent South African campaign had left their mark. Never again were they going to fight a war without a proper map, even if it now seemed that war in Somaliland might be some way off in the future. For Hassan had, in the meantime, concluded a treaty with the Italian government that gave him the protection of the Italian flag and the right to continue to govern his tribes in the interior of Italian Somaliland. Jack returned to Britain in April 1905, the month after the treaty was concluded, having finished work on a map whose most immediate use was to illustrate the military report and an official history of the 1901–4 operations.

For a few years British Somaliland was at peace. The Mad Mullah's Dervish army was so quiet that the British even felt confident enough to withdraw its garrisons from the interior, maintaining a presence only in the coast towns. To guard against any possible attack that Hassan might undertake, they armed the tribes so that they could protect themselves. Soon the tribes used the weapons to fight each other instead, and the Mullah took advantage of the dissension to attack the coastal towns, in 1912 occupying the outpost of Bohotle.

To restore order and to deter further Dervish raids, the British formed a 'Somaliland Camel Constabulary'. The years of fighting that followed would not finally come to an end until after the First World War, when a new weapon, every bit as terrifying as the Maxim, helped the British to finish off this most stubborn of enemies.

On 21 January 1920, six de Havilland DH9s took off on the first of a series of sorties against the Dervish strongholds of Medishe, Jidali and Taleh. Hassan had never seen an aeroplane in his life before and, considering their approach to be a sign from God, put on his finest clothes to greet them. The first bomb killed his uncle Amir and ten riflemen, while he himself only narrowly escaped. Over the next three weeks the daily bombardments and strafing of the aeroplanes wiped out all that remained of his army.

With a handful of followers he fled into Abyssinia, where he died of the famine and sickness that overwhelmed his camp towards the end of the year.

The crushing nature of the victory made it easy for the British to consign the Mad Mullah to the history books, but they might have done better to try to understand the passion that had over twenty years enabled him to sustain his struggle against overwhelming odds. They dismissed him as mad for his religious fanaticism, and called Somaliland 'uncivilised' because it was so resistant to modern progress, but Mohammed Abdullah Hassan believed that he was answering the voice of the Prophet, that he was fighting the unbelievers who had invaded Muslim lands and desecrated the Muslim faith. 'The Kafirs are our enemies,' he complained on the eve of his rebellion. 'Do you not see that they have destroyed our religion and made our children their children?'

I couldn't help but think that my own age – so weary of intractable jihadist conflicts, of headlines documenting yet another atrocity or drone attack – has much to learn from the details of this earlier time, especially when I read of a young man in Kansas, John T. Booker Jr, who was charged in April 2015 of attempting to detonate a bomb at Fort Riley military base and providing material support to Islamic State. Quietly spoken, when he was brought before a judge, he was concerned to correct the spelling of his assumed name, Mohammed Abdullah Hassan, of which no one in the Topeka District Court seemed to appreciate the significance.

The Mad Mullah was one of the first of the twentieth century's rebel leaders to challenge the Empire's grip. Others would soon follow, some of them in the Lynch brothers' own country of Ireland. But it was only in the last years of their service that the edifice of the Empire began to show serious signs of cracking.

The brothers' service had coincided with the high point of the Empire's power, but also its arrogance. As I followed the trail of their postings up to the eve of the Great War, I was struck by how any significant change that did take place seemed only to entrench an underlying assumption that the right to govern was chiefly the prerogative of the white man. The racist complexion of the Empire was inescapable. While the white-settler colonies of Canada, Australia and New Zealand had already evolved into self-governing, quasi-independent nations by the end of the nineteenth century, the non-white populations of Africa, India and the Far East faced years of struggle to win their political freedom.

It was the growing independence of Canada that accounted for why Michael Lynch returned to England with the 40th Submarine Company from Halifax on 16 March 1906, but also why Jack went out there less than a month later. The Mother Country wanted to give Canada the kind of assistance that would help her to stand on her own two feet. Three years earlier, the founder of the Colonial Survey Section, Major E. H. Hills, who was the head of the Topographical Section of the War Office, had written a report called 'The Military Survey of the Dominion of Canada'. Before submitting it, he erased the word 'Military' from the title. In a preliminary note, he explained: '[T]he only satisfactory and economical procedure is to plan the survey of a country on such comprehensive lines that the resulting maps will be of value for all purposes for which accurate knowledge of the features of the ground is required.' He recommended a systematic survey of the whole of Canada (nearly four million square miles), although it was the military need that would determine the early expenditure.

Canada's Department of Militia and Defence, which had commissioned the report, had been established in the aftermath of the American Civil War, when the United States was regarded as a potential enemy. The fear that the victorious Union army might turn northwards had been an important factor in the original confederation of the Crown colonies, which became the self-governing Dominion of Canada in 1867. Forty years on, Canada had developed cordial relations with its powerful southern neighbour, but the Boer War had brought home to senior officers that the lack of any decent military mapping would be a grave weakness should relations ever turn hostile again.

Without waiting for the report to receive government approval, the survey branch of Canada's newly established Military Intelligence Department began topographical mapping in the Niagara Peninsula in 1904. But progress was slow for the lack of trained surveyors and a plan of systematic primary triangulation – the essential basis for any accurate map. So in April 1905, Canada's Chief of General Staff, Brigadier General Percy Lake, wrote to the minister of defence, Sir Frederick Borden, to expedite matters:

1. I have already brought to your notice the great disadvantage under which the Militia force of Canada would labour in consequence of the non-existence of proper maps of the country, in the event of that force unhappily being required to repel invasion.

2. That an army should not be able to command the use of good maps of its own country is not only a reflection upon the progress of the nation, but is a defect which directly tends to invite defeat, more especially in a case such as ours where a Canadian force would have to face superior numbers and would need every advantage it could get from science to enable it to cope with them.

3. Yet it may with truth be said that, with the exception of a survey of a portion of the Niagara peninsula and of one or two other small areas, there is not in existence a map of any part of Canada good enough for military purposes.

4. Canada is probably the only civilized country in the world which does not possess or endeavour to produce a reliable survey representing the topographical features of the main roads within, at least, the settled portions of its area.

5. I know no Canadian map which attempts to delineate the contours of the ground in the manner adopted by the Ordnance Surveys of European countries and of the United States.

6. The main reason for this is that any survey, to be accurate, must be based upon the exact determination – by astronomical observation and triangulation – of certain selected points within its area, on which the actual surveyors can 'close,' i.e., verify their work. These hardly exist in Canada.

Agreeing to commence a topographical survey of the country based on the primary triangulation that the general was calling for, the Canadian government turned to Britain for help. An arrangement was reached under which the War Office loaned a team of topographical surveyors each year from the beginning of spring to the onset of winter. The maps themselves were printed at the Ordnance Survey headquarters in Southampton because Canada did not have the specialist presses necessary for such work.

Jack Lynch was among the first team of four military surveyors to set out for Canada on 12 April 1906. When they began their topographical work in the Ottawa area, a priority was to establish a framework for all subsequent surveys, by making a link to Canada's first geodetic triangulation point, which had been established the previous summer on the top of King Mountain outside the capital.

Jack made the annual trip to Canada four years in a row. Patrick travelled out with him for the second season of 1907. Both received the same note of special merit, which was included in their service records: 'Commended by the Governor General of Canada for satisfactory work done in connection with the Topographical Survey of Canada 1907'.

If ever there was a moment when their work for the Intelligence Division of the War Office could be said to have passed from surveying into spying, this was the most likely time. Some years later, I was interested to discover, their section of Intelligence would be called MI4. In the first years of the Canada survey, the prime mission of the War Office topographers was to map the areas of strategic importance in a frontier strip that stretched from Quebec through Montreal, Ottawa and Toronto down to Lake Erie, but they also crossed the border.

Two maps, marked 'Secret' and dated 1904–7, chart the railway networks in the north-eastern and north-western corners of the United States. I can find nothing other than the maps themselves to explain their purpose, but a wartime scenario that involved a British attack on America was considered within the realm of possibility long after the maps had been made. In 1921, Canada's director of military operations and intelligence, Colonel James 'Buster' Sutherland-Brown, devised a contingency plan, 'Defence Scheme No. 1', which entailed a surprise attack on precisely the parts of US territory that had been shown on the Intelligence Division maps. In the face of the insuperable odds of America's

ten-to-one advantage in men, the goal was to create enough of a
diversion to win time for the Empire to come to Canada's aid.

Ten years later, America devised its own scheme for a pre-emptive
strike against the British Empire, 'War Plan Red'. Both plans may
seem with hindsight to have been little more than war games at a
time when the Empire was beginning to feel its age, but the imperial
habit was a difficult one to shake off. And certainly when Jack and
Patrick were in Canada before the First World War, Britain and her
dominions had yet to awake from Britannia's dream.

If anything, the idea of Empire seemed to be enjoying a second
wind. In the spring of 1907, at about the same time as the two
brothers set off for that year's trip to Canada, the Imperial Conference was taking place in London. Attending were the leaders of
the Empire's self-governing colonies, Canada, Australia and New
Zealand, but also Cape Colony and the Transvaal, which, after
three years of British rule following its defeat in the Boer War, had
recently been given self-governing status. An extraordinary sight,
suggesting the continuing power of the *Pax Britannica*, was to see
the Boer general, Louis Botha, sitting down to lunch with Dr Leander
Starr Jameson, the leader of the notorious Jameson Raid, which had
a decade earlier nearly triggered an anti-Boer uprising in the
Transvaal. The former bitter enemies were among the conference
guests of the Lord Mayor at a banquet in the Guildhall. A Boer
flag that had been captured at Jacobsdal usually decorated the hall,
but it was discreetly removed for the occasion.

'The relations between them were not always as cordial,'
commented Canada's prime minister, Sir Wilfrid Laurier, when
he gave a speech on behalf of the self-governing colonies.
'Who would have thought that five years ago, when we were
contemplating the Conference of 1907, that two members of that

Conference would be Dr Jameson and General Botha – one here as Prime Minister of the Cape and the other as Prime Minister of the Transvaal?' Of all the nations in the world, he went on, only England would have dared to grant the Boers self-government so soon after the end of the war. 'So long as the British Empire is maintained upon these lines, it will rest upon foundations firmer than the Rock and as enduring as the ages.'

Laurier celebrated an Empire that championed constitutional liberty, democracy and a respect for other traditions. Although he was himself from French-speaking Quebec, he could speak of the 'Mother Country', he said, because Britain was home to the mother of Parliaments which had provided the model on which Canada's own democracy was based. Ultimately, that was the root of the country's loyalty and its continuing commitment to an Empire that still seemed to offer the best guarantee of global order, progress and prosperity. But in praising Britain's respect for other traditions, Laurier was of course thinking only of European traditions.

The sixth day of the conference took place at the Colonial Office in Downing Street. The topic for discussion was emigration. To the agreement of all the other leaders present, the prime minister of Australia put forward the proposal that emigrants from Britain should be encouraged 'to proceed to British colonies rather than foreign countries'. In the discussion, he articulated the racial policy that underlay the development of all the self-governing colonies. The British government had an obligation, he argued, to encourage 'people of British stock' wishing to leave Britain to emigrate to the colonies of Empire with their boundless scope for settlement rather than 'other countries under other flags'. Their presence not only increased the prosperity of those colonies, leading to greater trade with Britain, but also offered 'a guarantee for the control of those great territories by our own people and our own race'.

Acknowledging the mixed traditions that existed in both Canada and South Africa, he offered some elaboration:

> I use the word 'race' here generally and in no invidious sense. We quite recognise that in Canada and in South Africa we have two races with whom we are most intimately associated. We look forward in those countries to gradual merging into a common stock. They are so closely akin to each other that there is no obstacle to a complete blending of the two. Ultimately, there will be a Canadian people, and a South African people, who, while associated with the Empire as closely as possible, will not have within themselves the consciousness of any division.

The two 'races' he was thinking of were, respectively, French and Dutch. As for the division between black and white, he was categorical: 'We are determined to have a white Australia and mean to keep it white.' To this end, he told the conference, Australia had decided to deport the 'Kanakas', the South Pacific islanders who worked on the Queensland sugar plantations. 'We believe it is good for the islands to have them back, and good for their people that they should return and live among them. For ourselves, we will have a white Australia, cost us what it may. We are anxious to let everyone know it.'

Dr Jameson was impressed that Australia had been able to attract white immigrants to replace such labour. Similar efforts in South Africa to replace black labour had failed. 'If we get a navvy out there, we pay the navvy under the circumstances in which the labour takes place – not under the ground, but on the surface in mining work – 10 shillings a day in the summertime; but he does exactly half the amount of work that the black man at three pounds a month does.'

In response to the fear that the desire for a white Empire was undermined by Britain's imprecise naturalisation laws, which did not explicitly exclude people of non-European descent, the Home Secretary Herbert Gladstone – son of Britain's great reforming prime minister William Gladstone – reassured the conference that it was not a serious issue because in practice Britain 'admitted extremely few persons of non-European descent'.

Such were the deliberations of the Empire's leaders on 25 April 1907, the eve of the Lynch brothers' departure for Canada. They may have come from a poor Roman Catholic family in the west of Ireland, but at least they could console themselves that they were just the kind of men that the Empire wanted. White.

On the last day of the conference, Laurier demonstrated his flare for the grand vision when he unveiled a proposal for an 'All Red Route' that would bind the Empire together all the more closely. A subsidised line of super-fast steamers would bear passengers and mail across the Atlantic at twenty-five knots. Canada's transcontinental railway would then whisk them across to Vancouver in only four days, from where another fleet of swift ships would take them to New Zealand and Australia. A passage of about forty days would be reduced to as little as twenty-five. No one could have known it at the time, but it turned out to be a fruitless dream that symbolises well this period of the Empire's last hurrah.

The All Red Line was not so much a new idea as an extension of an imperial goal that had been the talk of the Colonial Conference which had taken place at the end of the Boer War five years before.

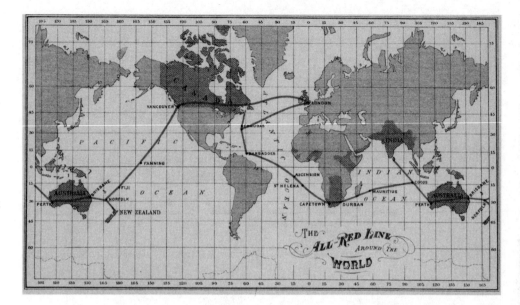

It was a project to encircle the globe with a cable that landed on only the territories of the British Empire.

In October 1902, the cable ship *Colonia*, which had been specially built with the capacity to lay the final 3,500-mile length of cable from Bamfield near Vancouver to Fanning Island in the mid-Pacific, completed the final section that connected Canada with Australia, but also inaugurated the world's first global system of instant communication.

In Ottawa, the Canadian surveyor and railway engineer, Sir Sandford Fleming, who had championed international telegraphy for a quarter of a century, celebrated the occasion by sending a message from Ottawa to Ottawa, which, arriving back in the office from where he had sent it ten hours before, was then delivered by messenger to Rideau Hall, the residence of the Governor General of Canada, Lord Minto: 'Receive globe encircling message

via England, South Africa, Australia and Pacific Cable, congratu-
lating Canada and the Empire on completion of the first segment
state controlled electric girdle, the harbinger of incalculable advantages, national and general.' Sir Sandford calculated that the
message had travelled around the world at about 3,000 miles an
hour.

Knighted on the occasion of Queen Victoria's Diamond Jubilee,
Sir Sandford Fleming was one of the Victorian age's great builders
of Empire, famous for feats which seemed calculated to stitch and
hold that Empire together. He designed Canada's first stamp, the
Threepenny Beaver; he was chief engineer of the Canadian Pacific
Railway; he had even tamed time itself. After missing a train in
Ireland because a guide had misprinted the departure time as p.m.
instead of a.m., he championed the adoption of a 24-hour clock,

which eventually became the basis for Universal Time with its adoption of Greenwich as the prime meridian.

Visionaries like Sir Sandford Fleming helped shape a world where anything seemed possible. He had arrived in Canada as a young emigrant from Kirkcaldy, Scotland, in 1845 when the trans-atlantic journey took four weeks. Sixty years later, the ships of the Canadian Pacific Steamship Company could make the crossing in only four days. When Sir Wilfrid Laurier was proposing the All Red Route in 1907, the 'World's Greatest Transport System' — as the Canadian Pacific called itself — had just put into service two of the fastest ships afloat, the *Empresses of Ireland* and *Britain*. More *Empresses* would follow — *Scotland*, *Canada*, *Australia*, even *Japan*, *China* and *France*. But the dream of the All Red Route ended for good on 29 May 1914 after the *Empress of Ireland* collided with a Norwegian collier and sank in the Saint Lawrence River with the loss of more than a thousand lives.

When Jack Lynch went to Australia, he travelled the other way round — east, through the Suez Canal and across the Indian Ocean. The RMS *Omrah* arrived in Port Philip, Melbourne, after a leisurely voyage of thirty-eight days on Monday 11 April 1910. 'Fine weather marked the whole trip,' reported the Melbourne *Argus*, 'which was consequently considerably enjoyed.' When the amenities of the ship included not only the excellent dining facili-ties that modern refrigeration made possible, but also a smoking room, bar and extensive library, the speed of the All Red Route was not necessarily an advantage.

A few months earlier, Australia had welcomed the most famous Royal Engineer of them all, Viscount Kitchener of Khartoum, who had been asked to write a report on the defence of the country.

Whatever fate awaited the All Red Route, the all red line of imperial defence policy still bound Britain and her self-governing dominions tightly together. Australia was even more short of military maps than Canada. So once again the War Office in London agreed to make available a team of Royal Engineers NCOs to help out, loaning them to the Australian government for a period of two years.

Just as Major Hills had written a report for the Canadians, five years later his successor at the War Office, Lieutenant Colonel Charles Close, wrote one for the Australians, in which he set out the essential principles of a successful mapping strategy. Recommending that the work should be confined in the first instance to areas around Australia's big cities, Brisbane, Sydney, Melbourne, Adelaide and Perth, he stressed the importance of an underlying framework of triangulation. 'It is fatal to accuracy to allow any compilation of sketches or other previously disconnected material.'

His advice was ignored. The Australians put the Royal Engineers team to work on mapping the cities, but when Jack and his comrades began their first assignments in the Melbourne area, they were told to add topographical detail to already existing parish maps, although no underlying framework of triangulation existed.

The Australian Intelligence Corps, which supervised the mapping effort, treated the presence of the British surveyors as a reluctant necessity. They acknowledged that the existing maps of their big towns lacked topographical detail, so they needed British military expertise to that extent, but to create totally new maps, as the War Office had been suggesting, seemed liked Pommy punctiliousness. When it was suggested that an Australian officer should be sent on a fact-finding mission to Europe, the head of the Intelligence Corps in Victoria, John Monash, who would later become the commander-in-chief of the Australian army, advised, 'We are aiming at no academic achievements. Our sole purpose is to produce, as quickly as possible, workable, useable, and sufficiently accurate and complete maps of our principal theatres for the use of our General Staff in war. Everything that does not directly contribute to this result should be neglected.'

Down under and down to earth, the Australians displayed a rivalry with the Mother Country that had already been expressing itself on the cricket field for some time. When another team of British surveyors was sent to map Adelaide, local members of the Australian Intelligence Corps made complaints that were raised in the federal Parliament. They believed, their MP explained to the House of Representatives, that 'while no doubt from a military point of view they may have much to learn, as surveyors they could not be taught very much about the work of map-making, and that they might very well have been entrusted with the preparation of a map of their own country'.

Meanwhile the British NCOs had plenty of their own reasons to feel aggrieved. They were being ordered, in effect, to build a house on sand, and they were answerable to inexperienced local surveyors with little or no military training, who, appointed as officers in Australia's part-time militia, worked only during weekends and holidays. While the British NCOs lugged their heavy equipment across often rough terrain, working day after day beneath the blazing sun, the Australian officers kept to the road in motor cars made available to them by the Royal Australian Automobile Corps. Making only occasional visits to the field, they would take a few spot levels from the shade of their cars, issue instructions to the NCOs about the next part of the parish plan to be surveyed, then leave them, as one brief put it, to do 'the slower and more laborious work of walking over the ground and filling in detail'.

The Australian Intelligence Corps were so proud of their first topographical map that they put it on public display. When the Army Survey Regiment reprinted it eighty years later to celebrate the formation of the Royal Australian Survey Corps, the National Library's catalogue attributed authorship to the Australian draughtsman: 'This map was drawn by W.O., Hon. Lieut. J.J. Raisbeck R.A.E. for an exhibition in 1910, and was designed as a standard for future one-inch military survey maps.' But no mention was made of the British NCOs who did the plane-table surveys on which the map was based.

In August 1910 Jack was posted to New South Wales to work on the coastline between Sydney and Newcastle. After he had completed his plane-table sheets, he sent them to the Survey headquarters for New South Wales at Victoria Barracks, Sydney, where they were put together with the sheets of other topographers to form an overall map of the region. The work of incorporation was undertaken by a locally recruited draughtsman, Warrant Officer George Constable, who did not realise that the lack of an underlying system of triangulation made his task next to impossible. As he laboured away fruitlessly, he became more and more despondent until, overwhelmed by despair at his failure to make the sheets fit together, he shot himself with his service revolver.

At least, his death was not in vain. The Australian General Staff at last accepted the advice that they had been given from the outset, and decided that all future topographical maps would have to be based on primary triangulation. Swallowing their pride, they made initial enquiries about whether the British War Office's Colonial Survey Section, which was in the Federated States of Malaya (Jack's brother Patrick was with them), might undertake the work, but then realised that, by a stroke of good fortune, the Australian army had just acquired a former Royal Engineers surveyor of nearly twenty years' experience, who had even served with the Colonial Survey Section when it was first formed back in 1902.

Jack, who had been due to return to England at the end of the two-year War Office agreement for the loan of its surveyors, found another reason to stay on when he fell in love with Mary Jane Kennedy. They married, according to his military service record, on 5 June 1912 in St Francis' Catholic Church, Melbourne. The following year he applied to be discharged from the Royal Engineers and, on 28 August 1913, re-enlisted in the Royal Australian Engineers. He was immediately appointed to set up a triangulation section, which in July 1915 became part of a new 'Australian Survey Corps'. A few months later, in January 1916, he was promoted to the rank of Lieutenant, becoming head of the corps. A Lynch had become an officer at last.

Many of the early plane-table surveys that the British NCOs did when they first arrived in Australia survive in the Australian National Library. They include Jack's map of the Lake Macquarie area south of Newcastle, drawn in India ink with extraordinary detail and precision. It not only records the lie of the land but also gives a summary of the work schedule. Beginning on 22 August 1910, Jack completed a topographical survey of eighty-one square miles on 21 December. Of 105 days' actual work, he spent sixty-six inking in the detail, and twelve on the levelling and contouring

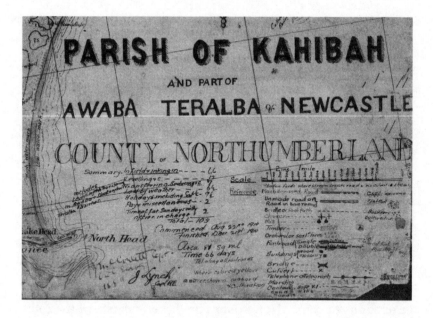

of an immensely varied landscape of lake, hill, forest and seashore, as well as the small town of Boolaroo, which stood at the foot of Brooks Mountain. It was a fast-growing community in 1910, with a range of industrial activity that included coal mining, lead smelting and timber.

On a scale of two inches to a mile, the map recorded every feature of military significance, both natural and man-made. It used different-style hatchings and symbols to distinguish between trees for timber and orchards, between flat rocks and boulders, between cultivated fields and marshland, between buildings of a masonry construction and those of wood. It picked out all the telegraph and telephone lines, the tracks, bridal paths, railways and roads. It specified whether the railways were one way or two way, whether the roads were 'macademised' or unmade, and where shallow streams crossed them in the absence of culverts. All the detail that an army could possibly need to defend Boolaroo – or besiege it – was shown, but the worst enemy of all was already there, defying any conventional defence, in the shape of the chloride works at the edge of town, which contaminated the soil with zinc and lead, poisoning the streams and rivers.

Overlooking Boolaroo, 'the place of many flies', Brooks Mountain is the highest point on the map. It was named after William Brooks, a settler who had opened a coal mine there on land that had been given to him as a Crown grant. The Awabakal Aborigines, who had been dispossessed of their land around Lake Macquarie many years earlier, would not have understood this kind of ownership, because they believed that the land, and all that was on it, belonged to everyone – to them, their ancestors and the generations to come. Nor would they have understood the folly of killing the land that provided sustenance – what the white man so often called 'progress'.

Today the place is known again by the name that the Aborigines used, Munibung Hill. It was here, according to legend, that, in the time of the Dreaming, a serpent filled the valleys with water to form the lake that was home to the Awabakal – 'the people of the flat surface'. Every hill, valley or river, every bird, beast or fish – even every fly in Boolaroo – was part of the network of life that their Great Spirit ancestors had created.

Jack's map showed the collieries, roads and railways of the new Australia, rendering accurately a terrain that the settlers understood in terms of coal and timber, but a different map was needed to reveal the hidden dimension that the Aborigines saw.

A little way up the Pacific coast from the lake entrance, was the small town of Belmont, with its school, post office and police station. This was where the Reverend Lancelot Threlkeld had set

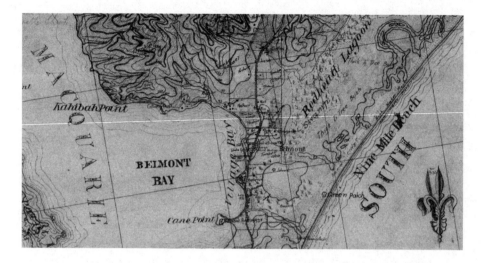

up a mission station in 1825 when no town yet existed. He had chosen the spot because many of the Awabakal still camped there by a lagoon between the lake and the Pacific shoreline. They belonged to the Bahtabah clan, which occupied a coastal strip of land between the entrance to the lake at Swansea and Charlestown further to the north.

But soon his wish to convert them took second place to wanting to understand them. It was the last possible moment to document a way of life that was being threatened by disease and the relentless encroachment of the European settlers. '[T]he decrease of the Aborigines proceeds rapidly,' Threlkeld wrote in 1839, 'in the elapse of a very few years, humanly speaking, the race will become extinct in these parts.' Threlkeld worked to salvage as many fragments of Awabakal culture while he could. To help him he had a native tutor, Biraban, who was one of the tribal leaders. Known as Johnny M'Gill to the settlers, Biraban had been a servant to an officer at Sydney barracks and had also worked as a bush constable, tracking down escaped convicts from the penal colony at Newcastle.

Biraban taught Threlkeld the Awabakal language and explained the myths and customs that were an inseparable part of the landscape in which they lived. His own name, Biraban, meant Eagle-Hawk, after the great bird who dropped the circles of stones that could be found on the hilltops around Lake Macquarie.

While Jack could record the swamp and forest that surrounded the lagoon at Belmont, it was an unwritten story that explained why it was a sacred place. A long time ago, the moon-man, Pontoe-Boong, became jealous of the sun-woman, Punnal. He was tired of having to cross the sky alone in the dark. The people below rarely saw his shining face, while they were able to admire Punnal every day, except when the cloud spirit Yura made the rain. The moon-man was so sad that he went far away and cried for many days. When he next visited the earth, he saw his face huge and silver in a large lagoon that his own tears had made. Filled with happiness, he shouted to the people on the surrounding hills, 'Don't be afraid. I have come to bring joy.' He returned to the sky, but never forgot the people of the lagoon, shining his very brightest whenever he visited them, so that it was almost like day. And to celebrate his return, the Awabakal danced by the lagoon in his honour.

Only the very early European settlers were lucky enough to catch a glimpse of the Aboriginal way of life that their arrival would soon destroy. Having no accurate maps, they relied on native guides like Biraban to show them the country. An unnamed Newcastle settler gave this account of an excursion to Lake Macquarie in 1821:

Our parson, the Rev F. A. Middleton, who was an especial favourite with the blacks, started with myself, with the whole tribe of

upwards of 100 on a walking trip to Lake Macquarie. Our necessary
supplies, blankets, &c, they carried on their heads. On arrival, I
was enchanted with its beautiful scenery, and can never forget it.
The whole surrounding country and lake were serene and still;
solitude reigned; no tree disturbed; no trace of white man's
civilisation, but all in its wild natural state. We enjoyed all the wild
sports of Australian bush life in its primitive state as the Aborigines
of that day (before they were contaminated with our vices) were
accustomed to enjoy them, shooting, fishing, kangarooing, and
hunting, our game was ample for us all. They supplied us also (by
diving) with the finest mud oysters for which the waters of the lake
are noted. These we scalloped on our bush fires, and we spent five
or six days of as much enjoyment as I have ever had in any part
of the world.

This ultimate tourist excursion took place when the lake was still
known to the white settlers as Reid's Mistake. In 1800, Captain

William Reid had embarked from Sydney in his schooner, the *Martha*, to bring back coal from the north. Discovering the long, narrow passage into the lake, he assumed that he had found the mouth of the Hunter River, which would take him up to Newcastle. The error turned out to be a piece of good fortune, as some friendly natives showed him where there was plenty of coal to be found near the lake entrance. The name Reid's Mistake stuck until the lake was renamed in honour of the governor of New South Wales, Major General Lachlan Macquarie, when settlers reached the area twenty-five years later.

Jack, who visited the place long after the white man's avarice had exhausted the natives' goodwill, had to rely on plane table and theodolite to find his way around, but he would surely have admired the Aborigines' peerless knowledge of topography. I wondered whether their fierce bond with the land ever reminded him of Ireland, where an eagle hawk might easily have dropped some of the stones that had been scattered with such mysterious design across the Burren. Clare's cairns and stone monuments may have been far less old, going back at most six thousand years instead of sixty thousand, but there was a similar sense of people, myth and land woven into one. How the Devil's marks came to be found on a bridge along the Tulla road, near the burial mound of the High Kings, was the kind of story that a Johnny M'Gill might have told.

Britain attempted to redress the wrongs that had been done to Ireland through the Land Acts of the late nineteenth century, giving security of tenure and then ownership to the tenant farmers. In Australia the first of the Aboriginal Land Rights Acts was passed in 1976 with a similar purpose of making amends. Seeking to reflect the Aborigine system of land ownership, the Act created the concept of inalienable freehold title to land held

on a communal basis and enabled Aborigines to claim back trad-
itional lands. The measures could never come close to making up
for the full scale of the wrong, but the effort of atonement was a
much truer measure of 'civilisation' than the fences the Europeans
put up when they first arrived in Australia.

The biggest fence of all arrived with the Second World War,
when the military value of Jack's map suddenly became apparent.
Fearing that the Japanese would attempt a landing on Nine
Mile Beach, the long beach that stretched from the entrance of
Lake Macquarie north towards Newcastle, the Australian army
erected concrete tank traps across Belmont Lagoon and cleared
many acres of scrubland to deny cover to an enemy invasion.
When the moon-man paid his monthly visit to the lagoon, he must
have felt more forgotten than ever.

The service records of the Lynch brothers swirl down finally into
the whirlpool of the Great War, after which 'all changed, changed
utterly'.

I turned away from Jack to his brothers, sketching in as best I
could the progress of their careers up to the banks of that Rubicon.
While James remained in Britain working for the Ordnance
Survey until he was posted to France in 1916, Michael continued
on his tour of the Empire's harbours – from Weymouth to Ceylon
in 1908, then on to Singapore in 1911.

When the youngest, Thomas, had finished his training at
Chatham, he joined the 14th Survey Company, which was based in
Ireland. Among his service papers was Army Form B. 221, which
he signed at the Cork Ordnance Survey office in 1906 to extend his
length of service. Some nameless clerk – no doubt with the rank and
pay of a sapper – had taken the trouble to give each stage of the

form's journey – from the Ordnance Survey regional office in Cork (30 January), to the Ordnance Survey headquarters in Southampton (1 February), to the 14th Survey Company headquarters in Dublin (3 February) and, finally, to the Corps Record Office at Chatham (is it 5 or 6 February?) – an official stamp even when there was no official stamp, drawing in its place a wobbly freehand ellipse in ink, but omitting the 'p' in Southampton. With such dogged respect for protocol the cogs of the military machine continued to turn and turn and turn, even into the years of the Apocalypse.

Thomas had his first taste of foreign service when he travelled out to the Gold Coast in 1911, arriving in Accra on 21 September. He was one of a detachment of thirteen sappers from the 14th Company who had been sent to survey the mining concessions in the Gold Coast Colony and its dependency of Ashanti, which had been annexed in 1901 after a series of wars.

It was in Accra, during the year of my birth, 1960, that a British prime minister conceded that the Empire had had its day. 'The wind of change is blowing right through Africa,' Harold Macmillan declared. When he repeated the comment in apartheid South Africa a few weeks later, he warned, 'Whether we like it or not, this growth of national consciousness is a political fact.' But a gentle breeze had in fact been blowing for some time, evident even in the very last years of the Lynch brothers' service.

The fate of the legendary Golden Stool, which was the symbol of Ashanti independence, offered some measure of how the change began to take root. In 1900, the then governor of the Gold Coast, Sir Frederick Mitchell, marched to the Ashanti capital of Kumasi demanding that the stool be given up to him. 'What must I do to the man, whoever he is, who has failed to give to the Queen, who is the paramount power in this country, the stool to which she is entitled? Where is the Golden Stool? Why am I not sitting on the Golden Stool at this moment? I am the representative of the paramount power; why have you relegated me to this chair? Why did you not take the opportunity of my coming to Kumasi to bring the Golden Stool and give it to me to sit upon?' Sir Frederick's boorish assertion of strength served only to trigger another war, in which a thousand British soldiers and two thousand Ashanti warriors lost their lives. The Golden Stool itself remained hidden. Indeed it would be the British Queen who would surrender her own stool first when she died the following year.

But twenty years later the Golden Stool was dug up from its hiding place by labourers who were building a new road. The Ashanti chiefs were appalled to discover that this stool containing the spirit of their nation had been desecrated and stripped of its gold. Suddenly the British authorities found themselves in a situation that could easily have triggered yet another war. This time round, however, they benefited from a willingness to understand the Ashanti point of view which included the recent establishment of an anthropology department under the direction of a Captain Robert Rattray. Consulting with an Ashanti elder about the significance of the stool, Rattray wrote a report that warned the British authorities against seeking the stool's custody, suggesting instead that the Ashanti chiefs should be allowed to conduct their own trial of the culprits. He argued, too, that even though the stool had been stripped of its gold, the fact that its wooden framework was still intact meant that its soul had not been destroyed.

Accepting the recommendations, the chief commissioner of Ashanti, Charles Harper, asked only that he should be allowed to review the verdict of the Ashanti court. Of the fourteen suspects accused of complicity in the crime, the native court sentenced six to death, seven to life imprisonment, and one to 'drink fetish'. With the agreement of the chiefs, Harper commuted the six death sentences to banishment, on the basis that the essential integrity of the stool had not been destroyed; discharged five others; and required the remaining three to 'drink fetish' before the chiefs. It was due to Rattray's investigations, Harper later wrote in his official report, 'that much that is new in the history of the "Golden Stool" has come to light and with such knowledge Government has seen the way to deal in a sympathetic spirit with the disturbing event of its desecration'.

In 1923, Captain Rattray published a book on the religion and customs of the Ashanti people, in which he made a plea for attempting to understand and value native beliefs and traditions that had previously been dismissed:

I approached these old people and this difficult subject (their religious beliefs) in the spirit of one who came to them as a seeker after truths, the key to which they alone possessed, which not all the learning nor all the books of the white man could ever give me.

I made it clear to them that I asked access to their religious rites such as are here described for this reason. I attended these ceremonies with all the reverence and respect I could accord to something which I felt to have been already very old, before the religion of my country had yet been born as a new thought; yet not so entirely new, but that even its roots stretched back and were fed from that same stream which still flows in Ashanti today.

The starting point of Captain Rattray's enquiry was one of shared humanity. His trust and respect were rewarded a few years later when an Ashanti elder took him to see what no European had seen before, in spite of all the force that the British Empire had brought to bear to make the Ashanti people reveal it: the Golden Stool. In the same visit, he saw other precious Ashanti relics, although not the skull of Sir Charles MacCarthy.*

Thomas returned to England from the Gold Coast in October 1912 to undertake Ordnance Survey duties with the 19th Company based at Southampton. He was sent out again to West Africa in September 1913, this time to Sierra Leone, where he remained until 12 July 1914. From the annual report of the Colonial Survey Committee for 1913, I learned that he was contributing to a survey of Freetown which was intended to provide a basis 'for a system of street construction and drainage'. If I felt little curiosity to find out any further details, perhaps it was because this

---

* 'Possibly because my friends did not want to hurt my feelings,' Rattray commented, 'but I was informed it still existed.'

second African trip seemed to pale in comparison to those storm clouds ahead. After only three months back in England he was transferred, on 20 November 1914, into the 11th Field Company, which was serving with the British Expeditionary Force in France. It turned out to be his last posting.

It remains only to fill in the final entries of my grandfather Patrick's military history sheet, which likewise ends with that posting to end all postings, 'B.E.F., France'. After returning from the Topographical Survey of Canada at the end of 1907, he was seconded to the Colonial Survey Department of Ceylon, where he served as Assistant Superintendent of Field Surveys for three years. Then, in May 1912, he was sent to the Federated States of Malaya. Here he was reunited with the Colonial Survey Section, which had just spent six years in South Africa making the detailed topographical maps whose absence had caused the British so much trouble during the Boer War.

The CSS was abruptly recalled on the outbreak of the European war in order to make a map of the British Expeditionary Force's base camp at Le Havre, but it returned to Malaya after the war was over, as if, for all the destruction in between, it could simply carry on from where it had left off. Patrick, by this time, had left the Royal Engineers and was working for the Land Commission in Ireland, which, incredibly, had just become an independent country. But if he had wanted to catch up with what his old comrades had been doing, he would have been able to do so at the Royal Geographical Society in London, where the commanding officer of the section, Captain Kirby, on his return from Malaya, gave a lecture on his experiences.

The published account of the proceedings offers a fascinating glimpse of the struggle between reactionary and progressive values as the Empire, unawares, began the final lap of its existence. In a withering estimate of native enterprise, the captain, clearly belonging very much to the old school of British army officer, said that the average Malay had adopted civilisation enough to appreciate the value of the motor car, but 'seldom understands what goes on underneath the bonnet'. He explained that he had given up trying to recruit Malays as 'survey coolies' because their dislike of routine work and poor physique made them 'a bad type of coolie for a Topographical Field Party'. Instead, he had the good fortune to employ a party of Dyaks from Sarawak. 'It is not so long ago that the Dyak was a head-hunter, but only on one occasion did any of my Dyak coolies show a tendency to relapse. One was discovered with a newly garnered human head as his pillow. On investigation I am glad to say this head was not taken from a member of the section, but that the coolie had found a dead Chinaman.'

The captain's second in command on the expedition, Lieutenant Willis, who was in the audience, intervened to speak up for his Dyak friends, insisting that they had been 'in no sense coolies' but were 'genial survey collaborators'. He told the following story to make clear what nice people they were to deal with and what an attractive mentality they had:

> I was walking along a very narrow jungle path. A Chinaman coming in the opposite direction required a great deal more than his fair share of the path. As we brushed past each other, four of my Dyaks pattered up with very broad smiles on their faces and very large knives in their hands and said, 'Did you see that man? He did not give you anything like enough room to walk; may we please cut his head off?' I had to act quite quickly, for silence is taken as consent, and it is somewhat awkward to explain afterwards that one did not really mean it.

I left these folk with very genuine regret, and, I may also add, with a certain amount of subterfuge, because six of them, having saved enough money for a journey to Europe and equipped themselves, with a general view of appearing well in London society, with one Homburg hat apiece, announced their intention of coming home with me.

Even if the lieutenant clearly did not underestimate the challenge of bridging the cultural difference, his wish to treat the Dyaks as collaborators rather than coolies offered a glimmer at least of a more enlightened age, when a new generation could begin to dismantle the iniquities of imperial rule and attempt a different kind of relationship on the basis of respect – an age when the Chinaman would eventually have the last laugh.

15

Things Fall Apart

The skip devoured objects that had once been the fabric of our lives. A childhood memory had rescued Rousseau's *Snake Charmer* but an equally cheap reproduction of John Piper's *Windsor Castle* was tossed on the heap. Had I known that it had once hung in my father's rooms in Oxford along with *The Snake Charmer*, I would have wanted to keep it too.

Only chance sentiment granted a reprieve to things that otherwise had no obvious value: a legless, one-eyed teddy bear; a ragged old seaside bag that my mother had made out of scraps of towelling; a rusty wheelbarrow in which she used to push her grandchildren around the garden. A few things saved from the bonfire of the past, which suddenly, in their isolation, evoked the scale of the break-up, exposing the illusion of permanence we had enjoyed until the death of our parents.

After my father died, it took more than a year to sell my parents' house. So my brothers and I had plenty of opportunity to explore what they had built during their life together before it was put asunder for ever. As we went through desks, drawers and cupboards that had been beyond bounds when they were still alive, old papers tumbled out from the time before we were born, raising as many questions as they answered now that our parents were no longer around to explain the significance of things.

I suppose every generation eventually makes enquiries about the previous generation. In a filing cabinet in my father's study I found an attempt at a family tree in which he had sketched the Lynches back to my great-grandparents. The familiar precision and tidiness with which he had set about the exercise made the errors in this example of genealogy before the World Wide Web all the more striking.

In my father's version of the family, my great-grandparents had only four sons: James, Michael, Thomas and Patrick – in that order as though James were the eldest and Patrick the youngest, while the son who was the eldest, Jack, had been left off the tree completely. In the next generation, James had been attributed children who in fact belonged to Michael, while Michael had some phantom child called 'Maeve'. As for whom each might have married, the best that could be done was '= ?', an equation that, in representing the general doubt over things, seemed to me to have a significance that went far beyond genealogy.

Although I never managed to figure out who Maeve was, some of the gaps I could fill in. So the two question marks after my mother's older sister Breda were twins Mary and Margaret who had both died within days of their birth in 1925. And not even mentioned – perhaps because not even known – was another child, Mary Margaret, who had died in February 1928, almost exactly a year before the arrival of my mother, Anne Patricia, on Valentine's Day in 1929.

From the absence of the generation that has since followed my own, I guessed that the tree had been drawn at some point during the 1970s – after we had become teenagers, when my parents had more leisure to think about such things, but also after the tolling of bells had begun for the departing members of their parents' generation. It would have been drawn just before my mother began to investigate the very first death from that generation, which had actually occurred a whole sixty years before.

'Thank you for your letter dated 14 August 1979,' replied the director general of the Commonwealth War Graves Commission to her letter enquiring about the burial place of her uncle Thomas during the Great War. 'From the cuttings you sent us we have been able to glean enough information to discover the identity of your uncle: Sapper Thomas Joseph Lynch, 13419, 11th Field Company Royal Engineers, died on 16 May 1915, age 32. Unfortunately, his grave was among those which the Army Graves Service was unable to trace after the War and he is therefore commemorated on Panel 1 of the Le Touret Memorial, France.'

My mother went out to Flanders to see the name a few months later. It only occurs to me now that, at fifty years old, she would have been almost exactly the age I was when I began to write this book. It was the end of a decade of deaths that only slightly registered on my teenage self but must have had a big impact on her – her mother in 1972, her aunt Annie in 1974, and her mother-in-law, Leah, with whom she formed a close bond after an unpromising start, in 1979. Little by little, the heavy door was closing on the previous generation. She wanted to find out what she could, although in the end she found out no more than a name: Thomas, the Unknown Uncle.

On 7 October 1914, Thomas joined the badly depleted 11th Field Company, which had gone out to France with the 2nd Division of the British Expeditionary Force nearly two months before. Since then they had been through the Battle of Mons, the Great Retreat to the Marne and the First Battle of the Aisne. Now, as the opposing forces sought to outflank each other in the race to the sea and the BEF took up a defensive position on the left flank of the French army, they were about to take part in what history would call the First Battle of Ypres.

Although Thomas himself remains as elusive as ever, I was able to follow the last few months of his service in the Royal Engineers through the 11th Field Company War Diary, which survives in the corps library at Chatham. The company commander Major Denis de Vitré had spent the train journey to the new front writing letters of condolence to the families of the men who had already been killed in the Aisne campaign. One of the company's four sections had come under heavy shellfire while repairing a bridge over a canal at Pont-Arcy, about fifteen miles east of Soissons. The section officer and three men were killed, while ten sappers and drivers were badly wounded.

Thomas was stepping into the shoes of one of these men, I suppose. The abbreviation 'T.R. 12704' had been entered into his service record next to the mention of his transfer to the 11th Company. If 12704 was a service number, then the man he replaced was Sapper Cecil Kempsell.

From the railhead at Saint-Omer the company marched towards the Belgian border, finding billets each night in the countryside. Reaching the front, near Saint-Jean, on 21 October, it was ordered to reconnoitre the right flank of the 4th Brigade with a view to strengthening it against attack. After all the back-and-forth movement of the first few weeks, it was the beginning of a new kind of war, which involved the Royal Engineers shoring up static positions – although, to the extent that any soldiers continued to move, the Engineers did so more than most, as they met the defensive needs of the different regiments along a line that was in effect taking shape for the very first time. There were still several stretches of open ground without any trenches at all, so it was sometimes difficult to know for certain where the line actually was.

Within the first twenty-four hours of their arrival, the 11th Field Company had made a fire trench for the Irish Guards, completed dugouts for the 2nd Battalion of the Grenadier Guards, built a brigade headquarters, and put up a double apron fence of three-strand barbed wire nearly two hundred yards long. They then made bombproof shelters in case the farm where they were billeted should be destroyed by shellfire.

Before they could settle in they were ordered to march to the next point along the line that needed strengthening. Although it was well after midnight when they reached the village of Zillebeke, the crowds of refugees on the road made their billets difficult to find. Not that there was too much opportunity for sleep in any case: the fear of a breakthrough was such that the company had been kept in a state of constant readiness for several days. The men had orders not even to take off their boots.

The gruelling pattern of these first days involved fetching material and equipment during the afternoon, then laying wire in front of the trenches at night. The sappers who ventured out on this most dangerous of tasks had the cover of darkness but were otherwise completely exposed. To deaden the sound of fixing the wire, they hammered the pickets that held it in place with wooden mallets. Every now and then a magnesium flare would go up, when the men would have to fling themselves on the ground until they were safe again with the embrace of the returning darkness.

In the series of attacks and counter-attacks that took place over the next month the sappers were often required to support the infantry. 'The fighting from 19th October to 22nd November, known as the First Battle of Ypres, was as critical as any in the war,' commented the *History of the Royal Engineers*. 'It was fought with the heaviest odds against the small British force and against a line which in some places was held even by cooks and batmen.'

The fierce fighting meant that the first trenches were necessarily hurried and makeshift. In the War Diary, Major de Vitré commented on their poor siting, which he attributed to '1) the men digging themselves in where they had got following the most convenient natural feature; 2) the officers and men being dead tired; 3) the inexperience of the officers that had only lately joined their regiments to replace casualties.' The impression is of a small, badly outnumbered army hanging on by the skin of its teeth.

Soon Major de Vitré himself became a casualty, wounded in both legs. A new commander, Major Charles Foulkes, took over on 10 November. He had with him a camera that captured some of the weary men of the 11th Field Company enjoying a brief moment of relaxation outside the farmhouse near Zillebeke which they had made their home. I can't help but wonder if one of those men might have been my great-uncle Thomas, and wish that my mother had been able to see the photograph.

In his memoirs, Foulkes recalled his arrival. The billet was half a mile behind the front line but exposed to incessant salvoes of German shells that burst day and night over the back areas, while the British artillery, which had run out of ammunition, seemed to him to be non-existent. When the fighting died down, on 20 November, Foulkes estimated that the British battalions

contained on average only one officer and thirty men out of
their original complement and that some of the units had been
completely annihilated. The successful defence at Ypres, he wrote,
was 'the proudest achievement of the British Army during the
whole war'.

In the comparative calm that followed, replacements arrived to
make good the company's losses. They included the future author
of *Bulldog Drummond*, H. C. McNeile, who used his pseudonym,
'Sapper', for the first time when he wrote a series of stories about
the front, which the *Daily Mail* began to publish in the new year
under the title 'Reminiscences of Sergeant Michael Cassidy'.

A heavy-drinking, heavy-fighting Irishman of the Royal Engineers, who is convalescing from his wounds in London, Cassidy
tells his stories of the war to a young officer of the corps about
to set off for France. The officer, whose chief role is to listen,

resembled McNeile's own situation in real life. When he joined the 11th Field Company just after the First Battle of Ypres, its survivors had plenty of reminiscences to share with him, none of which required any exaggeration.

The first story, 'Three to One', is set during the advance to the Aisne, when, explains Sergeant Cassidy, 'it wasn't like what it is now, all one long line – there was a chance of striking a stray Uhlan on his own'. Cassidy and an officer called Trentham come upon a patrol of six drunken Uhlans about to rape a young French-woman. Cassidy describes how he and Trentham come out top in the uneven 'box-up' that follows, killing all six:

> 'Ah! the devils, the swine: to think of it. It might have been one's own girl, sir; and the look in her eyes – I'll never forget it.'
>
> 'But you killed the lot, Cassidy. That's the main point: you killed the brutes,' I cried excitedly.
>
> 'And is not one officer of the British Army and one sergeant sufficient for six Germans when it comes to that sort of work, especially when the officer is such as Mr Trentham?' he answered with dignity.

Although the idea of a partnership between an English officer and an Irish sergeant would become increasingly untenable after the Easter Uprising of 1916, during this early stage of the war it still offered a positive model for collaboration. At the same time as Sergeant Cassidy was making his debut in the *Daily Mail*, the Irish revolutionary Sir Roger Casement was attempting to persuade Irish prisoners of war in Germany to join an Irish Brigade to fight against Britain. He found it tough going. When he visited their camp, they were uncompromisingly hostile to him. The German authorities, at Casement's suggestion, relaxed the conditions of their imprisonment, but the Irish NCOs wrote to the camp commandant: 'We must beseech his Imperial Majesty to withdraw these concessions unless they are shared by the remainder of prisoners as, in addition to being Irish Catholics, we have the honour to be British soldiers.' It would require another year of war for the two things to begin to seem incompatible.

'When one's motto is "Ubique,"' comments McNeile's narrator, 'it follows that one may, following the dictates of the Great Powers that be at the War Office, be rudely torn away from old friends and associations, whom one may never see again, and be hurled into the midst of new faces as well as new conditions.' After only a week with the 11th Field Company, the Great Powers at the War Office dictated that McNeile should move on again, and, on 30 November, he was posted to the 1st Field Squadron.

Major Foulkes made the most of the post-battle lull to try out some innovations. 'Started experimental trench,' he recorded in the War Diary for 28 November. 'Rifle pits, 8' × 2', about 4' apart, to be connected up later leaving traverse between them.' The general in command of the 2nd Division, Sir Charles Monro, inspected the trench the same afternoon.

'Experimented with barbed-wire fence on tripods,' recorded another entry. In the margin was a drawing of the arrangement by which the barbed wire would be attached across six tripods, with a length of eight feet between each. It was hoped that the new method would make wire-laying in no man's land much more swift and less costly in lives. But one had only to picture the ungainly caterpillar of men and wire venturing awkwardly over the parapet to appreciate the wishful thinking: 'No. 3 section carried wire across country and placed it in position in front of imaginary trench.

Quite feasible – one man per tripod with extra man on front one.' But the idea did not catch on.

Meanwhile a curious transformation was taking place. While the old world of farm buildings and countryside churches was being obliterated by shellfire, a labyrinth of trench systems was taking its place. The features of this new landscape soon began to be named, at first with descriptions that expressed the obvious wartime immediacies – First Aid Corner, Windy Corner, Cock Shy, Brewery Road – but later with names that offered a nostalgic nod to the places that the soldiers had left behind. A foreign field became a pastiche of England. So at the village of Cuinchy, which the Guards regiments had held, the road leading to the dressing station near Windy Corner became Harley Street; close by were communication trenches called Oxford Street and the Marylebone Road, while the bridge that went over the canal near the station was Vauxhall Bridge. When the Highland Light Infantry joined the line they dug a trench called Glasgow Street.

In the 'English–Trench' dictionary that would help a visitor to understand the language of this new country, words could be found for every aspect of daily life. To take two fairly routine examples, 'whizz-bangs' meant the high-velocity shells that gave you no time to duck, while the much larger 'Jack Johnsons', after the American heavyweight champion of the world, gave you plenty of time to duck but much less chance of survival. 'A big black brute who gives you a thick ear if you're not very handy with your feet,' explained *The Sapper*, adding this overheard remark from a cockney soldier: 'It looks like a bloomin' four-an'-'arf Barclay Perkins comin' at yer, but it ain't all Barclay & Perkins when it busts.' Barclay & Perkins was a well-known London brewery that delivered its beer in four-and-a-half-gallon casks.

The year 1915 began quietly enough for the 11th Field Company. But even between offensives the rate of attrition was relentless. The company spent New Year's Day making the loopholes that enabled soldiers to fire from the trenches without having to raise their heads above the parapet. On Tuesday the 5th, all four sections went out under cover of darkness to lay a thousand yards of wire. One sapper hurt his knee and another dislocated his shoulder, but all returned safely. When they went out the next night, Sapper Scott was wounded by a bullet. On the 7th, they went out again to lay yet more wire. This time 2nd Lieutenant Matthews was wounded in the left shoulder by rifle fire from his own line. On the 8th, they built a new high parapet trench: Sapper Holbrook was wounded in the back, and Sapper Calwer in the thigh. The 10th was spent filling shell holes and no casualties were reported.

But the 11th was an especially bloody day. Over the past few weeks the company had been making improvised hand grenades, packing jam tins with high explosives. When an NCO went into the shed in which the hand grenades and gun cotton were stored, the candle of a hurricane lamp ignited two huge explosions:

> The whole of no. 1 Section who were on duty were either killed or injured. Sappers Brown, Bastable, Coppin and Edwardes were removed dead, and Sapper Collett was found dead under water in the pond close by the next morning. The wounded were given first aid in the billet and were removed by motor ambulance to Bethune. The following is the list of injured. Sergeant Doree, Corporal Roper, 2nd Corporal Gilbert and Sappers Beaumont, Campbell, Church, Cook, Clancy, Jarvis, Rouse, Wiles and Trail. 2nd Corporal Gilbert died next morning, making up to the 12th, 6 dead and 11 injured.

On the 25th, the Germans captured some trenches at Cuinchy. The Coldstream Guards, who had held them, were forced back into a keep that had been improvised among the giant brick stacks that crossed the lines. One of the most notorious spots on the Western Front, the Cuinchy brick stacks were a sort of heaven for poets imagining hell. It was a 'slaughter-yard', wrote Edmund Blunden. 'One could never feel at ease in the Cuinchy sector', which 'was as dirty, bloodthirsty and wearisome a place as could well be found in ordinary warfare'. Robert Graves remembered a 'most confusing' place, where the trenches had 'made themselves rather than been made', running in and out of the stacks that thwarted any attempts at system. 'The Germans are very close: they have half the brick-stacks; we have the other half. Each side snipes down from the top of its brick-stacks into the other's

trenches.' While the walls of Flanders' cathedrals and churches had been reduced to rubble, the bricks of Cuinchy, massed into stacks of about thirty feet high, had proved near indestructible, affording great tactical advantage to whichever side best commanded them.

The 11th Field Company arrived on the 31st to fortify the new position. While sections 1, 2 and 4 laid barbed wire around the keep, section 3 barricaded a railway embankment and culvert. In the early hours of 1 February, the section was still working on the fortifications, when the Germans launched a surprise attack on the trenches at the bottom of the embankment. The sappers joined the Coldstream Guards in an attempt to hold the line, but the Germans successfully pressed forward their advantage, compelling the defenders to give up the trenches under heavy gunfire.

The successful recapture of the trenches later in the day became a fabled exploit of Irish martial valour. After a heavy artillery barrage had been directed on the Germans in the trenches, about fifty Coldstream and thirty Irish Guards made a bayonet charge. Lance Corporal Michael O'Leary, from Macroom in County Cork, sprinted to a barricade where five German soldiers were about to put a machine gun into action. He took aim with his rifle and picked off the men one by one. Leaving his comrades to secure the gun, he then sprinted to a second barricade about sixty yards further on, where he killed three more Germans and took another two prisoner. In the words of the official dispatch, 'Lance-Corporal O'Leary thus practically captured the enemy's position by himself and prevented the attacking party from being fired upon.' Even the exploits of Sergeant Cassidy seemed tame by comparison.

In the summer, O'Leary was presented with the Victoria Cross at Buckingham Palace, and was the subject of many tributes from notables of the time. 'No writer in fiction would dare to fasten such an achievement on any of his characters,' commented Sir Arthur Conan-Doyle, 'but the Irish have always had a reputation of being wonderful fighters.'

One of the few people to remain unimpressed was O'Leary's own father, a fervent nationalist. 'I am surprised he didn't do more. I often laid out twenty men myself with a stick coming from Macroom Fair, and it is a bad trial of Mick that he could kill only eight, and he having a rifle and bayonet.'

The British recruitment campaign manipulated the occasion to persuade other Irishmen to enlist. 'AN IRISH HERO! 1 IRISHMAN DEFEATS 10 GERMANS,' a poster declared. Beneath a picture of Sergeant O'Leary, newly promoted for his exploits, it went on: 'Have you no wish to emulate the splendid bravery of your fellow countryman?'

Later in the year, George Bernard Shaw wrote a short play, *O'Flaherty VC*, which suggested that appealing to an Irishman's pride in King and Country was a poor method of persuading him to fight. Shaw's O'Flaherty fights to rid the world of the virulent nationalism that had driven the Kaiser's Germany to war. 'You'll never have a quiet world till you knock the patriotism out of the human race,' he declares. But the message was too subtle for 1915. After pressure from the authorities, the play was dropped from the schedule of the Abbey Theatre in Dublin. It would not be performed until 1920, when, in the latest twist of history, the din of patriotism, as loud as ever, was expressing itself in the Anglo-Irish war.

In a preface to the published play, Shaw wrote:

The Irish were for the most part Roman Catholics and loyal Irishmen, which means that from the English point of view they were heretics and rebels. But they were willing enough to go soldiering on the side of France and see the world outside Ireland, which is a dull place to live in. It was quite easy to enlist them by approaching them from their own point of view. But the War Office insisted on approaching them from the point of view of Dublin Castle. They were discouraged and repulsed by refusals to give commissions to Roman Catholic officers, or to allow distinct Irish units to be formed. To attract them, the walls were covered with placards headed REMEMBER BELGIUM. The folly of asking an Irishman to remember anything when you want him to fight for England was apparent to everyone outside the Castle: FORGET AND FORGIVE would have been more to the point.

But back among the brick stacks at Cuinchy on the day that Michael O'Leary won his VC, there was little time to think about patriotism or heroism. The War Diary of the 11th Field Company gave this terse summary: 'Guards Brigade counter-attacked Germans in position lost the previous day in railway hollow.' Much more attention was given to the work the Engineers put in to save the Guards from the poor position they had taken up at the foot of the embankment, which offered them practically no field of fire. They moved the Guards to a position on higher ground, they made sandbag barricades, put up wire entanglements, constructed shell-splinter-proof dugouts, as well as a reserve position to which the Guards could fall back. This work had to be carried out under heavy shell- and rifle-fire. Three sappers were wounded.

A week later, the 11th Field Company took part in an attack intended to tidy up the line even further. The British trenches and brick stacks were still dangerously entangled with those of the opposing army. One German trench even ran right up to Cuinchy Keep, so that a party wall of heaped-up sandbags had been improvised at the meeting point between the two lines. The divisional commander ordered an assault to take back the trench and gain some ground in order to bring more of the brick stacks within the British line.

On Saturday 6 February, about a hundred sappers readied themselves for action. Fifty rounds of ammunition were issued to each man, along with a shovel, a pick and twenty empty sandbags. After a fifteen-minute artillery bombardment, the Coldstream and Irish Guards stormed the German trench, captured the brick stacks nearest the British keep, and established a new line at a much more defensible distance from the other stacks that the Germans continued to hold.

The Engineers immediately joined them. While two sections dug a trench at the new position, a third went back and forth bringing sandbags to the infantry. A small party of sappers then crawled into the area in front of the newly dug trench to make a wire entanglement, but soon had to stop because of heavy fire from the brick stacks that the Germans still held. A sapper was hit when they tried to get back to cover.

In his report on the assault, Major Foulkes recorded the details of the unsuccessful effort that was made to rescue the man: '[A]s the firing continued we had to drag him back to the trench, four of my men following me out to do this, although not asked to. One man had a bullet through his cap.* The Sapper (W. Webb) died and this was our only casualty of the day.'

The 11th Field Company were at last able to bid farewell to the brick stacks of Cuinchy on 22 March 1915, when they handed over responsibility for the sector to a territorial unit of the Royal Engineers, the 1st East Anglian Field Company, and moved on to the Givenchy sector, a mile further to the north. They arrived there about a week after the first large-scale British offensive of the war, at Neuve-Chapelle, had subsided into renewed deadlock between the opposing armies.

Among Major Foulkes's papers was what with hindsight seems like a madly hopeful 'special order' for the attack, dated 9 March 1915, from the commander of the 1st Army. 'At no time in this war has there been a more favourable moment for us,' wrote General Haig. 'Although fighting in France, let us remember that we are fighting to preserve the British Empire and to protect

---

* At this stage of the war soldiers still wore cloth caps. Steel helmets would not be in general issue until 1916.

our homes against the organised savagery of the German Army. To ensure success, each one of us must play his part, and fight like men for the Honour of Old England.' The human cost of defending Old England's honour had been 12,000 men killed or wounded, of which about 4,000 were Indian soldiers who had never seen England.

The 11th Field Company's own casualty figures, after weeks of ordinary attrition, would spike when they took part in the British army's next big attack. In the six weeks between the company's arrival in Givenchy and the beginning of the Battle of Festubert on the night of 15 May 1915, the War Diary recorded two men killed and four wounded; when Major Foulkes calculated the casualties of the week-long battle itself, the figures were five men killed, twenty-two wounded and two missing.

One of those missing was my great-uncle Thomas. His eleven years with the Royal Engineers ended with this entry in his service record: 'Officially considered as having died on or since 16.5.15', although this date must be in some doubt because of the time of the opening night attack. The 11th Field Company went into battle with the 6th Brigade of the 2nd Division, which moved forward from the Rue du Bois at 11.30 p.m. on 15 May. The battalion advanced in four waves, two sections of the 11th Company joining the third. 'Distance to be traversed was nearly 400 yards,' wrote Major Foulkes in the War Diary, 'therefore, all 4 lines were out in the open before leading line reached German trench. Hence losses of RE (and infantry).'

After the two lines of German trenches had been swiftly taken, the hard work began for the Engineers of adapting the newly won German positions and digging communication trenches back to the old front line across what had previously been no man's land. The company would only have got around to registering the disappearance of its missing men much later when things had quietened down, but around midnight seems the best estimate that can be given for when Thomas died, with Major Foulkes in the War Diary providing a diagram of where.

When my mother tried to find out about her uncle, she had to make do with the Names of the Missing on the stone wall in Le Touret Cemetery. If only she had known where to look, she would have been able to see the sketch map that Major Foulkes drew in the War Diary, showing where Thomas had died.

'There were no braver soldiers in the British Army,' he wrote of his company. '[O]n not one single occasion had they ever returned from a night's expedition with their set task unaccomplished, whatever the difficulties they had experienced or the intensity of the fire to which they had been exposed; and the losses they had suffered may be judged from the fact that among the officers alone, although the establishment of the unit was only six, there had been up till now no fewer than twenty-four casualties during eight months' fighting.'

Thomas was one of the many Old Contemptibles who did not grow old, a posthumous recipient of the '1914 Star', which was awarded to British soldiers who had served in France and Flanders between the beginning of the war and the end of the First Battle of Ypres on 22 November. I can't help but wonder what he would have made of how the world had changed between the day he left it and the day six years later, 14 April 1921, when the medal was finally delivered to the Lynch home in Deerpark, County Clare.

The war would continue to consume lives for another three and a half years. And even after the Armistice there was no peace to which he would have been able to return in his own country

Instructions regarding War Diaries and Intelligence Summaries are contained in F. S. Regs., Part II. and the Staff Manual respectively. Title pages will be prepared in manuscript.

WAR DIARY
or
INTELLIGENCE SUMMARY.
(Erase heading not required.)

Army Form C. 2118.

Hour, Date, Place	Summary of Events and Information	Remarks and references to Appendices

Sketch plan (from memory)

Scale about 300x = 1"

N

a, a – existing comm. trenches

b b, 4 new comm. trenches (dug for attack)

c Left comm. trench dug after attack

d Right comm. trench dug after attack

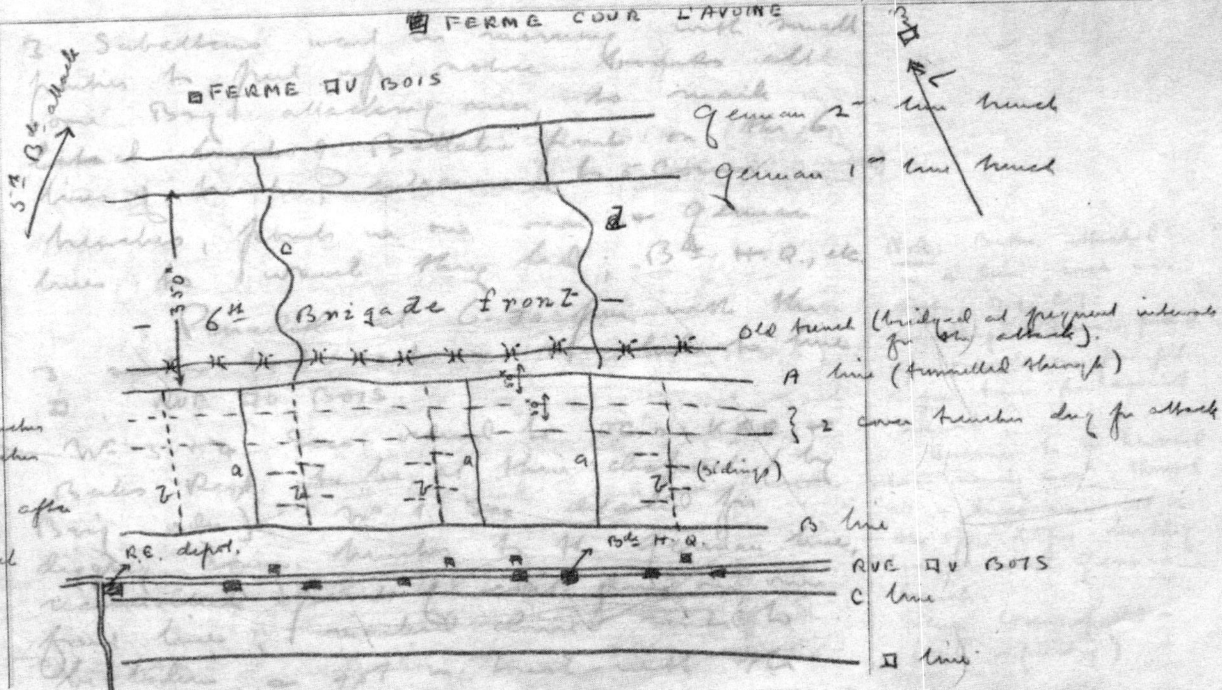

(73989) W4141—463. 400,000. 9/14. H.&J.Ltd. Forms/C. 2118/10.

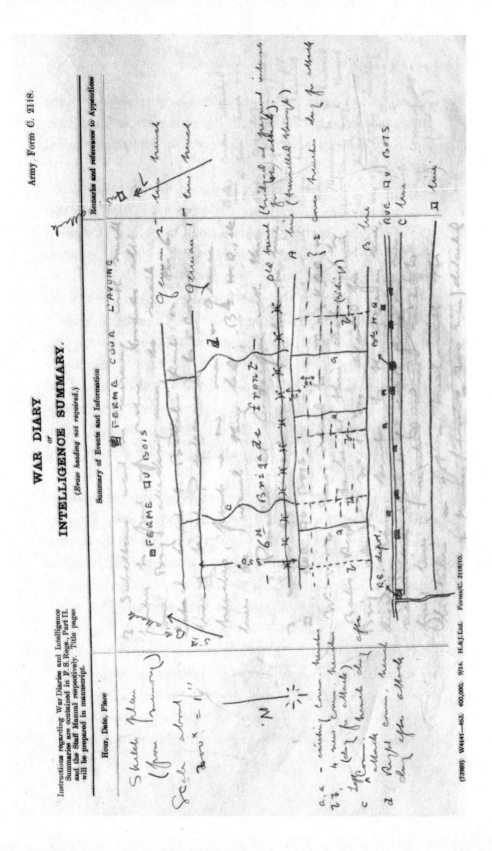

of Ireland. In 1915, he might reasonably have supposed that Home Rule would come to pass. Instead, there was the Easter Uprising; and then a guerrilla war, whose victors disowned all that his medal stood for.

While other nations honoured their dead, the new Ireland deliberately forgot the 50,000 Irishmen who had died in the Great War. Only in recent years has it become possible to give them the public honour they deserve, although their right to be remembered remains contested.

On the occasion of the war's centenary, the president of the Irish Republic attended a dedication of a Cross of Sacrifice at Glasnevin Cemetery. I had visited Glasnevin only about a year before with my aunt Joan and cousin Paula. We had come to pay our respects to my mother's older brother, Dermot. My aunt had bought some flowers from a stall by the entrance to the cemetery, which she arranged in front of her brother's headstone. Paula then said a prayer, in which she included my mother and other departed Lynches.

On our way to the graveside, we had passed many other families who had come to visit their loved ones in a place that is fondly known as 'the dead centre of Dublin'. And maybe it is the fact that remembrance is so central in Irish life that made the refusal to remember the dead of the First World War seem particularly cruel.

The president began his speech with these words:

It is important that the First World War, and those whose lives it claimed, be not left as a blank space in Irish history. Today therefore is a significant day, as we dedicate this Cross of Sacrifice – the first such Cross to be erected in the Republic of Ireland. On an occasion such as this we eliminate all the barriers that have stood between those Irish soldiers whose lives were taken in the war, whose remains for which we have responsibility, and whose memories we have a duty to respect. We cannot give back their lives to the dead, nor whole bodies to those who were wounded, or repair the grief, undo the disrespect that was sometimes shown to those who fought or their families. But we honour them all now . . .

My mother would have been proud to see the band of the Royal Engineers join Ireland's No. 1 Army Band in providing the music for the commemoration. Yet at the same time the hecklers beyond the cemetery railings, who interrupted the president's speech and chanted 'Shame, shame, shame on you' during the minute's silence, would have reminded her of why she had left Ireland for England.

When Thomas died, Kitchener's New Army divisions had yet to take the field and the war had some way to go to reach its full peak of industrial slaughter. He belonged to the old regular army whose traditions were becoming as much victim to the accelerated attrition of modern war as the men themselves. General Haig had asked his soldiers to fight 'like men for the Honour of Old England', but Old England no longer existed, and her honour was at risk too.

Quo Fas et Gloria Ducunt. Whether the Great War was just or not, it was much more difficult to uphold such a motto in the age of mass killing. Just a few days after the Battle of Festubert, on 26 May 1915, Thomas's company commander, Major Foulkes, was appointed to the staff of General Headquarters as a 'gas adviser'. The German army had used chlorine gas at Ypres in the previous month, and the commander-in-chief of the British Expeditionary Force, Sir John French, requested permission from the War

Secretary Lord Kitchener to respond in kind. 'The use of asphyxiating gases is, as you are aware, contrary to the rules and usages
of war,' replied Britain's most senior Royal Engineer. 'Before we
fall to the level of the degraded Germans I must submit the matter
to the Government.'

The necessity of war prevailed. Major Foulkes was asked to train
and organise gas troops who became known as the Special Brigade,
RE. The plans for retaliation were veiled in so much secrecy that
the new weapon, which evoked a visceral dislike among troops
from the outset, was referred to only as the 'accessory'. Robert
Graves's regiment took part in the Battle of Loos, where the 'accessory' made its debut. He recalled the reaction of a fellow officer
to the orders that detailed its use: 'It's not soldiering to use stuff
like that even though the Germans did start it. It's dirty and it'll
bring us bad luck. We're sure to bungle it.'

At just before 5.50 a.m. on 25 September 1915, a mixture of gas
and smoke was released from four hundred emplacements along
a 25-mile front. As the commander of the 1st Army, General Haig,
looked over the battlefield from a wooden tower in the grounds
of his headquarters in the château de Hinges, a thick cloud rolled
towards the German lines, but in some places the wind turned
and rolled the gas back to the British trenches. Graves witnessed
the gas cases that came stumbling into a dressing station, 'yellow-
faced and choking, with their buttons tarnished green'. So much
for the honour of Old England.

The British High Command continued to use gas until the end
of the war in spite of the widespread revulsion of its own soldiers.
There were hundreds of attacks. Under Foulkes's command, the
Special Brigade grew into sixteen companies with more than five
thousand men. In the words of the *History of the Royal Engineers*,

they 'turned the tables on the Germans and gave them far more gas than they ever gave the British', but there could be no glory in a weapon that remained, as the post-war treaty reaffirming the ban on its use said, 'justly condemned by the general opinion of the civilized world'.

It is beyond obvious logic why gas should be any more cruel than the death or mutilation that a soldier might suffer from a bullet, bayonet or high-explosive shell, but perhaps some of the taboo lay in the way it crept insidiously over its victims without warning. Impossible to see, gas denied agency, reducing the individual to a number.

Like the official statistics for the war's casualties. The final 'Statement of the Services' of 13419, Thomas Joseph Lynch, offered this brief summing-up:

Officially considered as having died on or since 16.5.15
Will – Not in military custody
Trade – Clerk
Next of kin – Father, Mr J. Lynch, Doora, Ennis, County Clare.
Total Service towards Engagement to 16.5.15 (date of discharge) –

Here the clerk had crossed out 'discharge', writing 'death' in its place, and added the figure 11 years 122 days. The only remaining piece of paper to complete the service record was the slip that Thomas's family had to sign to acknowledge receipt of his 1914 Star. Dated 14.4.21, it was signed 'J. Lynch'. The medal must originally have been addressed to Thomas's father, 'J. Lynch', at Deerpark, Doora, whom Thomas had designated his next of kin. But his father had died in 1913, so at first I thought that this

J. Lynch must have been Thomas's brother James, who had returned to Ireland an invalid after he was discharged with shell shock in 1918. But James died in September 1920, more than six months before the medal was signed for. When I looked more closely at the signature, I realised that it actually belonged to Thomas's oldest brother Jack, who had served with the Australian Imperial Force in France but had returned to Australia in 1919. What most likely happened offers an example of how difficult it is to make history tidy. With both his father and James dead, the parcel must have been sent on to the only 'J. Lynch' still surviving, Jack out in Australia.

While the great machine of military bureaucracy supplies an endless stream of dates and data, the human urge of course is always to want to find the traces of the person. I wondered where and how James had sustained the shell shock that ended his army career: 'Discharged – no longer physically fit for War Service, para 392 XVI King's Regulations, 15.11.18'. According to his statement of service, he was transferred from the 14th Survey Company into the 39th Company on 15 March 1916, but in the Royal Engineers library I could find no war diary with which to track the company's fortunes. Assigned to coastal defence at Sheerness, Kent, when the war began, the 39th was sent to France as a 'line of communications' company. It can only be speculation, but given the date of James's return to England in July 1918, I think a likely cause of his shell shock was one of the great bombardments with which the Germans opened their attacks during the Spring Offensive of 1918. On 21 March, the first of these, 'Operation Michael', flung three and a half million shells at the British lines in the space of only five hours.

Perhaps the only alternative to the mental collapse that my

great-uncle suffered was to practise the kind of dissociation typical of so many of the reports which were appearing in *The Sapper* that spring. 'Time has passed so quickly of late, to say nothing of the continuous order of "Move, move, move", that notes have not been kept quite as regular as they should be,' wrote the unnamed correspondent of an unnamed field company in a dispatch dated 17.4.18. 'Still, it's "Better late than never." The past month has not been all honey for the company. All ranks carried out their duty in a manner worthy of the Corps. Our deepest sympathy goes out to the relatives of those who fell in action.'

In an example of the stiff upper lip at its very stiffest, the correspondent quickly moved on to other matters. 'The "Roads of Life" may have been hard to travel these past weeks, yet that "Spirit of Sport" which has always been a predominant feature in the company has been well to the fore wherever possible. The football match with our sister company resulted in a 2–0 win in our favour.' And after the morning's match, further comfort arrived in a visit from the divisional band, 'whereby all could bask in the sun and listen to the excellent programme provided. At the conclusion of this, it was only a matter of a visit to the Canteen to satisfy our various needs, and so bring to an end "A Perfect Day".'

A perfect day of sangfroid somewhere in France. Gathering together the last loose ends, I wondered whether Michael Lynch had enjoyed as perfect a day when he married Ellen Josephine Cahill in Limerick on 27 July 1915. The circumstances suggested a hasty wartime marriage. From Cork Harbour, where Michael was serving with the 33rd Fortress Company, County Clare was just a short train journey away. During one of his visits to Deer-park, he would have found that Ellen, the youngest of the Cahill children, was back home from Scotland, where she had been

working as a schoolteacher in a Catholic school in Kilsyth near
Glasgow. There was every incentive for both of them to make the
most of a swift romance. Cork Harbour was a lucky wartime
posting, but Michael knew that there was no reason why he
shouldn't soon be posted to France like his brother Thomas. Meanwhile, as Ellen was thirty-four, it would not be surprising if she
had considered Michael to be pretty much her last chance to avoid
the fate that usually awaited the Cahills. Of her nine siblings, six
were missionaries in New South Wales: Minnie, Susan and Tillie
as nuns in the Order of Mercy, and Thomas, John and William as
ordained priests. Only two managed to escape the Church, but
they had to emigrate to the United States to do so.

Growing up in Clare in the 1930s, my mother might have
remembered 'Old Mrs Cahill' as a strict, unpleasant woman whom
she disliked visiting, but her uncle had had to put up with the even
older Mrs Cahill. When Michael went to live with his wife in the
Cahill house in Deerpark after the wedding, they shared it with
Ellen's mother Delia, a fervent churchgoer whose greatest pride
lay in the missionary endeavour of her large family. Michael
stayed only long enough to leave Ellen pregnant with their first
child. He was posted to Sierra Leone two months after the wedding.
When his son Michael Kevin was born on 3 June 1916, he was
still serving in the searchlight section of the 36th Fortress
Company, which defended Freetown harbour.

Not that the searchlights Michael operated could have been any
use against the German U-boats that in 1916 threatened to suffocate
Britain into submission. The strategic reality dictated the nature
of Michael's remaining service in the Royal Engineers. When he
returned to Britain at the end of the year, he was switched from
searchlight defence into one of the new forestry companies that

were established as heavy shipping losses in 1916 prevented Britain from importing enough timber supplies from overseas. He spent most of the rest of the war as Company Quarter Master Sergeant of the 368th Forestry Company, which was based in the Eawy forest near Rouen in Normandy.

Compared to James or Thomas, it was another lucky posting. The daily routine involved felling trees, which were then converted into telegraph poles or transported, by light railway, to a network of sawmills and charcoal kilns in the forest. The surviving war diary for the company details mostly uneventful work. In an exceptional accident that resulted in a court of inquiry a sapper was killed when a tree was felled, but otherwise absent was the weekly drip-drip of casualties that by the end of the war had decimated the 11th Field Company many times over.

With the arrival of spring 1918, when the Germans launched

their huge offensive, it briefly looked as though things were going to be different. The Forestry Directorate ordered that the men be armed and ready to march at short notice. Through most of April, each day's work ended with musketry drill, but by the end of the month the offensive had petered out and life in the forest returned to normal.

In June, Spanish influenza spread rapidly through the camp, until nearly half the strength of the company was too ill to work (60 out of 139 men). The absence of Michael's medical sheet from his service record means it is impossible to know whether he was one of the men who fell sick, but the overcrowded conditions of a camp where disease could be communicated so easily probably account for the tuberculosis he had when he came back to Ireland in February 1920. Life in the forest had turned out to be not so lucky after all.

Michael and Ellen had three more children, Paddy, Barney and Agnes, but soon Michael set off for Australia. Perhaps the trip was an effort to recover his health, but the family stories of the Cahills' piousness provide another reason for why he might have wanted to make the journey.

When I visited Clare, I had hoped to see inside the house where Michael had briefly lived. The only surviving building in Deerpark that still had a Lynch association, it was about a mile past St Brecan's Church, Doora, where I had found the graves of Michael and Ellen, and their son Paddy the priest. I turned off the road into a long, narrow lane that ran past a sun-dappled field with grazing horses. It was an idyllic, beautiful spot. The door was answered by Paddy's housekeeper, Mary Casey, an elderly, silver-haired woman who had continued to live in the house after his death.

'You might get a cup of tea if she's there,' I remembered my aunt Joan saying, while my cousin Paula told me, 'The sitting room is full of photographs of priests and nuns. It's like stepping back in time.' I thought here at last was an opportunity to see some old letters and photographs, maybe even to find some individual detail about Michael and his brothers that would make up for the spareness of the service records.

I explained who I was, Patsy's son over from England, but she didn't invite me in. Polite and a little wary, she gave me the name of someone who might be able to help me locate where the Lynch brothers' house had once been. It was only several months later that I learned from Pat Murphy that she thought I had come over from England to claim the house back.

Now Mary Casey herself is dead. The Church, to whom Paddy left the house in a final act of Cahill missionary endeavour, was able to auction it off at last. If my mother was still alive, I know that it would have been a cause of grievance for her to learn that Paddy had not left a penny to the Lynches, and it is perhaps just as well that she is not around to read this report of its sale in the *Clare Champion*:

A RECORD PRICE FOR DOORA PROPERTY

A record price of €390,000 was achieved for a house and 13.6 acres at a public auction in Ennis this week.

The house, located between the church and school in Deerpark, Doora, was the home of the late Fr Paddy Lynch. The house is set back some 350 metres from the road and is approached by a tree-lined avenue.

Dating to the 1700s, it is a small period house and is in need of refurbishment. Nevertheless, more than 35 parties viewed the house over the past five weeks and in excess of 60 people packed the Lemenagh Room in the Old Ground Hotel for the auction on Thursday afternoon.

'Bidding opened at €200,000 and briskly reached €370,000 in €10,000 increments. Five further bids brought down the hammer at €390,000,' auctioneer Paddy Darmody of Sherry Fitzgerald McMahon reported.

'I have been with Sherry Fitzgerald McMahon for more than 35 years and this house is unique . . .'

The only Lynch brothers to escape comparatively unscathed from the Great War were the two eldest. While the conflict tested as never before the ability of the Royal Engineers to be jacks of all trades, whether it was developing gas warfare or inventing the tank, Jack and Patrick remained topographical surveyors to the very end, although at first it appeared that there would not be much need for their expertise.

While the war, in its early weeks, was one of movement over large distances, existing maps sufficed. But once the two opposing armies found themselves squeezed into a narrow band, they changed the whole nature of the space they occupied, filling it with trenches and support trenches and ammunition dumps and dressing stations, creating vast fortress systems in what had once been empty fields. The sheer concentration of men and material meant that the battleground had to be charted in far greater detail than anyone had thought necessary before.

In August 1914, people had famously believed that the army would be home by Christmas; instead by Christmas they discovered that one army wasn't enough. The British Expeditionary Force in France had become so huge that, on Boxing Day 1914, it was divided into the 1st and 2nd Armies. The following summer, between the Battle of Festubert and the Battle of Loos, a third army was created. Topographical sections were attached to each of the three armies. It was at this point, in October 1915, that Patrick was sent to France, to join the topographical section of the 2nd Army which was in the north around the Ypres salient.

When the British Expeditionary Force set out for France at the start of the war, it was issued with maps that covered territory north of a line that ran from Le Havre to Luxembourg. One set comprised a strategic map showing the whole frontier area, and twenty-six larger-scale tactical maps. After the Great Retreat back to the Marne, maps of the area to the south had to be hurriedly printed and distributed. In October 1914, the line stabilised along the Western Front, but through much of 1915 the expectation was that there would soon be a breakthrough. So the British Expeditionary Force continued to use existing French and Belgian maps rather than make their own.

The diminishing hopes can be measured in the number of maps that were issued to the troops in the line. In February 1915, the allocation was a set of sixteen sheets; after the Battle of Loos in September, as another offensive came to nothing, it had dwindled to four. Soldiers arriving at the front from England received only two: Hazebrouck (sheet 5A) and Lens (11), which between them showed nearly all the railheads for the British sector. It was only once it was clear that the Western Front had become an indefinite feature that the topographical sections arrived to meet the need for more detailed maps. The tactical maps at the beginning of the war were on a scale of 1/80,000 and 1/100,000. When the war became static, the British first tried to enlarge existing French 1/80,000 maps to 1/20,000, but the gross distortions that resulted, throwing buildings many yards from where they appeared to be, meant that they were more dangerous than useful. The surveyors had no choice but to start again.

The standard scale for most tactical purposes was 1/20,000, but the topographical sections also produced trench maps on a scale of 1/10,000, and even larger scales for special operations. By the end of the war the eighty miles of the British Front Line had become a contender for the most heavily mapped place on earth. The military cartographers, producing endless, different versions of the same immovable line, offered a modern equivalent of the ancient philosopher's image of the river into which it is impossible to step twice. There was the flux of attack and counter-attack, of the artillery batteries blotting out villages, pockmarking the landscape with craters and ripping through the forests, yet through four long years the line remained virtually the same.

A relic of Patrick's time with the 2nd Field Survey Company is this letter of passage that, folded over three times, he must have carried in his top pocket:

The bearer, No. 28423, Sergt P. B. Lynch, R.E., is employed on survey work under the O.C., Topographical Section, R.E., 2nd Army. In carrying out his duties it may be necessary for him to use, from time to time, various instruments, such as plane table, clinometer, theodolite, etc., to take measurements with a tape and to enter houses or climb church towers to obtain a view. It is requested that he should not be hindered in his work if it can possibly be avoided.

Meanwhile whizzing over his head were the high-explosive shells of the Royal Artillery, who shared the sappers' motto of 'Everywhere' for good reason. I can imagine my grandfather at the end of a day's work, up some exposed tower with his plane table, strolling back to his billet through a landscape strewn with shell cases as plentiful as the dead leaves on the ground in autumn. I know that he must have picked up one of them as a souvenir from the battlefield, because many years later, suspended upside down from a brass frame, it served as the Lynch family's dinner gong. I last saw it in the hall of my uncle Dermot's house in Glasnevin. On the rim was the abbreviation 'CF 8/16 BSC': Cordite Filled, August 1916, Bethlehem Steel Company.

August 1916, the 31st to be precise, was the date of Patrick's discharge from the Royal Engineers, exactly twenty-two years after enlisting. From the perspective of corps bureaucracy, the date simply marked the termination of Patrick's 'second period of engagement', but I imagine he took some satisfaction from the

fact that he had more than done his bit at a time when there was good reason to think that the war would soon be over, even if we know now that it wasn't even halfway through. The BEF, swollen with new divisions that dwarfed the 'contemptible little army' with which Thomas had gone into battle, was two months into the 'Big Push' along the Somme, the headlines day after day promising the long-awaited breakthrough.

'The great British offensive has begun gloriously well,' wrote the *Daily Mail* on 3 July, 'and [what] we have now to bear in mind is that our troops do not expect to be in Berlin this week.'

'The tide has turned,' commented General Haig himself in an interview with *The New York Times* at the end of the month. 'It is only a question of more time till we win a decisive victory.'

The most famous Royal Engineer to leave the corps that summer was Field Marshal Lord Kitchener. On 5 June 1916 the ship that was carrying him on a diplomatic mission to Russia was sunk by a German mine off Orkney with the loss of nearly seven hundred lives. A black border surrounded the announcement of the news in the July issue of *The Sapper*. Noting that 'he of all men could least be spared', the editorial regretted the fact that he would not live to see the certain victory that his 'organising genius' had ensured. In less than two years, he had created the largest volunteer army the world had ever seen.

The sappers loved him because he epitomised so well their idea of what a sapper was. A favourite story among the rank and file went back to the days of Omdurman when he had built the desert railway that had defeated the Mahdi army. One day he arrived at the railhead wanting to go some miles back up the line, but there was just one rickety engine and no engine drivers. The only sapper he could find was a clerk who protested that he knew nothing about driving engines. 'Aren't you a Royal Engineer?' asked Kitchener. 'Well then, don't let yourself be defeated. Get up steam at once.' The clerk climbed up on the footplate after Kitchener and together they figured out how to get the locomotive going.

It was the kind of tale that might have helped Kitchener keep his own spirits going at the War Office. He had grown up in an age of Victorian heroes, but he came to represent the mass industrialised killing of the twentieth century, whether it was the concentration camps in South Africa or the New Army of 1914, although many argued that even its millions of men were not enough.

Only a week before Kitchener died, he was criticised in Parliament for his shortcomings. One MP even passed a motion that his pay should be cut. The prime minister, Herbert Asquith, had to come to his defence with words that only a few days later were able to serve as his epitaph: 'There is no other man in this country or in this Empire who could have summoned into existence in so short a time . . . the enormous armies which now, at home and abroad, are maintaining the honour of the Empire. I am certain that history will regard it as one of the most remarkable achievements that has ever been accomplished.'

Whether a mass volunteer army actually made any sense was another matter. The moral blackmail of young women handing out white feathers was hardly a sensible way of creating an effective war machine. Once it became clear that national survival was at stake, conscription was inevitable.

If the Military Service Act of January 1916 was a sad necessity, at least it curbed some of the bad poetry that patriotism so often inspired. In the same month that the Act was passed, *The Sapper* published a masterpiece of the genre:

> Shirkers of England, who're skulking at home
> And paying no heed to 'the call',
> How do you feel when you look at the men
> Who pass you in khaki again and again?
> Or have you no feelings at all?

And six more verses followed.

When Patrick returned home to Ireland in September 1916, he would have found no lack of feeling among his countrymen, but, in the aftermath of the Easter Uprising, England's call to Ireland had lost any appeal it might once have had. The Home Rule Act had been passed in the first days of the war only to be immediately suspended for the duration. The nationalist leader John Redmond had urged Irishmen to join Britain in a fight to defend the rights of small nations as the basis on which their own small nation could then hold Britain to account once the war was won. But there was a limit to how long a people could patiently wait for something that seemed so often promised to them only to be pushed ever further beyond their grasp.

The most recent debacle had occurred only weeks before Patrick's discharge. The Uprising caused the British government to initiate talks between Unionists and nationalists with a view to the immediate introduction of Home Rule, but the negotiations broke down towards the end of July over the proposed exclusion of Ulster. The atmosphere was further soured on 3 August when Sir Roger Casement became the last of the sixteen leaders of the Uprising to be executed.

A 'terrible beauty' was brewing, as more and more nationalists came to the conclusion that they should no longer depend on Britain's goodwill to fulfil Ireland's destiny. In his last speech to Parliament, in March 1917, a disillusioned John Redmond accused the government of a betrayal that would set Ireland on a different, more dangerous path.

'After fifty years of labour on constitutional lines we had practically banished the revolutionary party from Ireland. Now again, after fifty years, it has risen.' He ended with this warning:

> Any British statesman who by his conduct once again teaches the Irish people the lesson that any National leader who, taking his political life in his hands, endeavours to combine local and Imperial patriotism, endeavours to combine loyalty to Ireland's rights with loyalty to the Empire – anyone who again teaches the lesson that such a man is certain to be let down and betrayed by this course, is guilty of treason, not merely to the liberties of Ireland but to the unity, strength and best interests of this Empire.

It wasn't only the small nations of the Empire who were pondering the lesson. Among the troops fighting on the Western Front were four divisions of the Indian army, whose sacrifice created similar expectations of freedom. The Indian National Congress had been campaigning for self-government within the British Empire for many years, but the war created an extra impetus. When Sir S. P. Sinha gave the annual presidential address to the Congress at the end of 1915, he expressed the hope that it had changed the 'angle of visions' of Britain's rulers. The test before them was to prove the sincerity of the prime minister's assertion that the Empire rested not upon the predominance 'of race or class, but upon the loyal affection of free communities built upon the basis of equal rights'. Soon after the Easter Uprising, in August 1916, the All Indian Home Rule League was launched. It was impossible now to close the lid on the Pandora's box of liberty.

A civilian again after more than twenty years with the Royal Engineers, Patrick joined the Irish Land Commission, which, in supervising the redistribution of land from the Anglo-Irish gentry to the tenantry, presided over one of the most significant attempts to redress the past wrongs that England had inflicted upon Ireland. It was a quest for justice that any sapper who remembered his corps history lessons at Chatham would have known began with Captain Thomas Drummond, RE, who had first dared to take on the vested interests of the Anglo-Irish landowners: 'Property has its duties as well as its rights . . .'

With such examples even an Irishman could be proud of the corps, but in the immediate years of Patrick's return it was best to play down such connections. In June 1919, when Knockjames National School, near Tulla, appointed a teacher who had served in the British army, notices were sent to local parents with the warning, 'Keep your son from Knockjames, otherwise you will have reason to regret it. By Order of the Irish Republican Army.' Attendance plummeted. A father who defied the warning was badly wounded with shotgun pellets, while the teacher resigned and left for England.

The last of the five Lynch brothers to take part in the Great War, Jack joined the Australian Imperial Force at the end of 1917. If the dramatic effect that the passage of time had had on his physical appearance could be gleaned from a comparison of

Lieut. Lynch—Army Survey Corps.

the descriptions of him in his British and Australian service records – from 161 pounds in September 1894 to 224 pounds in December 1917 – nothing beats the caricature that the cartoonist Sam Wells drew of him for Melbourne *Punch* in February 1918 a few days after his arrival in England. He is a splendid, Falstaffian figure with a pipe who would have brightened up any mess room.

As befitting an Irishman abroad, Jack had set off on his long journey to England on a Royal Australian Navy transport ship called the *Ulysses*. After several months at Parkhouse Camp on Salisbury Plain, he was posted in May 1918 to the Depot Field Survey Company in France, where he spent the remainder of the war.

Ahead of him were millions of miles of Australia still waiting to be mapped. He retired in 1934 on his sixtieth birthday with the rank of Major. When he died a few years later, in July 1938, the *Melbourne Advocate* reported on a funeral in which his body was accompanied into the Catholic Church of the Holy Cross by a military guard of honour and then borne on a gun carriage to its final place of rest in the New Cheltenham Cemetery. 'He was a man of outstanding character,' reported the *Advocate*, 'and his ready Irish wit will be missed from many a gathering.'

The *Clare Champion* published its obituary of Jack a few months later with its romanticised account of his brothers' army service in which they received battlefield commissions that the British never gave them.

This was the version my mother knew. She may have gone to her grave with no more than the skimpiest idea of what they did, but from what I have discovered about them, there were many reasons why she could have been even more proud of them than she already was.

Epilogue

M y mapping of the past ended only a few days ago, when I took a photograph of the statue of Thomas Drummond in Dublin's City Hall. I arrived in the wake of the centenary celebrations for the Easter Rising. Emblazoned on billboards and on the sides of buses in stark, tinted colours that reminded me of 1960s Warhol, the rebels of Easter 1916 were being treated like rock stars. At this high point for Irish national pride, their blood sacrifice, which had led to the creation of the state, demanded wholesale celebration. The challenge of accommodating the more inconvenient truths was for another time.

Inconvenient truths like Drummond. A country that defined so much of its identity in opposition to England could not easily admit that a British Royal Engineer had done as much as anyone to redress its wrongs. But if Drummond himself had long been forgotten, at least his statue still stood among the pantheon of Irish heroes. To his right, as I entered the hall, was the equally massive statue of the Great Liberator, Daniel O'Connell, bearing in one hand a petition for the repeal of the Union.

PROPERTY HAS ITS DUTIES
AS WELL AS ITS RIGHTS.

Having paid my respects to Drummond, I made the pilgrimage
to the GPO Building on O'Connell Street, where a hundred years
ago, Patrick Pearse had read out the Proclamation of the Irish
Republic. As I reached the Liffey, I came upon a group of French
tourists who were gathered around a brass pavement plaque that
marked one moment in Leopold Bloom's wanderings through the
city: 'As he set foot on O'Connell Bridge a puffball of smoke
plumed up from the parapet. Brewery barge with export stout.
England. Sea air sours it, I heard.'

As I set foot on O'Connell Bridge, the 'Rise of the Rebels' tour
bus passed a city bus advertising a movie called *Bastille Day*.
Outside the GPO building, I found a wreath festooned with
wilting flowers, which the president of the Republic had placed
there a couple of weeks before on Easter Sunday. Although there
was still another fortnight until the calendar day on which the
rising itself had begun, 24 April, the revolution's shrine had already
gone back to being an ordinary post office again. What a piece of
Irish genius it had been to choose a movable feast day.

On the other side of the street, beyond the outstretched hands
of the statue of the trade union activist Jim Larkin, was Clery's,
where my mother had worked for three years before coming to
England. And just a little further, the Spire of Dublin. A hundred
and twenty metres high, the giant stainless-steel needle occupied
the spot that had once belonged to Nelson's Pillar. The IRA had
blown up the monument in March 1966, as their contribution to the
fiftieth anniversary of the Easter Rising. It would have been much
better if Nelson had been quietly shipped back to England, and one
of the many statues of O'Connell gently lowered in his place. He
already stood on a tall pillar in Ennis. So why not Dublin, too? The
thought took me back to a treasured memory from October 1966,

when after school one day my mother took me and my older brother Jonathan to see Nelson's Column in Trafalgar Square, just six months after the Irish one had been destroyed. I was only five, England had won the World Cup, and all was well with the world.

Back home in London, I have found some supporting evidence for the memory in the box of family photographs, but as timely a discovery is an old, broken-backed missal stuffed with prayer cards for the departed. If my mother had lived only a little longer and been able to look through them, eventually she would have found one 'in loving memory of Patrick Bennett Lynch, Bridge House, Quin, Co. Clare.' I can never know whether she ever saw it, but it is a good way to say goodbye.

London, April 2016

ST. PATRICK, APOSTLE OF IRELAND,
PRAY FOR US AND FOR THE DEPARTED.

R.I.P.

Notes

Prologue

'*The death has taken place*' (p.5): *Clare Champion*, 18 March 1939.

Chapter One: Carrying the Flame

'*the existence of human beings*' (p.20): 'Gogarty Here, Sees Ireland in the War', *New York Times*, 30 September 1939.

Chapter Two: An Irish Village

'*Despite the counter-influences of the modern era*' (p.36): Eddie Lawrence, foreword to *Quin, Clooney, Maghera: Our Living History* (Parish Newsletter, 2008), p.1.

Chapter Three: Only Yesterday

Conor Clune being shot thirteen times (p.46): Edward MacLysaght, *Changing Times: Ireland Since 1888* (Smythe, 1978), p.101.

Chapter Four: Across the Banner County

'There are other stories written daily' (pp.62–3): complete speech reproduced in the *Daily Telegraph*, 18 May 2011.

'the commencement of a salutary revolution' (p.77): Charles E. Trevelyan, *The Irish Crisis* (Longmans & Co., 1848), p.1.

Chapter Five: Esprit de Corps

'a High Priest offering an incantation at the altar' (p.91): Cyril A. Luckin, *1894 to 1984: One Man's Story, To My Family and Friends and the Corps of Royal Engineers*, unpublished manuscript (Royal Engineers Library, 1985), p.41.

Opening of the new military theatre at Chatham and Captain Brackenbury's lecture on 'Moral Force in War' (pp.93–94): *Daily News*, 20 December 1872.

'The first of these maxims is LOYALTY' (pp.94–5): Colonel B. R. Ward, 'Lecture 2', *Battalion Order* (School of Military Engineering, 1910), pp.6–7, RE Corps Library, 355.486 (RE)WAR.

'it is chiefly by the example of the actions of our forefathers' (p.96): *The Sapper*, April 1910.

Chapter Six: Everywhere

'Neither in this Cathedral, nor in any other Church' (pp.99–100): *The Sapper*, April 1910.

'revolted against dinner parties' (p.100): G. Lytton Strachey, *Eminent Victorians* (Penguin Books, 1948), p.233.

'The Church is like the British Army' (p.101): Gravesham Borough Council, 'General Gordon', *Discover Gravesham*. Web. 21 March 2016.

'The easy luxuries of his class' (p.101): Strachey, *Eminent Victorians*, p.234.

'When the Waters were dried an' the Earth did appear' (p.102): Rudyard Kipling, 'Sappers', *The Seven Seas* (Methuen & Co., 1896), p.175.

'*The question is one*' (p.103): *The Sapper*, October 1985.

'*its great extent, and the extraordinary levelness of its surface*' (p.104): Major-General William Roy, 'An Account of the Measurement of a Base on Hounslow-Heath', *Philosophical Transactions of the Royal Society of London* (Royal Society of London, 1785), vol.75, p.390.

'*Emigrant Soldiers' Gazette and Cape Horn Chronicle*' (p.107): The hand-written issues of the newspaper were gathered together and brought out in a printed version, which was printed by John Robson at the office of the *British Columbian* in 1863.

'*Mutton – Scarce. Porter and wine*' (p.108): *Emigrant Soldiers' Gazette*, 13 November 1858.

'*The name of the deceased is at present unknown*' (p.108): *Emigrant Soldiers' Gazette*, 13 November 1858.

'*I've lost a bunch of bright steel keys*' (p.108): *Emigrant Soldiers' Gazette*, 12 March 1859.

'*Hang me, old boy*' (p.108): *Emigrant Soldiers' Gazette*, 25 December 1858.

'*our readers will bear with us*' (p.109): *Emigrant Soldiers' Gazette*, 20 November 1858.

'*motley adventurers*' (p.109): Douglas to Labouchere 8657, National Archives, CO305/8, p.108.

'*It being also necessary*' (p.110): *Emigrant Soldiers' Gazette*, 20 November 1858.

Chapter Seven: The Queen's Shilling

Quin statistics (p.117): *The Parliamentary Gazeteer of Ireland* (Fullarton & Co., 1846), p.103.

'*What if I should give you your life?*' (p.117): Nigel Jones, *Tower: An Epic History of the Tower of London* (Hutchinson, 2011), p.370.

Chapter Eight: The Shadow of This Time

The unveiling of Gordon's new statue at Chatham on 19 May 1890 (pp.123–4): London *Standard*, 20 May 1890.

'*brave General Gordon*' (p.125): London *Standard*, 20 May 1890.

'*It makes one's heart burn to see such beauty destroyed*' (p.126): J. Wardle, *General Gordon: Saint and Soldier* (Henry B. Saxton, 1904), p.28.

'*I have got such a piece of plunder*' (pp.126–7): General Gordon, letter to Charles Harvey, 25 October 1860, 'General Gordon Letters', *Christie's: The Art People*, Christie's Sale 7590, Lot 122, 4 June 2008. Web. 23 March 2016.

'*the coup de grâce to their work*' (p.127): Lieutenant Colonel G. J. Wolseley, *Narrative of the War with China in 1860* (Longmans, Green and Roberts, 1862), p.279.

'*vengeance*' (p.127): Wolseley, *Narrative of the War with China*, p.280.

'*In their thirst after decoration*' (p.128): Wolseley, *Narrative of the War with China in 1860*, p.233.

The banquet at the Royal Academy of the Arts (pp.128–31): *Morning Post*, 6 May 1861.

'*One day two bandits*' (pp.131–3): Victor Hugo, letter to Captain Butler, 25 November 1861, quoted in Foster Stockwell, *Westerners in China: A History of Exploration and Trade, Ancient Times Through the Present* (McFarland & Co., 2003), p.79.

Chapter Nine: None That Can Compare

'*His name is far less well known*' (p.135): Bernard Roland Ward, *The School of Military Engineering* (Royal Engineers Institute, 1909), p.96.

'*only great effort*' (p.136): John F. McClennan, *Memoir of Thomas Drummond* (Edmonston & Douglas, 1867), p.iv.

'*a labour of love*' (p.136): R. Barry O'Brien, *Thomas Drummond: Under-Secretary in Ireland, 1835–40* (Kegan Paul & Co., 1889), p.vi.

'*was a gentleman of great ingenuity*' (p.137): David Malcolm, *Genealogical*

Memoir of the Most Noble and Ancient House of Drummond (G. Maxwell, 1808), pp.64–5.

'*making things*' (p.137): McClennan, *Memoir of Thomas Drummond*, p.7.

'*[A] glare shone forth,*' (p.139): McClennan, *Memoir of Thomas Drummond*, p.439.

'*inveterate haze and fogginess*' (p.140): J. H. Andrews, *A Paper Landscape: The Ordnance Survey in Nineteenth-Century Ireland* (Clarendon Press, 1975), p.42.

'*Your light has been most brilliant tonight*' (pp.140–1): McClennan, *Memoir of Thomas Drummond*, p.77.

'*[E]ngaged in the Ordnance Survey*' (p.141): quoted in McClennan, *Memoir of Thomas Drummond*, pp.248–9.

'*The world is the same everywhere*' (p.143): McClennan, *Memoir of Thomas Drummond*, p.132.

'*One room, spacious and lofty*' (p.143): McClennan, *Memoir of Thomas Drummond*, p.131.

'*The Chancellor seemed*' (p.144): McClennan, *Memoir of Thomas Drummond*, p.136.

'*in obtaining the correct data*' (p.144): *Morning Post*, 24 December 1831.

'*Reader, if thou canst boast the noble name*' (pp.145–6): *Morning Chronicle*, 30 August 1816.

Croker's coining of the term 'Conservative' (p.146): *Quarterly Review* (January 1830), p.276.

'*the victory of dispassionate opinion*' (p.146): *The Times*, 6 June 1832.

'*We hope this will be preserved*' (p.146): McClennan, *Memoir of Thomas Drummond*, p.161.

'*on fire with factions*' (p.150): David Knapman, *Conversation Sharp: The Biography of a London Gentleman Richard Sharp (1759–1835) in Letters, Prose and Verse* (Dorset Press, 2003), p.358.

'*partiality for Ireland*' (p.150): O'Brien, *Thomas Drummond*, p.75.

'*I am very busy*' (p.153): O'Brien, *Thomas Drummond*, p.232.

'*Sub-constables Ker and Keenan*' (p.153): O'Brien, *Thomas Drummond*, p.237.

'*As the party walked very close*' (pp.153–4): O'Brien, *Thomas Drummond*, p.238.

'*through the white liver*' (p.154): *Glasgow Herald*, 29 June 1829.

'*Sir, The state of the country*' (pp.154–5): O'Brien, *Thomas Drummond*, p.224.

'*As the proceedings*' (p.155): O'Brien, *Thomas Drummond*, p.225.

'*My Dear Drummond*' (p.156): O'Brien, *Thomas Drummond*, p.229.

'*Where the greater preponderance*' (p.157): Thomas Drummond, 'Report from Select Committee of the House of Lords on the State of Ireland in Respect of Crime', Minutes of Evidence before Select Committee, 19 June 1839, *Sessional Papers of the House of Lords* (1839), vol.20, p.1072.

'*Any time between*' (p.158): Charles Gavan Duffy, *My Life in Two Hemispheres* (T. Fisher Unwin, 1898), p.39.

'*It was like a cordial*' (p.158): Duffy, *My Life in Two Hemispheres*, pp.39–40.

'*a desire that a matter so serious*' (p.159): McClennan, *Memoir of Thomas Drummond*, p.316.

'*the tenure and occupation of land*' (p.160): O'Brien, *Thomas Drummond*, p.283.

'*the lamentably destitute condition*' (p.161): O'Brien, *Thomas Drummond*, p.283.

'*The deficiency of a demand for labour*' (p.161): O'Brien, *Thomas Drummond*, pp.283–4.

'*Property has its duties*' (p.161): O'Brien, *Thomas Drummond*, p.284.

'*in sales at a reduced price*' (p.162): O'Brien, *Thomas Drummond*, p.284.

'*I foretold*' (p.163): O'Brien, *Thomas Drummond*, pp.258–9.

'*Ireland, though for years past*' (p.164): *Reports from Commissioners, 1837–38: Second Report of the Commissioners Appointed to Consider and Recommend a General System of Railways for Ireland* (Her Majesty's Stationery Office, 1838), vol.47, p.92.

'*which it is more pleasing*' (p.165): McClennan, *Memoir of Thomas Drummond*, pp.373–4.

'*The mere bodily fag*' (p.166): O'Brien, *Thomas Drummond*, p.256.

'*[E]ven his every-day official business*' (p.166): McClennan, *Memoir of Thomas Drummond*, p.411.

'*but he is on thorns*' (p.167): McClennan, *Memoir of Thomas Drummond*, p.412.

'*Doctor, all is peace*' (p.167): McClennan, *Memoir of Thomas Drummond*, p.426.

'*I wish to be buried in Ireland*' (p.167): O'Brien, *Thomas Drummond*, p.387.

'*We have not often*' (pp.167–8): *Freeman's Journal*, 16 April 1840.

'*The death of Mr Drummond*' (p.168): *Morning Chronicle*, 20 April 1840.

Six lectures on 'Heroes, Hero Worship and the Heroic in History' (pp.168–9): The lectures were published in the same year as a book by Chapman, Hall.

'*The history of the world*' (p.169): Thomas Carlyle, *Heroes, Hero Worship and the Heroic in History* (Chapman, Hall, 1840), p.34.

'*for the loss of*' (p.169): *Freeman's Journal*, 20 April 1840.

'*a tribute of respect*' (p.169): *Freeman's Journal*, 22 April 1840.

'*It is right that*' (p.170): *Freeman's Journal*, 25 April 1840.

'*It is fortunate that*' (p.170): Charles Kegan Paul, *Maria Drummond: A Sketch* (Kegan Paul & Co., 1891), p.59.

'*a more public situation*' (p.171): *Illustrated London News*, 2 December 1843.

'*on subjects connected*' (p.172): The full title of the collection was: *Papers on Subjects Connected with the Duties of the Corps of Royal Engineers* (John Weale, 1840), vol.4.

'*For the example*' (p.172): Thomas Larcom, 'Memoir of the Professional Life of the Late Captain Drummond', *Papers on Subjects Connected with the Duties of the Corps of Royal Engineers* (John Weale, 1840), vol.4, p.xxiv.

'*to savour of the spirit*' (p.172): *Freeman's Journal*, 29 January 1853.

Chapter Ten: Home

'*For to admire*' (p.177): Rudyard Kipling, 'For to Admire', *The Seven Seas* (Methuen & Co., 1896), p.225.

'*To my mind*' (pp.179–80): *The Sapper*, May 1896.

'*open all the debatable questions*' (p.181): J. H. Andrews, *A Paper Landscape: The Ordnance Survey in Nineteenth-Century Ireland* (Clarendon Press, 1975), p.161.

Calls for native Welsh officers to accompany survey parties (p.181): *North Wales Chronicle*, 24 August 1895.

'*The illuminations that filled the streets of London*' (p.183): *Morning Post*, 23 June 1897.

'*I speak here for the Irish race*' (p.183): *Morning Post*, 22 June 1897.

The jubilee protest in Dublin (p.184): *Freeman's Journal*, 22 June 1897.

'*to be a true, brave and faithful soldier*' (p.185): Peter Karsten, 'Irish Soldiers in the British Army, 1792–1922: Suborned or Subordinate?', *Journal of Social History* (Autumn, 1983), vol.17, no.1, pp.31–64.

Chapter Eleven: Kitchener's Revenge

Exhibition at Royal United Service Institution (p.187): *Morning Post*, 12 March 1897.

'*the mischievous power*' (p.188): *Star*, 19 March 1896.

'*[T]he gentlemen who are constructing*' (p.188): *Daily News*, 13 September 1897.

'*the aboriginal natives*' (p.188): Winston S. Churchill, *The River War: an Historical Account of the Reconquest of the Sudan*, ed. Col. F. Rhodes, D.S.O., 2nd edn. (Longmans, Green & Co., 1902), p.7.

'*The qualities of mongrels*' (p.189): Churchill, *The River War*, p.8.

'*So 'ere's to you*' (p.189): Rudyard Kipling, 'Fuzzy-Wuzzy', first collected in *Barrack Room Ballads and Other Verses* (Methuen & Co., 1893), p.10.

'*By 6.45 more than 12,000 infantry*' (p.190): Churchill, *The River War*, 1st edn. (Longmans, Green & Co., 2 vols., 1899), vol.2, pp.118–19.

'*My boys, I am very glad*' (p.192): *Morning Post*, 9 November 1898.

'*They talk of "Tommy Atkins"*' (pp.195–6): *The Sapper*, May 1899.

'*As the Duke of Connaught*' (p.197): *Morning Post*, 30 October 1899.

The Royal Irish Fusiliers pelted with stones (pp.197–8): *Morning Post*, 26 October 1899.

'*sorrow and humiliation*' and '*It is to be hoped*' (p.198): *Freeman's Journal*, 2 October 1899.

'*on the basis of recognising*' (p.198): *Freeman's Journal*, 8 February 1900.

'*I assert without fear*' (p.199): Hansard, HC Deb, 25 February 1901, vol.89, c.1165.

'*a policy of extermination*' (p.199): Hansard, HC Deb, 17 June 1901, vol.95, c.580.

'*Knowing how eagerly any news*' (pp.201–2): *The Sapper*, June 1900.

'*By the time you receive this letter*' (pp.202–3): *The Sapper*, February 1900.

'*These Boers are stickers*' (p.203): *The Sapper*, April 1900.

'*took a rifle and waited*' (p.203): *Morning Post*, 17 November 1899.

'*27118, 2nd Corpl. E. O'Leary*' (pp.203–4): *The Sapper*, June 1900.

'*A lady missionary*' (p.204): quoted in *The Sapper*, February 1900.

'*cruel system*' and '*with crushing effect*' (p.205): Emily Hobhouse, *Report of a visit to the camps of women and children in the Cape and Orange River colonies* (Friars Printing Association, 1901), p.14.

'*I feel ashamed*' (p.205): quoted in Jane Meiring, *Against the Tide: A Story of Women in War* (iUniverse, 2009), p.201.

'*When the Children of Israel*' (p.206): Rudyard Kipling, 'Sappers', *The Seven Seas* (Methuen & Co., 1896), p.176.

Chapter Twelve: From Gibraltar to St Helena

'*superior in range*' (p.210): Vice Admiral Harry H. Rawson, 'Admiralty Report', para. 10, National Archives, WO32/6373.

'*The past history of Gibraltar*' (p.211): Sir George White, 'Covering Despatch of the Governor', *Gibraltar Defence Scheme* (Foreign Office, June 1901), p.2, National Archives, CAB11/66.

'*The growth of continental navies*' (pp.211–12): comments written on the summary of the military recommendations of the Gibraltar Committee, 'Works under construction at Gibraltar', National Archives, WO32/6373.

The account of the submarine miners (pp.212–14): W. Baker Brown, *History of Submarine Mining in the British Army* (Royal Engineers Institute, 1910), pp.73-121.

'*special military importance*' (p.215): E. H. Hills, *The Geographical Journal* (1908), vol.32, no.4, p.398.

Details of Jack's smoker (pp.215–16): *The Sapper*, April 1902, p.243.

'his work on malaria' (p.218): 'Ronald Ross – Facts', Nobel Prizes and Laureates, *Nobelprize.org*. Web. 27 March 2016.

Sir Ronald Ross's study (p.218): Sir Ronald Ross, *Report on the Prevention of Malaria in Mauritius* (J. & A. Churchill, 1908). See pp.73–4 for the figures cited.

'Dear Editor' (p.220): *The Sapper*, June 1901.

The account of Cronje's journey (p.221): *The Western Mail*, 9 June 1900.

'abruptly like a huge black castle' (p.222): Charles Darwin, *Journal of Researches into the Natural History and Geology of the Countries Visited during the Voyage of HMS Beagle Around the World*, 2nd edn. (John Murray, 1845), p.486.

'We beheld a kind of village' (p.222): Count de Las Cases, *Mémorial de Sainte Hélène: journal of the private life and conversations of the Emperor Napoleon at Saint Helena* (Henry Colburn & Co., 1823), p.128.

'On viewing the island' (pp.223–5): Darwin, *Voyage of HMS Beagle*, p.487.

'The English, or rather Welsh character' (p.225): Darwin, *Voyage of HMS Beagle*, p.487.

'respectable gentleman's country-seat' (p.225): Darwin, *Voyage of HMS Beagle*, p.491.

'After the volumes of eloquence' (p.225): Darwin, *Voyage of HMS Beagle*, p.486.

The sappers at Napoleon's funeral (p.226): *The Sapper*, September 1899.

'A pretty geranium hedge' (pp.227–8): *The Sapper*, September 1899.

'The town offers no attractions' (p.229): *The Sapper*, March 1902.

'For some reason or other' (p.230): *Sketch*, 8 November 1899.

'poor soldiers fatigued to death' (pp.230–1): Barry Edward O'Meara, *Napoleon in Exile: or, a Voice from St Helena* (Simkin Marshall, 1822), vol.1, p.80.

The Johnson submarine (p.231): Mike Dash, 'The Secret Plot to Rescue Napoleon by Submarine', *Smithsonian*, 8 March 2013. Web. 29 March 2016.

'The best position for his camps' (p.232): School of Military Engineering, *Notes on Plane-Tabling on Small Scales* (Royal Engineers Library, 1925), class no.526.9, accession no.1896, p.2.

'*As the winter has only just begun*' (p.233): letter from 2nd Lt F. B. Legh to
 Director-General Military Intelligence and Mobilisation, War Office,
 18 June 1903, National Archives, WO181/25.

'*The man who carried out the St Helena survey*' (p.233): letter from Major
 Charles Close to Sir David Gill, 11 January 1906, National Archives,
 WO181/251.

'*who knew every step*' (p.235): Darwin, *Voyage of the HMS Beagle*, p.487.

The move of the Colonial Survey Section to Freetown (p.236): Sir Charles
 M. Watson, *History of the Corps of Royal* Engineers, (Longmans &
 Co., 1914; reprinted, 1954), vol.3, pp.180–81.

'*While looking for marine animals*' (p.238): Darwin, *Voyage of HMS Beagle*, p.7.

Chapter Thirteen: Africa

'*I have been increasingly conscious*' (p.246): *New York Times*, 19 February 2015.

'*as trade increased*' (pp.250–1): Brigadier-General W. Baker-Brown, *History
 of the Corps of Royal Engineers* (Longmans & Co., 1952), vol.4, p.82.

'*In this respect they followed*' (p.251): Baker-Brown, *History of the Corps of
 Royal Engineers*, p.82.

'*for Survey work*' (p.251): Baker-Brown, *History of the Corps of Royal Engineers*, pp.82–3.

'*obnoxious tax*' (p.252): Hansard, HC Deb, 9 May 1898, vol.57, c.701.

'*A more criminal policy*' (p.252): Hansard, HC Deb, 9 May 1898, vol.57, c.703.

'*naked savages*' (pp.253–4): Baker-Brown, *History of the Corps of Royal
 Engineers*, p.90.

'*Tambi taken by assault*' (p.254): London *Standard*, 13 April 1892.

'*I don't think it's cricket*' (p.256): *Letters of Hugh Drummond Pearson*, unpublished manuscript, Royal Commonwealth Society Library, Cambridge
 University Library, letters, GBR/0115/RCMS356, fol. 91.

'*Somehow one never thought*' (p.257): *Letters of Hugh Drummond Pearson*,
 fols. 94–5.

'*going to turn out excellent*' (p.258): *Letters of Hugh Drummond Pearson*, fol. 135.

'Nothing makes him pleased' (p.258): *Letters of Hugh Drummond Pearson*, fol. 135.

'[O]ne of my men' (p.258): *Letters of Hugh Drummond Pearson*, fol. 135.

'No one knows' (p.259): *Letters of Hugh Drummond Pearson*, fols. 135–6.

'The doctor tells me' (p.259): *Letters of Hugh Drummond Pearson*, fol. 141.

'I am sorry to say' (pp.259–60): *Letters of Hugh Drummond Pearson*, fol. 143.

'I shook him off' (p.260): *Letters of Hugh Drummond Pearson*, fol. 146.

'In a weak moment' (p.260): *Letters of Hugh Drummond Pearson*, fol. 146.

'We get on here' (p.260): *Letters of Hugh Drummond Pearson*, fol. 143.

'they are beginning' (pp.260–1): *Letters of Hugh Drummond Pearson*, fol. 145.

'What noble ideas' (p.263): *Woodfall's Register*, 2 January 1792.

'We seem daily advancing' (p.264): Anna Maria Falconbridge, *Narrative of Two Voyages to the River Sierra Leone During the Years 1791–1793* (printed for the author, 1794), p.148.

'Involuntarily I strolled' (p.265): Falconbridge, *Narrative of Two Voyages to the River Sierra Leone During the Years 1791–1793*, p.32.

'[I]t was served to them' (p.267): Robert Thorpe, *Postscript to the Reply 'Point by Point': containing an Exposure of the Misrepresentation of the Treatment of the Captured Negroes* (Rivington, 1815), p.10.

'Since Governor Maxwell turned' (p.267): Robert Thorpe, *A Reply 'Point by Point' to the Special Report of the Directors of the African Institution* (Rivington, 1815), p.83.

'perfect Babel of confusion' (p.269): Robert Clarke, 'Sketches of the Inhabitants of Sierra Leone', *Transactions of the Ethnological Society of London* (1863), JSTOR Early Journal Content, www.archive.org, p.329.

'These men may' (p.269): James Holman, *Travels in Madeira, Sierra Leone, Teneriffe, St Jago, Cape Coast, Fernando Po, Princes Island, etc.*, 2nd edn. (George Routledge, 1840), p.193.

'The Krumen are a very peculiar race' (p.271): *British Parliamentary Papers: Appendix to Report from the Select Committee on the West Coast of Africa* (Irish University Press, 1842), vol.3, p.247.

Interview with the Kruman George Coffee (p.271): *Appendix to Report from the Select Committee on the West Coast of Africa*, p.281.

'appeared hardly to have ideas' (p.272): *Missionary Register for 1816* (L. B. Seeley, 1816), vol.4, p.240.

'Many of them, alas!' (p.273): *Missionary Register for 1816*, p.401.

The number of children in the colony's schools (p.273): *Appendix to Report from the Select Committee on the West Coast of Africa*, p.248.

'I pointed out how selfish' (p.274): *Letters of Hugh Drummond Pearson*, fol. 143.

'except through and with the consent' (p.274): quoted in Ade Renner-Thomas, *Land Tenure in Sierra Leone: The Law, Dualism and the Making of a Land Policy* (AuthorHouse, 2010), p.21.

'to keep constantly in sight' (p.275): Earl Grey, *The Colonial Policy of Lord John Russell's Administration* (Cambridge University Press, 2010; first published R. Bentley, 1853), p.286.

'[T]he aim of the Government' (p.275): quoted in Christopher Fyfe, *A History of Sierra Leone* (Oxford University Press, 1962), pp.261–2.

'reasonable dislike to being dispossessed' (p.276): Mary Henrietta Kingsley, *West African Studies* (Macmillan & Co, 1899), p.320.

'the people have by now' (p.276): T. J. Alldridge, *A Transformed Colony: Sierra Leone as it was and as it is* (Seeley & Co, 1910), p.39.

'to be free from' (p.276): Alldridge, *A Transformed Colony*, p.vii.

'improvements that would have' (p.276): Alldridge, *A Transformed Colony*, p.vii.

'[W]hen, on the morning' (p.277): Alldridge, *A Transformed Colony*, p.113.

'Wake! Every heart' (p.279): quoted in James W. St G. Walker, *The Black Loyalists: The Search for a Promised Land in Nova Scotia and Sierra Leone, 1783–1870* (Longmans & Co., 1976), p.145.

'Once you drink' (p.280): Alldridge, *A Transformed Colony*, p.66.

'Christianity without loyalty' (p.283): A. P. Kup, 'Sir Charles MacCarthy (1768–1824), Soldier and Administrator', *Bulletin of the John Rylands Library* (Autumn 1977), vol.60, no.1, p.78.

'Of course I immediately rose' (p.284): *Letters of Hugh Drummond Pearson*, fol. 140.

'*[R]ed hibiscus*' (p.286): *A Transformed Colony*, p.113.

'*maneless lion*' (p.286): Sir Richard Francis Burton, *To the Gold Coast for Gold: A Personal Narrative* (Chatto & Windus, 1883), vol.1, p.310.

Chapter Fourteen: The All Red Line

'*never-failing stream*' (p.294): George G. A. Skeen, *Guide to Colombo*, 6th edn., (A. M. & J. Ferguson, 1906), p.iii.

'*in an uncivilised and comparatively unknown country*' (p.296): Great Britain War Office General Staff, 'Prefatory Note', *Official History of the Operations in Somaliland, 1901–04* (HMSO, 1907), vol.1, p.3.

'*The Kafirs are our enemies*' (p.300): quoted in Roy Irons, *Churchill and the Mad Mullah of Somaliland: Betrayal and Redemption, 1899–1921* (Pen & Sword Military, 2013), p.133.

'*[T]he only satisfactory*' (p.301): Major E. H. Hills, *Report on the Survey of Canada*, 30 December 1903, p.4.

'*1. I have already brought*' (pp.302–3): letter from Brigadier General Lake to the Minister of Militia and Defence, Ottawa, 14 April 1905, *Sessional Papers of the Dominion of Canada 1909*, vol.9, no.145 (correspondence relating to the establishment of a Geodetic Service Bureau and the commencement of a Geodetic Survey in Canada).

The secret intelligence maps of the United States (p.304): War Office, Intelligence Division, British Library, IDWO1606.

'*The relations between them*' (pp.305–6): *Guardian*, 17 April 1907.

'*to proceed to British colonies*' (p.306): *Minutes of the Proceedings of the Imperial Conference 1907* (HMSO, 1907), p.155.

'*people of British stock*', '*other countries*' and '*a guarantee for*' (pp.306–7): *Minutes of the Imperial Conference 1907*, p.154.

'*I use the word "race"*' (p.307): *Minutes of the Imperial Conference 1907*, p.154.

'*We are determined*' (p.307): *Minutes of the Imperial Conference 1907*, p.175.

'*We believe it is*' (p.307): *Minutes of the Imperial Conference 1907*, pp.175–6.

'*If we get a navvy*' (pp.307–8): *Minutes of the Imperial Conference 1907*, p.164.

'admitted extremely few' (p.308): *Minutes of the Imperial Conference 1907*, p.181.

'Receive globe encircling message' (pp.309–10): quoted in George Johnson (ed.), *The All Red Line: The Annals and Aims of the Pacific Cable Project* (James Hope & Sons, 1903), p.462.

'Fine weather' (p.311): Melbourne *Argus*, 12 April 1910.

'It is fatal' (p.312): quoted in John D. Lines, *Australia on Paper: The Story of Australian Mapping* (Fortune Publications, 1992), p.43.

'We are aiming' (p.313): Lines, *Australia on Paper*, p.50.

'while no doubt' (p.313): C. D. Coulthard-Clark, *Australia's Military Map-Makers: The Royal Australian Survey Corps* (Oxford University Press Australia and New Zealand, 2000), pp.17–18.

'the slower and more laborious work' (p.314): Lines, *Australia on Paper*, p.49.

'[T]he decrease of the Aborigines' (p.319): quoted in *Newcastle Herald*, 29 July 1989.

'Our parson' (pp.320–1): quoted in John Maynard, *True Light and Shade: An Aboriginal Perspective of Joseph Lycett's Art* (National Library of Australia, 2014), p.17.

'The wind of change' and 'whether we like it or not' (pp.324–5): James Robertson, 'A Footnote for Historians: "Wind of Change" Harold Macmillan's Prime Ministerial Tour of Africa, 1960', www.jamesrobertson.com. Web. 29 March 2016.

'What must I do to the man' (p.325): quoted in Sir Francis Charles Fuller, *A Vanished Dynasty – Ashanti* (John Murray, 1921), p.188.

'that much that is new' (p.326): quoted in Noel Machin, *Government Anthropologist: A Life of R. S. Rattray* (Centre for Social Anthropology and Computing, University of Kent at Canterbury, 1998).

'I approached these old people' (pp.326–7): R. S. Rattray, *Ashanti* (Oxford University Press, 1923), p.11.

'seldom understands' (p.329): Captain S. W. Kirby, 'Johore in 1926: A paper read at the Meeting of the Society, 19 December 1927', *The Geographical Journal* (March 1928), vol.71, no.3, p.254.

'It is not so long ago' (p.329): Kirby, 'Johore in 1926', p.256.

'in no sense coolies' and *'genial survey collaborators'* (p.329): Kirby, 'Johore in 1926', p.259.

'I was walking along' (pp.329–30): Kirby, 'Johore in 1926', p.259.

Chapter Fifteen: Things Fall Apart

'The fighting from 19th October' (p.336): H. L. Pritchard (ed.), *History of the Corps of Royal Engineers* (Longmans & Co., 1952), vol.5, p.202.

'1) the men digging themselves in' (p.336): 11th Field Company Royal Engineers War Diary, Royal Engineers Library.

'the proudest achievement' (p.337): C. H. Foulkes, *'Gas!': The Story of the Special Brigade* (W. Blackwood & Sons, 1934), p.2.

'it wasn't like' (p.338): Sapper, *Sergeant Michael Cassidy, R.E.* (Hodder & Stoughton, 1916), p.6.

'Ah! the devils' (p.338): Sapper, *Sergeant Michael Cassidy, R.E.*, p.10.

'We must beseech' (p.339): quoted in *The Liverpool Echo*, 28 October 1915.

'When one's motto is' (p.339): Sapper, *Sergeant Michael Cassidy, R.E.*, p.3.

'Started experimental trench' (p.339): 11th Field Company Royal Engineers War Diary.

'No.3 section' (pp.339–40): 11th Field Company Royal Engineers War Diary.

Highland Light Infantry digging a trench called Glasgow Street (p.340): Colonel A. K. Reid, *Shoulder to Shoulder: The Glasgow Highlanders 9th Battalion Highland Light Infantry 1914–1918* (A. Aiken, 1988), ch.4.

'A big black brute' (p.340): *The Sapper*, February 1915.

'The whole of no.1 Section' (p.341): 11th Field Company Royal Engineers War Diary.

'slaughter-yard' (p.342): Edmund Blunden, *Undertones of War*, new edn. (Penguin Books, 1982), p.45.

'One could never' (p.342): Blunden, *Undertones of War*, p.43.

'was as dirty' (p.342): Blunden, *Undertones of War*, p.44.

'most confusing', *'made themselves'* and *'The Germans are'* (pp.342–3): Robert Graves, *Goodbye to All That* (Penguin Books, 1969), p.96.

'*Lance-Corporal O'Leary thus practically*' (p.344): *The London Gazette*, 16 February 1915.

'*No writer in fiction*' (p.344): quoted in the *Tablet*, 27 February 1915.

'*I am surprised*' (p.344): Peter Batchelor and Christopher Matson, *VCs of the First World War – The Western Front 1915* (Sutton Publishing, 1997), p.3.

'*You'll never have a quiet world*' (p.345): George Bernard Shaw, 'O'Flaherty V. C.: A Recruiting Pamphlet' in *Heartbreak House, Great Catherine, and Playlets of the War* (Brentano's, New York, 1919), p.195.

'*The Irish were for the most part*' (p.346): George Bernard Shaw, preface to 'O'Flaherty, V. C.: A Recruiting Pamphlet', p.179.

'*[A]s the firing continued*' (p.348): 11th Field Company Royal Engineers War Diary.

'*There were no braver soldiers*' (p.350): Foulkes, *Gas!*, p.14.

'*It is important that*' (pp.352–3): 'Speech at the Dedication of the Cross of Sacrifice', Glasnevin Cemetery, 31 July 2014, *President of Ireland* (media library of the Office of the President of the Irish Republic). Web. 25 December 2014.

'*The use of asphyxiating gases*' (p.354): quoted in Ulf Schmidt, 'Justifying Chemical Warfare: The Origins and Ethics of Britain's Chemical Warfare Programme, 1915–1939', in David Welch and Jo Fox (eds.), *Justifying War: Propaganda, Politics and the Modern Age* (Palgrave Macmillan, 2012), pp.132–3.

'*It's not soldiering*' (p.354): Graves, *Goodbye to All That*, p.123.

'*yellow-faced and choking*' (p.354): Graves, *Goodbye to All That*, p.127.

'*turned the tables*' (p.355): Pritchard (ed.), *History of the Corps of Royal Engineers*, vol.5, p.233.

'*justly condemned by*' (p.355): *Protocol for the Prohibition of the Use in War of Asphyxiating, Poisonous or Other Gases, and of Bacteriological Methods of Warfare*, presented at the Geneva Conference 1925 (HMSO, 1929).

'*Time has passed so quickly*', '*Still, it's "Better late than never."*', '*The "Roads of Life"*' and '*whereby all could bask*' (p.357): *The Sapper*, July 1918.

War diary of the 368th Forestry Company, Royal Engineers (p.359): National Archives, WO95/4059/4.

'A RECORD PRICE FOR DOORA PROPERTY' (pp.361–2): *Clare Champion*, 12 December 2014.

Mapping of the Western Front (pp.363–4): 'Geographical Section, General Staff', *Report on Survey on the Western Front 1914–1918* (HMSO, 1920).

'The great British offensive' (p.366): *Daily Mail*, 3 May 1916.

'The tide has turned' (p.366): *New York Times*, 1 August 1916.

'he of all men' (p.366): *The Sapper*, July 1916.

Anecdote about Kitchener at the rail-head in the Sudan (pp.366–7): *The Sapper*, July 1916.

'There is no other man' (p.367): Hansard, HC Deb, 31 May 1916, vol.82, c. 2806.

'Shirkers of England' (p.368): *The Sapper*, January 1916.

'After fifty years of labour' (p.369): Stephen Gwynn, *John Redmond's Last Years* (Edward Arnold, 1919), p.255.

'Any British statesman' (p.369): Gwynn, *John Redmond's Last Years*, p.256.

'angle of visions' (p.369): quoted in Sir S. P. Sinha, *Future of India: Presidential Address to the Indian National Congress* (J. Truscott & Son, 1916), p.26.

'Keep your son from Knockjames' (p.371): quoted in Robert Kee, *The Green Flag* (Penguin Books, 1989), vol.3, p.85.

'He was a man of outstanding character' (p.373): *Melbourne Advocate*, 11 August 1938.

Acknowledgements

The very nature of this book means that I owe the first debt of gratitude to my relations. So my thanks go to Christopher and Dinah; to my brothers Andrew and Jonathan and their families; to my aunts Joan Siohn, Theresa Heapes, Helen Maskatiya and their families; to my uncle Thomas Lynch and his family; to my cousins Theresa Walters and Paula Scully and their families; to Charles and Margaret Dupont; and to my Murphy cousins and their families.

I must single out one of the Murphys for special mention. When my mother began to talk about Ireland, she expressed the hope that one day I would meet someone who would explain in greater detail what she could remember only in scraps. I was lucky soon afterwards to meet my cousin Pat Murphy, who more than anyone else came to play that role during the research for this book. In the pursuit of forgotten history, he climbed over gates and walls, drove me across the Banner County and beyond, offering an inexhaustible source of enthusiasm, encouragement, good humour and – not least – a thirst for true understanding.

Although I had never been to Quin before, the welcome was

such that it was impossible to feel a stranger. On my first evening there, a memorable meal at Corbally as a guest of Lena, Niamh and Rory O'Loughlin made me feel I still belonged in a place that my family had left more than half a century ago. And I am grateful to them not only for a wonderful meal (ending with Irish coffee and fudge cake), but also for the way in which, over the days that followed, they showed me around Quin, made introductions, but also gave me my first taste of the magnificent, ancient landscape of the Burren, where the great tomb of Poulnabrone, five thousand years old, offered an early measure of what a map of the past could be.

Also in County Clare, I am grateful to Mary Casey, Mary Conlan, Una Chandler, Michael and Fanny Corbett, Carrie Clune, John Mungovan, Anne Marlborough, Flan McArthur, Father Michael McInerney, Ciss Chandler, Tom O'Loughlin; Antoinette O'Brien of the Clare Heritage Centre in Corofin; and to the staff of the Clare Museum, Ennis.

In England, thanks are due to my colleague at Queen Mary, Eddie Hughes, with whom I was able to share the coincidence of a family in Quin; to my agent Clare Alexander; to my editors at Heinemann, Tom Avery, Jason Arthur, Anna Argenio and Katherine Fry.

For help with maps, pictures and research, I am grateful to Christopher Coulthard-Clark, Jill Forrest, Tom Quinlan, Andrew Richardson, Nathan Sansom, James Scott, Lianne Smith, Sebastian Spencer, Tom Foulkes, Raymond Frogner and Kelly-Ann Turkington.

I would also like to acknowledge the assistance of the following institutions: the Australian Army Museum of Military Engineering, the British Library, Cambridge University Library, Dublin City

ACKNOWLEDGEMENTS

Hall, the Library of Congress, the Liddell Hart Centre for Military Archives at King's College, London, the National Archives at Kew, the National Library of Australia, the National Portrait Gallery, the Royal BC Museum, the Royal Commonwealth Society, the Royal Engineers Museum and Library, the University of Edinburgh, the Victoria and Albert Museum.

Last and far from least, I would like to record my appreciation for Elena Von Kassel Siambani, who reminds me most of that Royal Engineer's daughter.

Illustration Acknowledgements

Grateful acknowledgement is made for permission to use the following pictures. Every effort has been made to contact all copyright holders, and any error or omission brought to the publishers' attention will be corrected in future editions.

p.v,   Patsy as a small girl: family archive.

p.8,   advertisement for Drazin's shop in Hampstead: family archive.

p.9,   advertisement, 'Only 39 Steps to Drazin's': family archive.

p.13,   my Irish grandfather's suitcase: author's photograph.

p.26,   Patsy and Thomas as children: family archive.

p.27,   my mother on top of the tower of Quin Abbey: family archive.

p.27,   my father (smoking the pipe) with uncles Dermot and Jim: family archive.

p.32,   Quin Abbey: author's photograph.

p.37,   the schoolchildren at Quin National School: courtesy of the Quin-Clooney-Maghera Parish Pastoral Council.

pp.42–3, aerial view of Quin, *Life*, 24 July 1939.

p.44, 'An old Irish peasant with a child', cover of *Picture Post*, 27 July 1940.

p.45, cow in the meadow by Quin Abbey: *Picture Post*, 27 July 1940.

p.47, Amby Power planting potatoes in his garden: *Life*, 24 July 1939.

p.49, the old Catholic church, St Mary's, in the 1950s (since rebuilt): family archive.

p.49, the back of Fineen's Hall and the Protestant church: family archive.

p.50, Major Willie Redmond: copyright © National Portrait Gallery, London.

p.53, Sinn Féin banner in the Clare Museum, Ennis: author's photograph.

p.78, the famine monument at Ennistymon: author photograph.

p.92, postcard of the Royal Engineers in uniform: author's collection.

p.99, the Prince of Wales unveiling the statue of General Gordon at the Brompton Barracks, Chatham, *The Graphic*, 24 May 1890: author's collection.

p.107, front page of the *Emigrant Soldiers' Gazette*, 15 January 1859: courtesy of the Royal BC Museum and Archives.

p.113, stone pyramid on the 49th Parallel, photographed by the Royal Engineers 1860–61: copyright © Victoria and Albert Museum, London.

p.121, statue on the Kilrush Road, Ennis, 'A Soldier Remembers' by Shane Gilmore, limestone, 1999: author's photograph.

p.132, 'New Elgin Marbles', cartoon from *Punch*, 24 November 1860: author's collection.

p.139, diagram of the Drummond Light: courtesy of the Royal Society.

p.148, Captain Thomas Drummond, R.E., by Henry William Pickersgill: copyright © the University of Edinburgh.

p.180, A Royal Engineer enjoys his luncheon hour 'on the survey', cartoon from the *Sapper*, August 1900: copyright © The British Library Board, P.P.4038.cc.

p.191, General Kitchener on the frontispiece of Winston Churchill's *The River War*: copyright © The British Library Board, 09061,cc.4.

pp.193, 194 and 195, menu of the dinner to Lord Kitchener at the Royal Engineers' Mess, Chatham, on 8 November 1898: copyright © The British Library Board, P.P.4050.m.

p.199, two Irish soldiers during the Boer War, cartoon from the *Sapper*, August 1900: copyright © The British Library Board, P.P.4038.cc.

p.209, map of Gibraltar, 1903: copyright © National Archives.

p.210, table of guns defending Gibraltar: copyright © National Archives.

p.219, map of St Helena: copyright © The British Library Board, Maps MOD IDWO 1853.

p.222, aerial photograph of St Helena taken by a visit to the island by the French navy in 2014: © S.M. Brebel, Marine nationale.

p.223, Jamestown, St Helena: copyright © The British Library Board, Maps MOD IDWO 1853.

p.224, postcard of Jacob's Ladder, Jamestown: author's collection.

p.228, French sailors visiting Napoleon's empty tomb in 2014: © S.M. Brebel, Marine nationale.

p.235, escape route from Longwood to Prosperous Bay: copy-right © The British Library Board, Maps MOD IDWO 1853.

p.241, locket with picture of Patrick Lynch: family collection.

p.241, Patrick's St Benedict's medal: family collection.

p.247, my father as a young man attempting to blow the perfect smoke ring, 1953: family archive.

p.247, Oliver Sacks looking Brando-like in his biker's jacket: family archive.

p.248, Oliver, with Rousseau's *The Snake Charmer* behind him: family archive.

p.261, the Colonial Survey Section's map of Freetown: copyright © The British Library Board, Maps GSGS 2404.

p.277, Cotton Tree Station, Freetown: courtesy of the Gary Schulze Collection, the Sierra Leone Web.

p.278, the Sierra Leone Mountain Railway: courtesy of the Gary Schulze Collection, the Sierra Leone Web.

p.281, Wilberforce Memorial Hall and St George's Cathedral, Freetown: Delcampe.net.

p.287, survey stone, Sugarloaf mountain, Sierra Leone: copyright © Nathan Sansom.

p.290, Patrick Lynch with the Colonial Survey Section in Ceylon, 1913: family archive.

p.293, James, Michael and Thomas Lynch: family archive.

p.293, Michael Lynch: family archive.

p.297, map of the Haud, British Somaliland: copyright © The British Library Board, Maps TSGS 1781(a).

p.309, map of the 'All Red Route': copyright © The British Library Board, 8758.cc.32.

p.310,   the 'All Red Line' globe: copyright © British Library
Board, 8758.cc.32.

p.316,   the Parish of Kahibah, New South Wales: copyright ©
National Library of Australia.

p.317,   Jack Lynch's notes of his schedule: copyright © National
Library of Australia.

p.319,   detail from map of Kahibah Parish showing Belmont and
Lake Macquarie: copyright © National Library of
Australia.

p.321,   Joseph Lycett, 'Aborigines resting by camp fire, near the
mouth of the Hunter River, Newcastle, New South Wales':
© National Library of Australia.

p.337,   11th Field Company, Royal Engineers, outside their farm-
house bivouac near Zillebeke: Charles Foulkes Collection,
Liddell Hart Centre for Military Archives, copyright ©
Tom Foulkes.

p.342,   some improvised hand-grenades: Charles Foulkes Collection, Liddell Hart Centre for Military Archives, copyright
© Tom Foulkes.

p.343,   one of the brick-stacks at Cuinchy: Charles Foulkes Collection, Liddell Hart Centre for Military Archives, copyright
© Tom Foulkes.

p.345,   poster of Sergeant O'Leary: courtesy of the Library of
Congress.

p.346,   'For the Glory of Ireland' poster: courtesy of the Library
of Congress.

p.351,   Charles Foulkes' sketch of the opening Festubert attack in
the 11th Field Company War Diary: copyright © Royal
Engineers Museum and Library.

p.359, the Eawy forest in Normandy, January 1918: copyright ©
        Imperial War Museums (Q 10252).

p.365, Patrick Lynch's shell-gong: author's photograph.

p.370, Patrick Lynch's reference on leaving the Royal Engineers:
        family archive.

p.371, cartoon by Sam Wells of Lieutenant Jack Lynch, Imperial
        Australian Force, February 1918: © National Library of
        Australia.

p.372, Major Jack Lynch, Australian Survey Corps: copyright ©
        Australian Army Museum of Military Engineering.

p.376, the statue of Captain Thomas Drummond in City Hall,
        Dublin: author's photograph.

p.378, Trafalgar Square, October 1966: family archive.

p.379, prayer card with St Patrick: family archive.